Shakespeare & the First *Hamlet*

Shakespeare &
Series Editor:
Graham Holderness, *University of Hertfordshire*

Volume 9
Shakespeare & the First Hamlet
Edited by Terri Bourus

Volume 8
Shakespeare & Biography
Edited by Katherine Scheil and Graham Holderness

Volume 7
Shakespeare & Money
Edited by Graham Holderness

Volume 6
Shakespeare & His Biographical Afterlives
Edited by Paul Franssen and Paul Edmondson

Volume 5
Shakespeare & the Ethics of War
Edited by Patrick Gray

Volume 4
Shakespeare & Creative Criticism
Edited by Rob Conkie and Scott Maisano

Volume 3
Shakespeare & the Arab World
Edited by Katherine Hennessey and Margaret Litvin

Volume 2
Shakespeare & Commemoration
Edited by Clara Calvo and Ton Hoenselaars

Volume 1
Shakespeare & Stratford
Edited by Katherine Scheil

Shakespeare & the First *Hamlet*

Edited by
Terri Bourus

berghahn
NEW YORK · OXFORD
www.berghahnbooks.com

First published in 2022 by
Berghahn Books
www.berghahnbooks.com

© 2022 Berghahn Books

Originally published as a special issue
of *Critical Survey*, volume 31, numbers 1 and 2,
unless otherwise noted.

All rights reserved. Except for the quotation of short passages
for the purposes of criticism and review, no part of this book
may be reproduced in any form or by any means, electronic or
mechanical, including photocopying, recording, or any information
storage and retrieval system now known or to be invented,
without written permission of the publisher.

Library of Congress Cataloging-in-Publication Data

A C.I.P. cataloging record is available from the Library of Congress

Library of Congress Cataloging in Publication
Control Number: 2022012980

British Library Cataloguing in Publication Data

A catalogue record for this book is available from the British Library

ISBN 978-1-80073-553-8 hardback
ISBN 978-1-80073-554-5 paperback
ISBN 978-1-80073-555-2 ebook

https://doi.org/10.3167/9781800735538

Contents

List of Figures	vii
Introduction **Is Q1 *Hamlet* the First *Hamlet*?** Terri Bourus	1
Chapter 1 **Shakespeare's Early Gothic *Hamlet*** Gary Taylor	7
Chapter 2 **The Hybrid *Hamlet*** *Player Tested, Shakespeare Approved* Christopher Marino	35
Chapter 3 **Ofelia's Interruption of Ophelia in *Hamlet*** Michael M. Wagoner	55
Chapter 4 **Beautified Q1 *Hamlet*** Douglas Bruster	73
Chapter 5 **The Good Enough Quarto** Hamlet *as a Material Object* Terri Bourus	90

Chapter 6
Harvey's 1593 '*To Be* and *Not To Be*'   109
The Authorship and Date of the First Quarto of Hamlet
Dennis McCarthy

Chapter 7
'To Be, or Not To Be'   126
Hamlet *Q1, Q2 and Montaigne*
Saul Frampton

Chapter 8
Shakespeare, Virgil and the First *Hamlet*   141
John. V. Nance

Chapter 9
Unique Lines and the Ambient Heart of Q1 *Hamlet*   162
Laurie Johnson

Chapter 10
'Brief Let Me Be'   180
Telescoped Action and Characters in Q1 and Q2 Hamlet
Tommaso Continisio

Chapter 11
Q1 Hamlet   192
The Sequence of Creation and Implications for the 'Allowed Booke'
Charles Adams Kelly and Dayna Leigh Plehn

Chapter 12
What Doesn't Happen in *Hamlet*   211
Rory Loughnane

Afterword   234
Q1 *Hamlet*
Graham Holderness and Bryan Loughrey

Index   247

List of Figures

Figure 1.	Set for *Hamlet*, UNCW Department of Theatre, 2015 (note galleries on sides). Hamlet (Luke Robbins) and Laertes (Sean Owens). Courtesy Photo/2015 © University North Carolina Wilmington.	38
Figure 2.	Hamlet (Luke Robbins) and the Ghost (Kaleb Edward Edley), UNCW Department of Theatre, 2015. Courtesy Photo/2015 © University North Carolina Wilmington.	39
Figure 3.	Entrance of the court, UNCW Department of Theatre, 2015. Photographs by Belinda Keller for the University of North Carolina Wilmington. Courtesy Photo/2015 © University North Carolina Wilmington.	41
Figure 4.	Luke Robbins as Hamlet, UNCW Department of Theatre, 2015. Courtesy Photo/2015 © University North Carolina Wilmington.	42
Figure 5.	Hamlet (Luke Robbins) considering killing Claudius (Phil Antonino). Courtesy Photo/2015 © University North Carolina Wilmington.	50
Figure 6.	A formal stemma for Q1 *Hamlet*. Figure created by Madeleine Bruster, used with permission.	85

Figure 7. Hamlet from Saxo's Danish History to known texts of the play, through the extant texts. Figure by Charles Adams Kelly and Dayna Leigh Plehn-Peavyhouse.   197

Figure 8. The nature of the text of Q1 vs. Q2. Degrees of Q1 vs. Q2 concordance and passages unique to the text of Q1. Figure by Charles Adams Kelly and Dayna Leigh Plehn-Peavyhouse.   206

Introduction

Is Q1 *Hamlet* the First *Hamlet*?

Terri Bourus

Many of the questions that we ask about Shakespeare's *Hamlet* depend on what we mean by 'first'. In a book published in 1589, Thomas Nashe refers to a play about 'Hamlet'.[1] Earlier texts by Saxo Grammaticus and François Belleforest told the tragic story of a medieval Danish prince named 'Amlethus', 'Amleth' or 'Amleto', but Nashe is the first known printed occurrence of the Anglicized name 'Hamlet'. Nashe's 'Hamlet' is therefore, in one sense, the first *printed* 'Hamlet'. But at the same time Nashe's text clearly demonstrates that an English play about 'Hamlet' was already circulating and was familiar to Nashe's readers. Did Shakespeare write the early play that Nashe was mocking? Whoever wrote it, was that play being performed in the late 1580s printed at some later date? Is it the same play that was performed by the newly formed Lord Chamberlain's Men in 1594 at the theatre in Newington Butts?[2] Is it the same play that Thomas Lodge assumed would be familiar to his readers in 1596, a play about 'Hamlet', 'revenge' and a 'ghost' being performed

Notes for this section begin on page 5.

at the 'Theator' (the venue normally used by the Chamberlain's Men between 1594 and 1598)?³ Or were the performances in 1594 and/ or 1596 based on a revised version of the 1580s play? If so, who wrote the revision? Does any aspect of the German play *Tragoedia der Bestrafte Brudermord oder Prinz Hamlet aus Dännnemark* (first printed in German in 1781 from a manuscript dated 1710, and first translated into English in 1865) derive from performances by English actors, touring in Germany, of the English play of the 1580s, or from the performances in the mid-1590s?⁴

The answers to all those questions depend on our interpretation of another 'first'. The first known printed edition of *Hamlet* was published in 1603. The title page of the 1603 *Tragicall Historie of Hamlet Prince of Denmarke* explicitly attributes the play to 'William Shake-speare' and claims that it was performed by the company of actors to which Shakespeare belonged. That edition is often called 'Q1', shorthand for 'first quarto' (referring to the bibliographical format most often used for early editions of plays, a quarto). It was followed by an expanded second edition, also a quarto, also attributed to 'William Shakespeare' ('Q2'). After Shakespeare's death, another distinct version of the play was included in the big, expensive, hardbound 1623 'folio' collection of thirty-six of Shakespeare's *Comedies, Histories, and Tragedies* ('F', 'F1' or 'the Folio'). Q1 is the rarest of these three important early editions of Shakespeare's most famous play; it survives in only two known copies. It has had less influence on critical and theatre history than the other two early versions. In fact, all three early versions have been eclipsed by a fourth version, created by eighteenth-century editors, which combined material from both Q2 and F. That 'conflated' editorial version is the text that almost all readers and performers think about when they think about *Hamlet*. In the overwhelming majority of editions of Shakespeare from the last three centuries, that omnibus, conflated edition of the tragedy, the *last* version to appear in any surviving printed or manuscript text, is assumed to be the *first Hamlet*. As a result, the three editions printed between 1603 and 1623 are all dismissed on the assumption that, in different ways and to different degrees, each is a defective derivative from Shakespeare's hypothetical first manuscript of the play.

The foundations of modern Shakespeare scholarship were established before editors and critics were even aware of the existence of Q1. In 1823, a defective copy of the first edition was discovered, and a reprint of that version was published in 1825, introducing it to a wider circle of scholars and fans. Since 1992, Q1's version of the play has been made available in many different formats and publications: free online digital facsimiles and transcripts, inexpensive paperbacks, scholarly editions with textual notes and dense introductions, a paperback anthology of revenge plays, and textbooks designed for college students. Early in 2015, Zachary Lesser wrote a groundbreaking, award-winning history of the effect – on criticism, scholarship and performance – of the rediscovery of Q1 in 1823.[5] Three months earlier, I had published a very different book, not on the nineteenth- and twentieth-century reception of Q1 but on the circumstances surrounding its creation.[6] These two books were conceived and written independently of each other; they address different issues in different styles; they have tended to appeal to different readers. But they both challenged the orthodox assumption, which had dominated Shakespeare scholarship for a century, that Q1 could simply be ignored.

What the editions and monographs of the last thirty years have done, collectively, is to begin to canonize Q1 *Hamlet*. No one can claim that there is now a universal consensus about what Q1 is, or what it means, or how it came to be. In fact, the canonicity of works of art is usually accompanied by intense disagreements about how to interpret them. For most of the twentieth century, Shakespearians who agreed about nothing else agreed that they didn't need to worry much about the first edition of Shakespeare's most famous play. Q1 *Hamlet* is now becoming canonical because of an increasing recognition that it is *worth arguing about*. Rather than asking, 'What's the matter with Q1 *Hamlet*?', this book attempts to answer a much more interesting question: 'Why does Q1 *Hamlet* matter?'

Q1 obviously matters to our understanding of *Hamlet*, but what we make of it also shapes our understanding of the trajectory of Shakespeare's career and of early modern theatre history more generally. Even before Q1 was rediscovered, Edmond Malone had decided that Nashe and Lodge were referring to a lost play by Thomas Kyd.[7] According to this hypothesis, the 'first Hamlet' therefore had nothing to do with Shakespeare, except insofar as the lost play by Kyd might have influenced the surviving play that Shakespeare wrote more than a decade later. Kyd was first; Shakespeare was second. Recent scholarship has demonstrated how many plays performed before 1642 have perished, and the *Hamlet* play of the 1580s might be one of them.[8] We cannot rule out that possibility. But we also should not rule out, a priori, the possibility that Q1 is Shakespeare's first surviving version of his most famous play.

The thirteen chapters in this book all demonstrate, from different angles and in different voices, what happens when critics, performers, scholars and editors decide *not* to ignore the first edition of *Hamlet*. The table of contents arranges these chapters in order to juxtapose different approaches to similar problems. The first three chapters (Taylor, Marino, Wagoner) all draw on personal experiences of Q1 in performance; the next two (Bruster, Bourus) focus on the production of the 1603 quarto from the perspective of book history; the next three (McCarthy, Frampton, Nance) situate Q1 in early networks of reading and reaction; and the three that follow (Johnson, Continisio, Kelly and Plehn) all consider patterns of verbal variation between Q1, Q2 and F. The next chapter (Loughnane) also focuses on an analysis of verbal variants, but transforms the question of what happens in Q1 to the question of what does not happen in *Hamlet*. Finally, the afterword (Holderness and Loughrey) returns us to 1992, when the *Shakespearian Originals* edition of Q1 provoked an angry backlash that exposed the theoretical assumptions and emotional investments behind twentieth-century editorial orthodoxy.

But the contents could have been arranged in other ways, and I suspect that the chapters will be read, in print and online, by different readers in different combinations. Anyone fascinated by Shakespeare's dramaturgy might go first to Marino's illustrated description of the production he directed, but they will also be interested in Loughnane's analytical history of the whole genre of dumb shows, in Wagoner's exploration of interruptions in the structuring of dialogue, in the new kind of hybrid performance text that Kelly and Plehn propose and in the examination by Holderness and Loughrey of early modern collective creativity and the complex relationship between texts and theatres. Both Taylor and Marino analyse Scene 14 at length; like Holderness and Loughrey, Nance engages deeply with postmodernist theory; Taylor, Wagoner and Bourus all consider Q1 as a particularly gendered problem. Readers who like charts, tables and numbers may skip from Taylor to Bruster to Kelly and Plehn. Interested in Shakespeare's relationships with classical writers? You can find in Q1 links to Seneca (Taylor) and Virgil (Nance). Interested in Shakespeare's relationships with his contemporaries? You'll discover that Q1 connects *Hamlet* to Nashe,

Harvey and Jonson (McCarthy), to Kyd and Lodge (Taylor), to Florio (Frampton) and to Drayton (Bourus) – but not to Marlowe (Nance). Those chapters combine with Kelly and Plehn's statistical analysis of variants to challenge traditional assumptions about Shakespeare's artistic development from the early 1580s to the accession of James I. Some chapters (Bruster, Bourus, Kelly and Plehn) specifically address technical issues of textual transmission; but more fundamentally, all the chapters show that the traditional invocation of 'bad quartos' is an impediment to thought: it is an obfuscation, rather than an instrument of analysis. *Hamlet* as a play and a character is famous for the way that it makes the act of thinking dramatic. And Q1 *Hamlet*, if we actually read or perform it rather than gesturing at it dismissively, *makes us think*.

Attention must be paid to such a first.[9]

Terri Bourus is Professor of English and Professor of Theatre at Florida State University, where she teaches English and Irish drama in performance and on the page. She is one of the General Editors of the *New Oxford Shakespeare Complete Works* (2016–17) and the *Complete Alternative Versions* (forthcoming), in print and online. Her monograph, *Young Shakespeare's Young Hamlet* (2014), delves into the textual and staging quandaries of the first quarto of *Hamlet*. She has written essays on stage directions, the performance of religious conversion, Shakespeare and Fletcher's *Cardenio*, the role of Alice in *Arden of Faversham*, and Middleton's female roles. Bourus is an Equity actor, and has directed two very different productions of *Hamlet*, both based on Q1.

Notes

1. Thomas Nashe, 'To the Gentlemen Students of Both Universities', in Robertus Greene, *Menaphon* (1589), sig. **3r–3v.
2. Dulwich MS VII, fol. 9; transcribed in *Henslowe's Diary*, ed. R. A. Foakes and R. T. Rickert, 2nd edn (Cambridge: Cambridge University Press, 2002), 21–22.
3. Thomas Lodge, *Wits Miserie* (1596), sig. h4v.
4. See *Fratricide Punished (Der bestrafe Brudermord)*, trans. H. Howard Furness, rev. Geoffrey Bullough, in Geoffrey Bullough (ed.), *Narrative and Dramatic Sources of Shakespeare*, vol. vii (London: Routledge and Kegan Paul, 1973), 128–58.
5. Zachary Lesser, *Hamlet after Q1: An Uncanny History of the Shakespearean Text* (Philadelphia, PA: University of Pennsylvania Press, 2015).

6. Terri Bourus, *Young Shakespeare's Young Hamlet: Print, Piracy, and Performance* (New York: Palgrave Macmillan, 2014).
7. Edmond Malone, *The Life of William Shakspeare*, ed. James Boswell (1821), 295–96, 369–73. For a critique of Malone's foundational assumptions, see Bourus, *Young Hamlet*, 137–66.
8. See the Lost Plays Database, and in particular its 2012 entry for *Hamlet*: https://lostplays.folger.edu/Hamlet (retrieved 19 January 2022).
9. Attention should also be paid to Aaron Rodriquez, a doctoral candidate in English at Florida State University, who compiled the Index for this book.

Chapter 1
Shakespeare's Early Gothic *Hamlet*

Gary Taylor

In the beginning was the Ghost.

In every text of Shakespeare's *Tragedy of Hamlet, Prince of Denmark* we hear about, and see, the Ghost of Hamlet before we hear about, or see, Prince Hamlet.

The first known quotation from a play about Hamlet quotes the Ghost, and only the Ghost. Twenty-three seventeenth-century allusions to the play mention the Ghost.[1] Theatrical tradition claims that 'the top of [Shakespeare's] Performance was the Ghost in his own *Hamlet*'.[2] Shakespeare played the Ghost better than any other role.

Our assumptions about the literary, theatrical and textual history of *Hamlet* are quotations from the ghost of the eighteenth-century scholar Edmond Malone, telling us a story about a ghost play, an allegedly lost 'Ur-Hamlet' written in the 1580s.

The Ghost is male, Hamlet is male, the first Elizabethan writers to mention Hamlet are male. Shakespeare is male, Malone is male, Malone's ghost play was allegedly written by the English male

Notes for this section begin on page 31.

playwright Thomas Kyd, inspired by the Roman male playwright Seneca. Saxo Grammaticus (who Latinised the medieval Scandinavian myth) and François Belleforest (who translated that story into French) were male. Contemplating *Hamlet*, we seem to be trapped in a haunted men's club, or a haunted all-male English grammar school, or a haunted all-male university, like Wittenberg – or like 'the Universities of Cambridge and Oxford', where Shakespeare's *Hamlet* was performed in Shakespeare's lifetime, according to the title page of the first edition.

But the ghost does not appear in the stories told by Saxo or Belleforest, and the ghost in the Elizabethan *Hamlet* fundamentally differs from all the ghosts dramatised by Seneca or Kyd. If you want to understand any of *Hamlet*'s ghosts, you would be better off paying attention to the words of six women: Belsey, Bourus, Gertred, Kristeva, Montagu and Radcliffe.

Women's ghosts

The most important source of Shakespeare's ghost, Catherine Belsey tells us, is not Seneca, not a writer, and almost certainly not a man. *Hamlet*'s first scene dramatises 'a dark winter night', Belsey reminds us, where 'three seated figures are absorbed by a ghost story', a story interrupted by the arrival of an actual ghost. That Ghost's description of his torments owes something to Seneca and to medieval depictions of purgatory, but 'the ghost lore and the storytelling skills that make the apparition in *Hamlet* chilling grow out of the conventions of popular narrative', which Shakespeare would have learned from 'the old wives' tales and fireside stories of his Warwickshire childhood'.[3] In *Macbeth*, Shakespeare acknowledges such sources: Banquo's ghost is compared to something out of 'A woman's story at a winter's fire, / Authorized by her grandam' (*Macbeth* 3.4.63–64). Hamlet's ghost rises from the same matriarchal font. More generally, Belsey argues that what most distinguishes Shakespeare from his contemporaries is his incorporation and transformation of the fundamentally oral, fundamentally rural and popular, tradition of fireside tales.[4]

In another essay, published in 2014, Belsey more explicitly and systematically contrasts Shakespeare's populist Ghost in *Hamlet* to Kyd's elite Ghost of Andrea in *The Spanish Tragedy*. Andrea 'does not interact with the participants in the plot' and 'he is not uncanny';

the role of the former King of Denmark 'is unlike Andrea's in almost every way'. In particular, Kyd's Andrea and other Elizabethan ghosts 'may have frightened playgoers but, even when they participate in the action of the play, there is little evidence that they had the same effect on the fictional characters they haunted'.[5] The Ghost in *Hamlet* represents not only a departure from the precedent created by Kyd, but an innovation in early modern drama. No stage ghost before Shakespeare resembles the 'thing' that walks the battlements of Elsinore.

Belsey sustains this argument across three different publications, not because she particularly cares about nailing down every possible 'source' for Shakespeare's plays, but because she is challenging a long patriarchal scholarly tradition that emphasises Shakespeare's connections to classical literature and the Protestant Reformation. Connecting Shakespeare to Seneca situates him as a 'Renaissance' superman, capable of leaping across centuries with a single bound, and worthy of comparison to the intellectual and aesthetic giants of the Roman Empire. Connecting Shakespeare to the Reformation endows him with the intellectual seriousness of theology, the moral authority of Christianity, and the imperial nationalism of an England independent of Rome or any other European obligations. Both connections link Shakespeare to the educated male elite that dominated the editing and interpretation of his work from the early eighteenth century to the end of the twentieth.

Belsey does not deny that Shakespeare owes something to Seneca. But she does make that Senecan connection secondary, and dissociates it from the most interesting features of King Hamlet's Ghost. As A.J. Boyle observes, Seneca gave Renaissance dramatists, in and out of England, models for 'vivid and powerful declamatory verse, psychological insight, highly effective staging, an intellectually demanding verbal and conceptual framework, and a precocious preoccupation with theatricality and theatricalization'.[6] Seneca's plays do contain ghosts, which did influence the drama of the European Renaissance, beginning with Gregorio Correr's neo-Latin *Procne* in the 1420s.[7] But only two of Seneca's ghosts talk, and neither directly engages with the play's 'living' characters.

All the features of the Ghost that Belsey describes occur in all three early versions of the play, and she does not commit herself to a particular textual hypothesis about the origins of Q1 *Hamlet*. Nevertheless, she makes a number of standard assumptions about

Shakespeare's play. 'Hamlet must have been written between 1599 and 1601', she states, without feeling the need to cite any evidence for this traditional date, which goes back to Malone; likewise, she suggests that Shakespeare's *Hamlet* and Marston's play *Antonio's Revenge* may well draw on 'a common source, probably Kyd's lost *Hamlet*' – thus assuming, like most scholars since Malone, that Shakespeare was influenced by a lost play about *Hamlet*, written in the late 1580s by Thomas Kyd.[8]

Belsey accepted those assumptions in 2014, but they were not important to her argument, and they were systematically demolished that same year. Terri Bourus, re-examining the long scholarly history of claims about the chronology of Shakespeare's works, including all early references to 'Hamlet' in the theatre, demonstrated that 'Malone's insistence that the 1589 *Hamlet* cannot have been written by Shakespeare is unwarranted'.[9] She also argued that Q1 *Hamlet* could be the tragedy about Hamlet that Thomas Nashe mocked in 1589, that the Chamberlain's Men performed in 1594 and 1596, that Thomas Lodge mocked in 1596, that was performed in the City of London and the universities of Oxford and Cambridge in the late 1580s or early 1590s.

In 2014, Belsey had not read Bourus, and Bourus had not read Belsey. But their separate claims strengthen each other. Belsey's evidence that the Ghost reflects provincial folk tales and Shakespeare's own 'Warwickshire childhood' reinforces the evidence, marshalled by Bourus, that links Q1 *Hamlet* to events in Warwickshire between 1579 and 1585 (and to texts, political events and theatrical fashions of the 1570s and 1580s). Shakespeare's best performance as an actor was a role inspired by stories that laid the first foundations of his imagination. Likewise, if Shakespeare wrote his first *Hamlet* in late 1588 or early 1589 (as Bourus argues), then 'Shakespeare's own first sad tale of and for winter' (as Belsey calls *Hamlet*) is a defining 'first', an authorial signature, from the outset of his career.[10]

That authorial signature, in turn, explains the caustic tone of early references to Hamlet in the theatre. Bourus brilliantly and originally analyses Thomas Lodge's 1596 pamphlet, which alludes to 'the Vizard of the ghost which cried so miserably at the Theater like an oyster wife, *Hamlet, revenge*'.[11] But if Bourus had read Belsey, she might also have recognised the particular resonance of Lodge's otherwise superfluous 'oyster wife'. Lodge associates the Ghost in *Hamlet* with a source, and a stereotype, that is female, oral and uneducated – just like the 'old wives' who were associated with the telling of ghost stories. University-educated critics like Lodge (in 1596) and Thomas Nashe (in 1589) mocked the early *Hamlet* play precisely because it did not uphold the elite male values of their own classical education. But Lodge specifically tells us that, in the original *Hamlet* performed at the Theatre, the Ghost spoke directly to Hamlet. It thus engaged directly with the play's living characters – as Seneca's ghosts do not, as Kyd's ghost does not, but as the ghosts of traditional stories did. That early Hamlet ghost was typical not only of Shakespeare's other ghosts, but of his many portrayals of other 'ontological outliers': weïrd sisters, fairies, a puck like Robin Goodfellow, a spirit like Ariel, a 'monster' like Caliban.[12] These hybrid beings all draw upon medieval storytelling, and all initiate interaction and dialogue with humans. Lodge was mocking a characteristically Shakespearian ghost.

The mother's scene

Like Belsey, Bourus challenged the patriarchal scholarly tradition that has governed interpretation of *Hamlet*; but unlike Belsey, Bourus was primarily interested in textual and theatrical issues. *Young Shakespeare's Young Hamlet* seems to me the single most important book in Shakespearean textual criticism since *The Division of the Kingdoms*, published thirty years earlier – and it has provoked similarly hostile reactions from self-appointed guardians of Shakespeare's reputation.[13] But Bourus, in reframing the textual issues, also reinterprets the role of Hamlet's mother, Gertred, the Queen of Denmark. The Q1 version of that role significantly differs from the familiar Queen of the second quarto, of the Folio, and of the conflated editorial text created by combining them. Bourus has played, directed and written about Q1's Gertred. While Belsey upends traditional interpretation by calling attention to the rural 'old wives' and 'grandams' who told ghost stories on winter evenings, Bourus upends it by calling attention to the young wife Gertred, mother to a teenage prince but still young enough, and sexual enough, to hold out the possibility of giving birth to another son, another heir, who could displace Hamlet and put his uncle's offspring on the throne.[14]

This difference between Q1's Gertred and the corresponding character in the expanded canonical *Hamlet* is, unsurprisingly, connected to differences in the Ghost. After all, Gertred and the

Ghost were married. In Q1, their son Hamlet reacts to the Ghost's revelations by exclaiming, 'Yes, yes, by heaven, a damned pernicious villain' (Sc. 5.78) – presumably a reference to his uncle. But in the canonical text he instead exclaims, 'Yes, yes, by heaven! O most pernicious woman!' (1.5.104–105) – undoubtedly a reference to his mother.[15] The canonical texts emphasise the Queen's guilt; Q1 does not. It can hardly be a coincidence that Q1 alone contains two lines by Gertred that explicitly and solemnly assert her innocence: 'But, as I have a soul, I swear by heaven / I never knew of this most horrid murder' (11.85–86). She speaks these lines shortly after the Ghost's last appearance in the play, where Q1 alone specifies that he enters '*in his night-gown*' (11.57), a costume change that emphasises his relationship to his wife, rather than the military career foregrounded by all his previous appearances in armour.

Overall, Q1 is much shorter than the other texts, but – against the grain of its own brevity – it gives Gertred an additional scene. If Q1 contained an additional scene for Hamlet, do you think that scene would have been ignored by editors and critics? But an extra scene for a woman has been of little interest to the haunted men's club of *Hamlet* interpreters. What editors label Scene 14 in Q1 is a sequence of continuous writing for which there is no equivalent in our canonical texts of *Hamlet*. That scene makes it absolutely clear that the Gertred of Q1 actively conspires with Horatio and Hamlet against her second husband, Hamlet's uncle, the new 'King' of Denmark: she accuses him of 'treason' and 'villainy', and calls his mind 'murderous'. Her allegiances are not nearly so transparent in later texts of the play. Q1's unique Scene 14 – like Q1's unique variants in Sc. 5 and Sc. 11 – creates a much more sympathetic mother, with a much closer relationship to her son.

How are we to account for this scene? To answer that question, we have to shift gears, stylistically and methodologically. Before returning to the larger interpretive issues involving the Ghost, we must detour into an examination of the editorial and bibliographical assumptions that have justified traditional dismissals not only of this scene but of the entire text of Q1 *Hamlet*. (Anyone who is more afraid of data than of ghosts may prefer to skip to the next section.)

The theory of memorial reconstruction, which dominated twentieth-century Shakespearian textual criticism and editing, asserts that a text like Q1 reflects the imperfect memory of an actor, who played a small part in early performances of the play. If that hypothesis is true, then Q1 has been corrupted by an imperfect memory, and where it differs from the other early texts it therefore cannot be an accurate reflection of the language of the playwright.[16] The alternative theory of shorthand, or of rapid note-taking by members of the audience, posits that one or more spectators, attending one or more performances, quickly wrote down words as they were being spoken, and then after the performance went back over those notes in an attempt to recreate a text that they had never read. Consequently, again, when Q1 differs from the other early texts it cannot be an accurate reflection of the language of the playwright.[17] Both these theories, both these scenarios, assert – and depend upon the assertion – that the verbal texture of Q1 is not Shakespearian, whenever it departs from the other early texts. Likewise, the revisionist theories of Lukas Erne and Andrew Gurr posit that Q1 represents what was performed, but not what Shakespeare himself wrote: Shakespeare's original text was extensively modified by the actors, in order to radically abridge and popularise it. Thus, according to Erne and Gurr, whenever Q1 differs from the other early texts, it reflects the style of one or more other members of the Chamberlain's Men, rather than of Shakespeare himself.[18] Whatever the historical or logical merits of these different claims, what they all have in common is a shared conviction that, wherever Q1 differs from the other early editions, its detailed verbal texture is the product of writing by someone other than Shakespeare.

Scene 14 departs from all other texts of *Hamlet*, and it is a large enough sample to be tested by twenty-first-century micro-attribution techniques. Such tests tabulate strings of consecutive words, called 'n-grams'; sequences of two words (bigrams), three words (trigrams), or four words (quadgrams) seem to be the most reliable. The tests identify rare phrases, testing a sample passage against large databases of early modern plays and/or even larger digital databases of early modern printed texts of all kinds. Such tests have successfully identified sample passages by Dekker, Fletcher, Greene, Heywood, Jonson, Kyd, Marlowe, Middleton, Nashe, Peele, William Rowley, Shakespeare, Theobald, Webster and Wilkins.[19] Such methods have also successfully distinguished Shakespeare from writers consciously trying to imitate him. 'Identity is systemic and cellular; imitation is selective and semiotic.'[20] The things that stand out to us, in reading or listening to an author's work, are conspicuous features of style, easiest to remember and to imitate; they are features that the

Renaissance humanist classroom taught sixteenth-century English schoolboys to spot and to copy. But automated searches of very large databases pay no attention to whether a phrase is memorable or extraordinary. Instead, computers can systematically search for word sequences of two to four words. These are inconspicuous linguistic idiosyncrasies that our brains are not capable of registering, or computing, at such scales. If we paid attention to such patterns, we could not possibly understand what we are reading or hearing. Moreover, before the creation of very large databases, no imitator could have known whether such linguistic fragments were unique across hundreds of plays or thousands of printed books. Early modern imitators could not possibly identify, or duplicate, such personal verbal idiosyncrasies.

Consequently, such tests should be able to tell us whether Scene 14 of Q1 *Hamlet* was written by Shakespeare, or by someone ineptly trying to imitate Shakespeare.

In its 271 consecutive words, there are 2,419 possible word sequences of two, three or four consecutive words. These 2,419 possible word sequences were checked against 346 works in the *Literature Online* database of drama first performed between the years 1564 and 1614.[21] I chose that fifty-year period (twenty-five years either side of 1589) because we need a range that does not unduly favour the 1600 or 1601 date (traditionally assigned to Shakespeare's canonical *Hamlet*), or the 1602 or early 1603 date (of the writing down by an actor or a note-taker of a bad imitation of a performance of Shakespeare's play), or the 1589 or 1588 date (when the original *Hamlet* play, mentioned by Nashe, was probably written). Bourus thinks the original *Hamlet* play was written by Shakespeare, and is preserved in Q1; most scholars think that the early *Hamlet* was written by someone else, and is entirely lost. In order to treat all these possibilities equally, we don't want to limit ourselves to plays from the early seventeenth century, or to plays from the 1580s. Moreover, the fifty-year range includes material that Shakespeare had not yet written in 1589, or 1600, or 1603; such material could not possibly have been anticipated by an actor or a note-taker in the last years of Elizabeth I's reign.

This test generates an Excel document with 2,419 rows (representing possible sequences of two, three or four consecutive words) and 346 columns (representing surviving plays in the *Literature Online* database for the years 1564–1614). Such an Excel document contains 836,974 data points: each data point represents the appearance of one of the lexical sequences found in the 271 words of this scene with one of the plays in the *Literature Online* database. Although 271 words may not seem to be a very large sample of text for the purposes of attribution analysis, in fact it contains a massive amount of data, much more than can be found in the tabulations of traditional authorial markers (metrical features, linguistic forms, contractions or oaths) in an entire play. Other studies have shown that the most reliable evidence comes from verbal sequences that appear in only one other dramatic text. The 271 words of this scene contain thirty-three such unique phrasal parallels to dramatic texts that premiered between 1564 and 1614.[22] (Full details of this and the following tests are given in the Appendix.)

> **Shakespeare: 12:** *Two Gentlemen of Verona, Taming of the Shrew, 2 Henry VI* (Shakespeare?), *3 Henry VI* 3.2, 5.1 (two unique parallels, both in Shakespeare scenes), *Richard II* (two unique parallels), *Romeo and Juliet* (Q1), *Much Ado, Julius Caesar, Hamlet* (Q2), *Pericles* Sc. 20 (Shakespeare).
> **Jonson: 3:** *Poetaster, King's Entertainment, Haddington Masque.*
> **Chapman: 2:** *May Day, Bussy D'Ambois.*
> **Heywood: 1:** *If you know not me, you know nobody.*
> **Heywood(?), Dekker (?) or Drayton (?):** *Edward IV.*[23]
> **Dekker: 1:** *Old Fortunatus.*
> **Playwrights with one parallel:** Thomas Hughes, Greene, Lodge, Samuel Rowley, Chettle-or-Munday, Beaumont-or-Fletcher, Middleton, Lording Barry.
> **Anonymous plays with one parallel:** *Mucedorus, Caesar and Pompey, Stuckley, London Prodigal.*

Thomas Kyd, the alleged author of the 1589 'Ur-Hamlet', has no parallels at all, in this test or the additional tests I describe below. We cannot explain Scene 14 by supposing (as I once did) that an actor or other reporter was remembering Kyd's lost play about Hamlet.[24] Shakespeare has four times as many unique parallels as any other single playwright. He wrote the only dramatic texts with more than one unique parallel (*3 Henry VI* and *Richard II*). All these parallels come from the thirty-eight most canonical Shakespeare plays (the thirty-six collected in the 1623 First Folio, plus the collaborative *Pericles* and *Two Noble Kinsmen*). Those thirty-eight plays constitute only 11% of the works included in the dramatic database used for this study; but that 11% contains 35% of all the unique dramatic parallels. Moreover, because the test records only parallels unique to a single *text*, it does not count parallels unique to a single *author*; as it happens, only one n-gram in Scene 14 is unique to two or more dramatic texts by a single playwright (Shakespeare's *Antony and Cleopatra* and *The Winter's Tale*). And the test does not register that some unique n-grams are, because of their context, closer to this scene than others. Contextually, the strongest of these thirty-four unique parallels comes from *3 Henry VI*, in a scene (3.2) attributed to Shakespeare even by those who believe that the play was written in collaboration. The Queen in Q1 *Hamlet* says, '*I take my leave, / With thousand* mother's blessings to my son'; the soon-to-be Queen in *3 Henry VI*, who also is primarily interested in protecting her children, says, '*I take my leave with* many *thousand* thanks' (my italics).[25]

Either the author of this scene was Shakespeare, or he was someone with an extraordinary knowledge of the idiosyncratic verbal minutiae of Shakespeare plays. We can imagine such a Shakespeare-obsessed actor or reporter, because in subsequent centuries there have been such obsessives. But we don't know of any in Shakespeare's own lifetime. Moreover, seven of the unique Shakespeare links to this scene were not in print in 1603, when Q1 was published. So the mythical reporter or note-taker must be remembering most of these passages from having heard them performed. But the one play that the alleged reporter might be expected to know best is the canonical text of *Hamlet*, preserved in the long second quarto, printed a year or two *later*, but which all traditional scholarship assumes was written and performed *before* the printing of Q1. So why is there only one unique link, here, to Q2 *Hamlet* (one of the longest dramatic texts in the period)? And why, more generally, are so few of the parallels from the period closest in date to the alleged composition of the unauthorised Q1 text? *Much Ado* and *Julius Caesar* are the closest, chronologically, to the traditional date of *Hamlet*, and to the traditional date of the writing down of the allegedly reported, allegedly remembered, or allegedly shorthanded manuscript behind Q1. Why are there so few parallels from the years 1596 to 1605? The traditional date of *Hamlet* sits right in the middle of that decade, but that decade produces only two unique parallels to other Shakespeare plays. By contrast, the eight years from 1588 to 1595, inclusive, generate eight unique Shakespeare parallels. Two plays from that early period, *3 Henry VI* and *Richard II*, each contain two parallels, more than any other plays from the whole fifty-year period; those two early plays together contain four unique parallels, more than the entire canon of any other playwright. This scene is much more closely linked to the beginning of Shakespeare's career than to the middle.

In this first test, I limited myself to dramatic texts, because theories about bad quartos have always assumed that the compilers of those unauthorised texts were people particularly obsessed with plays: either they were actors, or they were regular playgoers who knew enough about the London theatre to be able to pick out the plays that would be most attractive to booksellers and playbook-buyers. But the theory of note-takers in the audience does not require us to believe that the compilers were playwrights, or even regular playgoers; they might theoretically have been hired by a publisher to produce an illicit text of a play that he had heard would be vendible.

In order to avoid any such bias, I tested the same 271 words against the database of *Early English Books Online-Text Creation Partnership* (*EEBO-TCP*), again limiting the search to the years 1564 to 1614. But whereas my test of *Literature Online* is based on the presumed date of composition and performance of the plays, my test of *EEBO-TCP* instead is based on the years when a text was *printed*. Thus, the *EEBO-TCP* test eliminates from consideration all the Shakespeare texts first published after Shakespeare's death. This second test thus automatically removes five of the twelve unique Shakespeare parallels found in the first test, because those parallels came from texts first published in 1623 (*Two Gentlemen of Verona, Taming of the Shrew, 2 Henry VI, 3 Henry VI, Julius Caesar*). This second test is, if anything, biased *against* Shakespeare, because it removes from consideration half his dramatic canon (and six of his plays from 1588 to 1595). It also greatly increases the number of texts. Although there were only 346 dramatic texts for comparison in the *Literature Online* database, there are 15,109 in the same half-century of the *EEBO-TCP* database.

Again, 271 consecutive words produce 2,419 potential word sequences for testing; but now those 2,419 sequences are all checked against 15,109 texts, thereby producing 36,548,671 data points. The larger the database, the more difficult it is to generate a unique parallel. Nevertheless, this passage contains thirty-seven unique parallels to *EEBO-TCP* texts of 1564–1614. That's close to one unique parallel for every million data points; by contrast, in the test of dramatic texts there was about one unique parallel for every twenty-five thousand data points. Comparing this scene to these fifteen thousand books, Shakespeare still has the most unique parallels. He has more than twice as many parallels as any other writer, even though his canon has, by this test, been cut in half. The first quarto text of his *Richard II* is the only one of the fifteen thousand books to contain more than one unique parallel. Indeed, only three writers certainly have, in their entire canons, unique links to more than one text.[26]

> **Shakespeare: 5:** *Love's Labour's Lost, Richard II* (two), *Much Ado, Hamlet* (Q2).
> **Greene: 2:** *Friar Bacon and Friar Bungay, A disputation between a hee coney catcher and a she-coney catcher.*
> **Edward Grimeston: 2:** *History of France, History of the Netherlands.*

Greene's canon, in this database, has more individual titles and contains more words than Shakespeare's; Grimeston has fewer titles, but most of his works (including both the translated histories with unique links) contain far more words than any Shakespeare text. Moreover, three of the other works with unique parallels come from books that Shakespeare almost certainly read. Grafton's *Chronicle* (1569) is apparently a source for the *Henry VI* plays, and it contains a unique parallel to this scene in its account of Cnut (King of England, Denmark and Norway). Most scholars also believe that Shakespeare read both Painter's *Palace of Pleasure* (1566) and Bandello's *Certain Tragical Discourses* (1567).[27]

Finally, we can combine the tests from these two databases, and thereby produce a record of unique parallels in dramatic texts that do not occur in other texts printed during the same half-century. Again, there are 2,419 possible sequences of two, three or four words in this scene; if we combine the total number of *EEBO-TCP* texts printed between 1564 and 1614 with the total number of plays performed between 1564 and 1614 (but *not* printed in those decades), we have a total of 15,246 texts that can be checked for those sequences. That gives us a total of 36,880,074 data points. Only twelve phrases in the scene remain unique, measured against this combined database; that works out to less than one unique parallel in every three million data points. Shakespeare is the only writer who certainly has more than one parallel; *Richard II* remains the only single text with two.

> **Shakespeare: 6:** *Two Gentlemen, 3 Henry VI* (Shakespeare), *Richard II* (two), *Much Ado, Hamlet* (Q2).
> **Dekker: 1:** *Old Fortunatus.*
> **Heywood(?), Dekker (?) or Drayton (?): 1:** *Edward IV.*
> **Heywood: 1:** *If you know not me, you know nobody.*

Greene: 1: *Friar Bacon and Friar Bungay.*
Middleton: 1: *Trick to Catch the Old One.*
Chapman: 1: *May Day.*

Shakespeare has as many unique parallels as all other playwrights, and all other dramatic texts, combined.

The only hypothesis that plausibly accounts for all this lexical evidence is the one also independently supported by the documentary evidence of the title page: this additional scene was, like the rest of Q1 *Hamlet*, written 'By William Shakespeare'. It is not an imitation of Shakespeare. It is not a bad transcript of Shakespeare. There is no way somebody other than Shakespeare, working at the beginning of the seventeenth century, could have produced so Shakespearian a text. This is exactly the kind of lopsided result that we get when we test the authorship of passages known to be by particular early modern dramatists: the known author overwhelmingly dominates the results, just as Shakespeare dominates these results.

But no one who reads this scene will believe that Shakespeare wrote it at any time between 1599 and 1602. Verbally and dramatically, it is far less sophisticated than anything Shakespeare composed at the turn of the century. The theories about memorial reconstruction and bad quartos have convinced so many people because they reflect a shared experience. Anyone who brings to their reading of Q1 *Hamlet* a deep, sustained familiarity with the canonical texts of Shakespeare will conclude that it cannot have been written by Shakespeare *in the early seventeenth century* – which is when the experts, since Malone, have all told us that Shakespeare wrote *Hamlet*.

This is true not only of the play as a whole, but of Scene 14 in particular. There is only one way to reconcile the strong lexical evidence for Shakespeare's authorship of this scene with its self-evidently elementary artistry. If Shakespeare wrote it, it must have been written *very* early in his career. He could only have written so primitive a text before he wrote his earliest known tragedy, *Titus Andronicus*. In other words, if Shakespeare wrote Q1 *Hamlet*, he must have written it at about the same time that the so-called 'Ur-Hamlet' was written.

Killing the mother

Sir Stanley Wells was not knighted for contributions to mathematics. For readers sceptical of databases, numbers and empiricist claims about literature, Wells is a reliable, cautious, humanist guide.

In a characteristically compelling critical essay, published in 1997, Wells analyses the integration of violence in Shakespeare's works. Throughout Shakespeare's career as a playwright, he departed from classical precedent by putting acts of violence on stage; this theatrical violence dismayed neoclassical critics, and led Voltaire to describe *Hamlet* as a 'monstrous farce' that was also objectionably 'Gothic'. But Wells argues that, although there is violence in all Shakespeare's tragedies (and many of his other plays), the nature of that violence changes over time. Wells agrees with Ben Jonson's claim that *Titus Andronicus* was written in 1589; this is also the date that the New Oxford Shakespeare assigns to *Titus*. When Shakespeare was writing (most of) *Titus Andronicus*, he had not yet learned to integrate acts of onstage violence into the poetic texture of the work. As an example, Wells cites this passage from the final scene of the first quarto of *Titus*.[28]

> Die, die, Lavinia, and thy shame with thee,
> And with thy shame thy father's sorrow die. [*He kills her*]
> SATURNINUS What hast thou done, unnatural and unkind?
> TITUS Killed her for whom my tears have made me blind.
> I am as woeful as Virginius was,
> And have a thousand times more cause than he
> To do this outrage, and it now is done.
> SATURNINUS What, was she ravished? Tell who did the deed.
> TITUS Wilt please you eat? Will't please your highness feed?
> TAMORA Why hast thou slain thine only daughter thus?
> TITUS Not I; 'twas Chiron and Demetrius.
> They ravished her and cut away her tongue,
> And they, 'twas they, that did her all this wrong.
> SATURNINUS Go, fetch them hither to us presently.
> TITUS [*revealing the heads*]
> Why, there they are, both bakèd in this pie,
> Whereof their mother daintily hath fed,
> Eating the flesh that she herself hath bred.
> 'Tis true, 'tis true, witness my knife's sharp point.
> *He stabs the Empress* [*Tamora*].
> SATURNINUS Die, frantic wretch, for this accursèd deed.
> [*He kills Titus*]
> LUCIUS Can the son's eye behold his father bleed?
> There's meed for meed, death for a deadly deed.
> [*He kills Saturninus*]

Within 171 words of dialogue, four main characters are murdered, on stage, in front of the audience. Three of them die within four lines. Shakespeare eventually learns to dramatise violence, in masterpieces like *Richard II*, *Romeo and Juliet*, *Othello* and *King Lear*. But in *Titus*, it is hard to do anything poetically or philosophically with these four rapid deaths, and they are difficult to stage in a way that modern audiences find convincing.

Wells specifically contrasts these four deaths at the end of *Titus* with the four deaths at the end of *Hamlet*. He celebrates 'the thoroughness of the preparation for the deaths of Gertrude, Laertes, Claudius, and finally Hamlet himself' and 'the steadiness of the pacing by which these deaths are spaced out' over 425 words.[29] But Wells is contrasting *Titus* with the final scene of the *Hamlet* we all know, the expanded canonical version first published in late 1604. By contrast, this is what those four deaths look like in the first edition of *Hamlet* (17.85–111).

> *They catch one another's rapiers and both are wounded.*
> *Leartes falls down, The Queen falls down.*

KING	Look to the Queen.
QUEEN	O the drink, the drink! Hamlet, the drink! [*Dies.*]
HAMLET	Treason, ho! Keepe the gates!
LORDS	How is't, my lord Leartes?
LEARTES	Even as a coxcomb should:
	Foolishly slain with my own weapon. Hamlet,
	Thou hast not in thee half an hour of life –
	The fatal instrument is in thy hand,
	Unbated and invenomed. Thy mother's poisoned.
	That drink was made for thee.
HAMLET	The poisoned instrument within my hand?
	Then venom to thy venom – die damned villain!
	Come, drink – here lies thy union, here!
	The king dies.
LEARTES	O he is justly served.
	Hamlet, before I die, here take my hand
	And, withal, my love. I do forgive thee.
	Leartes dies.
HAMLET	And I thee.
	O I am dead, Horatio, fare thee well.
HORATIO	No, I am more an antique Roman, than a Dane.
	Here is some poison left.
HAMLET	Upon my love I charge thee let it go.
	O fie, Horatio. An if thou shouldst die
	What a scandal wouldst thou leave behind?
	What tongue should tell the story of our deaths
	If not from thee? O my heart sinks, Horatio.

> Mine eyes have lost their sight, my tongue his use.
> Farewell, Horatio. Heaven receive my soul.
> *Ham[let] dies.*

Here, four main characters die in the course of only 189 words of dialogue. (One of the murdered characters is a queen and a mother, whose death is directly related to what she has just swallowed.) Wells does not make this connection between the first quartos of these two tragedies, because he assumed (just as, in the late 1990s, I assumed) that Q1 *Hamlet* was a 'bad quarto'. But if we do not make that assumption, it is hard not to notice how similar the dramaturgy of the final scene of *Titus Andronicus* is to the dramaturgy of Q1 *Hamlet*. As Wells shows, the treatment of violent action in *Titus* is less sophisticated, verbally and theatrically, than the treatment of violence in the *Henry VI* trilogy. The same can be said of Q1 *Hamlet*.

One other detail of *Titus Andronicus*, not noticed by Wells or (apparently) anyone else, also suggests that it was written at about the same time as Q1 *Hamlet*. When Marcus realises that someone has viciously mutilated Lavinia, by cutting off her hands and cutting out her tongue, he says,

> O, had the monster seen those lily hands
> Tremble like aspen leaves upon a lute
> And make the silken strings delight to kiss them,
> He would not then have touched them for his life.
> Or had he heard the heavenly harmony
> Which that sweet tongue hath made,
> He would have dropped his knife . . .
> (Sc.4/2.4.44–50)

Marcus here remembers Lavinia singing in harmony with the lute she was playing. There is no opportunity for her to do so in *Titus*. But this moment would have been more powerful for the original audience if they had heard (and the playwright was reminding them of) the same boy actor, in another play, performing as a young female character, singing while s/he played the lute. The only such character in the Shakespeare canon, or in any play known to have been performed by Shakespeare's acting company, is Ofelia in Q1 *Hamlet*, which specifies that she enters '*playing on a lute, and her hair down, singing*' (Sc.13.14.1). All scholars agree that the canonical, expanded *Hamlet* could not have been written until years after *Titus Andronicus*, so this apparent metatheatrical allusion only works if Q1 *Hamlet* represents the 1589 *Hamlet*.

The similarities between Q1 *Hamlet* and *Titus* extend to their association of northern Europe with military conquest and violent revenge. Both plays end with a northern invasion, led by a son in defence of his father, which overthrows the reigning dynasty: the invaders are Goths in *Titus* (led by the avenging son Lucius) and Norwegians in *Hamlet* (led by the avenging son Fortinbras). But for sixteenth-century Englishmen, Norwegians and Danes were Goths. Early modern maps of the Baltic world identify a number of place names that are probably unfamiliar to twenty-first-century readers of Shakespeare: Gothia, Gotlandia, Mare Gothicum. Those names all reflect standard medieval and Renaissance assumptions about the Goths, which derived from Jordanes' *Getica*, a sixth-century Latin history of the Goths; Jordanes claimed that the Goths originated north of the Baltic Sea, in 'Scanza' (modern Scandinavia).[30] Thus, Robert Fabyan's *Chronicle*, which seems to have influenced Shakespeare's early history plays, recorded that the 'Normans or Danys' are 'descended of the nacyon called the Gothes, which ... nowe ben inhabyted in Dacia, whych in our speche is called Denmarke'.[31] Peter Martyr's *History of Travayle* (1577) likewise situated the Goths who conquered Rome in 'Gothia or Gothlande' alongside the Swedes and Norwegians and other 'people of these North partes of the worlde'.[32] *Batman upon Bartholme* (1582) noted that the original Ostrogthes, who conquered Rome, were 'now under the government of the kings of Denmarke'; he also cites Isidore of Seville's conclusion that 'Danes came of Gothes'.[33] In 1588, *The Mariners Mirror* tells readers that 'The famous Isle of Gotland part of the dominion of the king of Denmarke ... took name of the Gothes, which did once inhabit it'.[34] All these recycled stories about the Goths (called 'Geats' in *Beowulf*, and Gots, Jutes, Gets and Getae in Elizabethan texts) identified them as barbarian warriors who conquered Rome (like the Goths in *Titus Andronicus*) and who also invaded and subjugated England (like the Danes in *Hamlet*).

Of course, this might all be a coincidence. No text of *Hamlet* calls the Danes 'Goths'. But Ben Jonson, in 1614, remembered *Titus* as a play of the second half of the 1580s, no later than 1589, and Thomas Nashe in 1589 alluded to a play about 'Hamlet' (or 'Hamlets') full of 'tragical speeches'. Both the extant *Titus* play and the *Hamlet* narratives in sixteenth-century editions (of Saxo Grammaticus and Belleforest) are 'historical' and 'medieval' in a messy, mythical way; both are tragedies about revenge, dynastic collapse, the second marriage of a northern European widow-queen with adult male offspring from her first marriage, and a great father-warrior whose violent achievements haunt a younger generation. And both plays are stylistically uneven: we can glimpse in both of them the great poet and playwright that Shakespeare would become, but those anticipations of a future Shakespeare are mixed with fossils of the clumsy twenty-something start-up of the 1580s. Just as most scholars of the nineteenth and twentieth century denied Shakespeare's responsibility for Q1 *Hamlet*, so most Shakespeare scholars of the eighteenth and nineteenth centuries denied his responsibility for *Titus*. Malone denied Shakespeare's authorship entirely, relegating the play to an appendix in his landmark 1790 edition. As Stanley Wells writes about another early play (*The Two Gentlemen of Verona*), Shakespearians may be tempted to a 'too easy dismissal' of apprentice work because 'it does not provide the critic with what he wants, and finds elsewhere' in later Shakespeare texts.[35] We judge the ghost of Shakespeare Past by the ghost of Shakespeare Future. *Titus* suffers from comparison with *King Lear*, and Q1 *Hamlet* suffers from comparison with Q2 and the Folio.

The two most prominent eighteenth-century critics who defended Shakespeare's authorship of *Titus Andronicus* were both women, and they defended it by embracing Shakespeare's medieval Gothic credentials. Elizabeth Montagu, who celebrated Shakespeare as 'our Gothic Bard', could not imagine anyone but Shakespeare having written *Titus Andronicus*. In 1794, four years after Malone's edition had denied Shakespeare's authorship, the great Gothic novelist Anne Radcliffe, in *The Mysteries of Udolpho*, quoted *Titus Andronicus* and attributed the quotation to 'Shakespeare'.[36] And both these women also appreciated the Gothic elements of *Hamlet*, derided by Voltaire. The phrase 'our Gothic Bard' appears in Montagu's chapter on Shakespeare's treatment of 'Praeternatural Beings', which she attributes to the influence of 'Gothic manners, and Gothic superstitions' that 'still maintained a traditional authority among the vulgar'; she associates that authority not only with oral tradition, but with women in particular: 'The genius of Shakespear ... adorns *the Beldame*, Tradition, with flowers gathered on classic ground, but still wisely suffering those simples of *her* native soil, to which the established superstition of *her* country has attributed a magic spell, to be predominant'.[37]

Montagu's method and style is very far from the academic, documented prose of Belsey. What stands between them is Julia Kristeva, who in 1980 provided the first sophisticated theoretical analysis of what she called 'powers of horror', which she linked to the 'abjection' of the body, including in particular the dead body.[38] Thomas Nashe and Thomas Lodge, who so contemptuously rejected the original *Hamlet*, were harbingers of the middle-class aesthetic sensibility that would dominate the elite male club of English literary criticism from Jeremy Collier to John Dover Wilson, which dismissed Gothic fiction and horror films as the most disreputable of genres. *Hamlet*, like *Titus Andronicus*, works 'by putting grotesquely horrible images into the cozily familiar world of home': a meat pie, a nap in the garden, a nightgown.[39] In a book focused on Dostoyevsky, Proust, Artaud and Céline, Kristeva laid the foundations for twenty-first-century scholarship that has historicised and theorised Shakespeare in terms of Gothic tropes and the aesthetics of horror.[40] Shakespeare was first dismissed as 'Gothic' by a French male theorist (Voltaire); it seems appropriate that the celebration of him as Gothic should be made possible by a French female theorist.

Across the stylistic and theoretical gap from Enlightenment to postmodernism, Montagu and Belsey both insist upon the essentially female, essentially oral, essentially rural origins of Shakespeare's ghosts. They also insist that this Shakespearian effect differs fundamentally from the treatment of ghosts in most other Elizabethan plays, including those by Thomas Kyd. What the ghost in Kyd's *Spanish Tragedy* has in common with the ghosts in Seneca is that their importance does not depend on their encounters with a human being. They provide a frame. They do not dramatise the experience of a human being encountering a ghost, and being terrified by that encounter. Although I am not an actor, due to a last-minute emergency I was drafted to play the Ghost in Terri Bourus's 2011 production of Q1 *Hamlet*. Because we limited ourselves to early modern performance practices, we had no fancy special effects to make me spooky. A little make-up gave my face an unusual pallor; that was all. What I learned from performing that primarily silent role is that my function was to generate a response from the other actors: *their* response convinced the audience that something uncanny and terrifying was happening, right in front of them.

When the Ghost first enters, the voluble scholar Horatio is conspicuously stunned into silence; only after four speeches by Marcellus and Barnardo is Horatio able to speak, and what he says is 'It horrors me'. Those three words are the play's first description of the effect that an undefined inhuman 'it' has upon an all-too-human 'me'. The verb 'horrors' here has to mean 'horrifies', and editors committed to theories about bad quartos conjecture that the rare verb 'horrors' is just an 'aural error'.[41] But a basic principle of textual transmission is that a copyist is likely to substitute something commonplace for something idiosyncratic and exceptional, which means that 'the rarer reading' is more likely to reflect the author's intention.[42] That 'rarer reading' is perfectly intelligible to modern actors and audiences. And two seventeenth-century writers familiar with Shakespeare did not consider it an error. Shakespeare's fellow playwright and occasional collaborator Thomas Heywood used the same three-word phrase ('it horrors mee') in a later pamphlet, describing devilish blasphemies that 'not only ... make the eares to tingle, but the heart to tremble'.[43] Sir Edward Dering adapted Shakespeare's two *Henry IV* plays; writing in a scholarly way about 'Divinity', Dering also used the same three-word phrase ('it horrors me').[44] Maybe the Q1 phrase was an oral idiom, which first appeared in print in 1603; maybe Shakespeare invented it; maybe Heywood and Dering had read the 1603 edition of *Hamlet*, or heard a performance that contained the phrase. What is beyond conjecture is that Q1's phrase made sense to Shakespeare's contemporaries – and to contemporaries who knew Shakespeare's own work well.

In William Gibson's formula, 'The future is already here. It is just not evenly distributed'.[45] The educated ruling class in sixteenth-century England can be appropriately defined as 'early modern', but the overwhelming bulk of the population, including the rural, non-aristocratic, poorly educated female population, was still living in the middle ages. If you doubt this, you need only look at the medieval carvings that still survive in the misericord in Holy Trinity Church in Stratford-upon-Avon, with their vividly frightening mythical beasts and their rats gnawing on human corpses that seem to be still alive as they are eaten.[46] You need only look at the nineteenth-century engraving of Stratford's now-demolished, medieval charnel house, with its Gothic arches over the human debris of parishioners not important enough to be buried in the church or the graveyard.[47] You need only walk, alone, through Holy Trinity churchyard on a dark winter night when a power outage has temporarily shut down the electrical grid.

Shakespeare did not need Thomas Kyd to teach him anything about Gothic ghosts. And we do not need a lost play by Thomas

Kyd, or elaborate theories of unauthorised transmission, to explain anything in the text of Q1 *Hamlet*, or anything in the references to a play about *Hamlet* between 1589 and 1596. We need to exorcise those ghosts.

Gary Taylor is Robert O. Lawton Distinguished University Professor at Florida State University, where he chairs the Department of English. He is one of the General Editors of the *New Oxford Shakespeare Complete Works* (2016–17) and *Complete Alternative Versions* (forthcoming). He previously general edited Thomas Middleton's *Collected Works* (Oxford, 2007), which won the MLA prize for a Distinguished Scholarly Edition. He has published widely on textual and editorial problems in early modern drama since 1979, but has also written on the history of Shakespeare's reception (*Reinventing Shakespeare*, 1990), the history of masculinity (*Castration: An Abbreviated History of Western Manhood*, 2000), and the origins of the metaphorical racial category 'white' (*Buying Whiteness: Race, Culture and Identity from Columbus to Hip-Hop*, 2005).

Appendix: Unique N-grams in Q1 *Hamlet*, Scene 14

I. *Literature Online*, dramatic works first performed 1564–1614.

I have checked all the works identified by Literature Online as first performed during those years against the dates given to them in Wiggins's *British Drama*, and removed thirty-five texts that Wiggins dates before or after those years. Asterisked items are also unique in the *EEBO-TCP* test, below. Dates record year of publication. Differences in spelling are not indicated. Parallels that are not grammatically exact are recorded in parentheses.

Madam your son] Barry, *Ram Alley*, 1611 (Madame your sonne in law).

*is safe arrived] Shakespeare, *Richard II*, 1597.

now received] Shakespeare, *Antony and Cleopatra*, *Winter's Tale*, 1623. This phrase occurs in one playwright, but two plays; it is therefore not included in my totals.

*he writes how] Shakespeare, *Two Gentlemen of Verona*, 1623.

how he escaped the] Samuel Rowley, *When you see me, you know me*, 1605 (how he escapes the).

being crossed] Shakespeare, *Julius Caesar*, 1623.

the winds, / He] Shakespeare, *Pericles* 20.13, 1609.

*packet sent to] Robert Greene, *Friar Bacon and Friar Bungay*, 1594. The bigram 'packet sent' is also unique among dramatic texts (but not in *EEBO-TCP*). My totals are based on 'maximalist' criteria, and so record only one unique link to Friar Bacon; if we use 'formalist' criteria, there are two.

saw himself] Thomas Hughes et al., *Misfortunes of Arthur*, 1587. This is the only dramatic parallel with no grammatical variant in the verb.

*conversion with your grace] Shakespeare, *Richard II*, 1597 ('To have some conference with your grace alone'). The phrase in *Richard II* is the only parallel in *LION* or *EEBO-TCP* where the word preceding the trigram 'with your grace' is a noun, begins with 'con' and means 'conversation, conference'. For the legitimacy of Q1's noun 'conversion', see Thompson and Taylor, *Texts of 1603 and 1623*, 149.

*your grace he will] Heywood, *If you know not me, You know no bodie*, 1605. The trigram 'grace he will' is also unique in the test for drama, but not in *EEBO-TCP*.

*I perceive there's] Middleton, *A Trick to Catch the Old One*, 1608. The bigram 'perceive there's' is unique only in drama.

*there's treason] Heywood, Dekker or Drayton, *Edward IV*, 1600.

treason in his] Jonson, *Haddington Masque*, 1608.

that seemed to] Anonymous, *Caesar and Pompey*, 1607.

*sugar o'er] Shakespeare, *Hamlet*, 1604 (Q2), Sc.9/3.1.49 (do sugar ore). In Q2 this phrase is spoken by Polonius to Ophelia; neither Horatio nor the Queen is on stage.

*and please him for] Chapman, *May Day*, 1611.

him for a time] Jonson, *Poetaster*, 1602.

murderous minds] Chapman, *Bussy D'Ambois*, 1607 (murtherous mindes). Only drama parallel without grammatical variants.

hath appointed me to] Shakespeare, *Taming of the Shrew*, Sc.13/4.5, 1623. The trigram 'hath appointed me' is also unique.

side of the city] Jonson, *Part of the King's Entertainment*, 1604.

me a mother's] Beaumont and Fletcher, *Cupid's revenge*, 1615 (me a Mother).

that he goes about] Anonymous, *The London prodigal*, 1605 (that he went about).

king and you shall] Anonymous, *Mucedorus*, 1598.

and you shall quickly] Shakespeare, *3 Henry VI*, 5.1/Sc.23, 1623.

you shall quickly find] Anonymous, *Captaine Thomas Stukeley*, 1605.

things fell] Shakespeare, *Romeo and Juliet*, 1597.

*there writ down] Dekker, *Old Fortunatus*, 1600.

*writ down that] Shakespeare, *Much Ado*, 1600.

pointed for] Chettle and Munday, *The Death of Robert, Earl of Huntington*, 1601.

father's seal] Lodge, *The Wounds of Civil War*, 1594.

take my leave with] Shakespeare, *Richard Duke of York* (1595), Sc. 12, identical to *3 Henry VI* (1623), 3.2. In *EEBO-TCP*, there are three other examples of 'I take my leave with', but none is followed by 'thousand'.

blessings to my] Shakespeare (?), *2 Henry VI*, 1623 (1.1.22). In *Contention* this scene seems not to have been written by Shakespeare; but in *Contention* the line reads 'pleasures to my'. The change from 'pleasures' to 'blessings' might therefore belong to Shakespeare's adaptation of the original scene.

II. *Early English Books Online-Text Creation Partnership*, works first published 1564–1614

*is safe arrived] Shakespeare, *Richard II*, 1597.

arrived in Denmark] Richard Grafton, *History* (1569), p. 175 ('he was sodeinly certified of the inuasion made by them of Norway into Denmarke ... Canutus ... tooke shipping, and ... arriued in Denmarke').

in Denmark. This] Caradoc, *Historie of Cambria*, trans. H. Lhoyd (1584). Both passages have a sentence-break, indicated by punctuation, at the same point in the trigram.

treason that the king] Castanheda, trans. Nicholas Lichefield, *First booke of the ... conquest of the East Indias*, 1582.

*packet sent to] Robert Greene, *Friar Bacon and Friar Bungay*, 1594.

*saw himself betrayed] Calahorra, trans. 'R. P.', *The second part of the first booke of the Myrrour of knighthood*, 1599. Only exact match without grammatical variants.

*death, / As at his] John Keltridge, *Two godlie and learned sermons*, 1581 (death, as at his).

*conversion with your grace] Shakespeare, *Richard II*, 1597.

*your grace, he will] Heywood, *If you know not me, You know no bodie*, 1605.

*will relate the circumstance] Emanuel Ford, *Parismus*, 1605.

*the circumstance at] Bandello, trans. Geoffrey Fenton, *Certaine tragicall discourses*, 1567 (the circumstance at). Only match without grammatical variants.

*I perceive there's] Middleton, *A Trick to Catch the Old One*, 1608.

*there's treason] Heywood, Dekker or Drayton, *Edward IV*, 1600.

*in his looks / That] Robert Greene, *A disputation*, 1592 (in his lookes, that).

*sugar o'er] Shakespeare, *Hamlet*, 1604 (Q2), Sc.9/3.1.49 (do sugar ore).

*will sooth and] Arthur Hall, *A Letter*, 1576.

*and please him for] Chapman, *May Day*, 1611.

*him for a time / For] Robert Allen, *Doctrine of the Gospel*, 1606 (him, for a time, for).

*are always jealous] William Watson, *Decacordon*, 1602.

Yes madam, and] Shakespeare, *Loves Labours Lost*, 1598. This is not unique in *Literature Online* for plays performed in 1564–1614. But the other dramatic examples did not reach print until after 1614.

*presence lest that] Barleti, trans. Zachary Jones, *Scanderbeg*, 1596.

*to court he is] Serres, trans. Edward Grimeston, *History of France*, 1607 (to Court. Hee is). Only example without grammatical variants.

*observe the king] Thomas Ireland, *The oath of allegiance*, 1610. Only exact match which also has the trigram in one sentence; it occurs three times in this text. So it is not technically 'unique', though it is unique to a single author and single text.

*fell not to his] Bullinger, trans. 'H. I.', *Fiftie godlie and learned sermons*, 1577.

*went for England and] William Clark, *A replie vnto a certaine libell*, 1603.

in the packet] Ulpian Fulwell, *The flower of fame*, 1575.

*packet there] Teixeira, trans. Anthony Munday, *The strangest aduenture that euer happened*, 1601.

*there writ down] Dekker, *Old Fortunatus*, 1600.

*writ down that] Shakespeare, *Much Ado*, 1600.

*them pointed] William Samuel, *An abridgement of all the canonical books*, 1569. The only example with the same meaning.

*him and by great] William Painter, *The palace of pleasure beautified*, 1566.

*by great chance he] Robert Anton, *Moriomachia*, 1613.

*so all was done] Robert Horne, *The Christian gouernour*, 1614.

*done without discovery] Jean François Le Petite, trans. Edward Grimeston, *A generall historie of the Netherlands*, 1608.

*once again I take] William Bishop, *The copies of certaine discourses*, 1601 (once againe I take my leaue).

*thousand mother's] Michael Drayton, *Englands heroicall epistles*, 1597 (a thousand mothers curses).

*mother's blessings to] Thomas Lupton, *A persuasion from papistrie*, 1581.

Notes

'Q1' refers to the 'first quarto' or 'first edition' of *Hamlet*, printed in 1603.
This chapter began as a talk at the Kingston-upon-Thames conference on Shakespeare and Scandinavia (8 October 2015). It has profited from feedback from the audience there and another at the University of Kansas. I am particularly indebted to Terri Bourus, Richard Wilson, Keegan Cooper, Michael Wagoner, John V. Nance, Gabriel Egan, and MacDonald P. Jackson.

1. Paul S. Conklin, *A History of Hamlet Criticism 1601–1821* (London: Routledge and Kegan Paul, 1957), 10n6.
2. Nicholas Rowe, 'Some Account of the Life ... of Mr. William Shakespear', in *The Works of Mr. William Shakespear*, ed. Nicholas Rowe, 6 vols (London: Tonson, 1709), 1: i–xl, here vi. For a defence of such oral traditions, see Gary Taylor, 'Shakespeare's Illegitimate Daughter', *Memoria di Shakespeare* 2 (2015), 177–194, and particularly 193 ('Ghosts fall between the cracks of our legal, textual, and editorial bureaucracies').
3. Catherine Belsey, 'Shakespeare's Sad Tale for Winter: *Hamlet* and the Tradition of Fireside Ghost Stories', *Shakespeare Quarterly* 61 (2012), 1–27, here 4, 24.
4. Catherine Belsey, *Why Shakespeare?* (Basingstoke: Palgrave Macmillan, 2007), 12–15, 65–67.
5. Catherine Belsey, 'Beyond Reason: *Hamlet* and Early Modern Stage Ghosts', in *Gothic Renaissance: A Reassessment*, ed. Elizabeth Bronfen and Beate Neumeier (Manchester: Manchester University Press, 2014), 32–54, here 33, 38.
6. Seneca, *Thyestes*, ed. and trans. A.J. Boyle (Oxford: Oxford University Press, 2017), xviii.
7. Gregorio Correr, *Procne*, in *Humanist Tragedies*, trans. Gary R. Grund (Cambridge, MA: Harvard University Press, 2011), 110–187.
8. Belsey, 'Beyond Reason', 35, 36. She also refers to 'Kyd's *Hamlet*' in endnote 16 (p. 51).
9. Terri Bourus, *Young Shakespeare's Young Hamlet: Print, Piracy, and Performance* (New York: Palgrave Macmillan, 2014), 137–180, here 166. For further evidence

in support of her revised chronology, see Gary Taylor and Rory Loughnane, 'The Canon and Chronology of Shakespeare's Works', in *The New Oxford Shakespeare: Authorship Companion*, ed. Gary Taylor and Gabriel Egan (Oxford: Oxford University Press, 2017), 417–602, esp. 542–548.
10. Belsey, 'Sad Tale for Winter', 5.
11. Bourus, *Young Shakespeare's Young Hamlet*, 144–151; Thomas Lodge, *Wits Miserie, and the World's Madnesse Discovering the Devils Incarnat of This Age* (London, 1596), 56 (sig. H4v).
12. For 'ontological outliers', see Gary Taylor, 'Empirical Middleton: *Macbeth*, Adaptation, and Microattribution', *Shakespeare Quarterly* 65 (2014), 239–264.
13. Gary Taylor and Michael Warren, eds, *The Division of the Kingdoms: Shakespeare's Two Versions of King Lear* (Oxford: Clarendon Press, 1983).
14. Bourus, *Young Shakespeare's Young Hamlet*, 117–126, and 'Enter Shakespeare's Young Hamlet, 1589', *Actes des Congrès de la Société Française Shakespeare* 34 (1 March 2016), esp. paras 33–35, doi:10.4000/shakespeare.3736, http://journals.openedition.org/shakespeare/3736.
15. Quotations from Q1 (and the Folio) cite *Hamlet: The Texts of 1603 and 1623*, ed. Ann Thompson and Neil Taylor (London: Arden Shakespeare, 2006).
16. The most systematic exposition of this view is G.I. Duthie, *The 'Bad' Quarto of Hamlet: A Critical Study* (Cambridge: Cambridge University Press, 1941); its last influential defender was Harold Jenkins in his Arden edition of *Hamlet* (London: Methuen, 1982). For a rebuttal, see Bourus, *Young Shakespeare's Young Hamlet*, 35–68.
17. For the most recent exposition of this Victorian theory, see Tiffany Stern, 'Sermons, Plays, and Note-takers: *Hamlet* Q1 as a "Noted" Text', *Shakespeare Survey* 66 (2013), 1–23; for a rebuttal, see Bourus, *Young Shakespeare's Young Hamlet*, 69–94.
18. Andrew Gurr, 'Maximal and Minimal Texts: Shakespeare v. the Globe', *Shakespeare Survey* 52 (1999), 68–87; Lukas Erne, *Shakespeare as Literary Dramatist*, rev. ed. (Cambridge: Cambridge University Press, 2013), 218–263; for rebuttals, see Bourus, *Young Shakespeare's Young Hamlet*, 94–99.
19. For a survey of all these tests, see Taylor and Loughnane, 'Canon and Chronology', 437–438.
20. Gary Taylor and John V. Nance, 'Imitation or Collaboration? Marlowe and the Early Shakespeare Canon', *Shakespeare Survey* 68 (2015), 32–47.
21. These tests were run in September and October 2015, when the New Oxford Shakespeare still had access to a version of *Literature Online* that allowed searches that included variant spellings. The searches were limited to exact word sequences; they do not include collocations ('disjunct n-grams'), because there is less agreement about the criteria for collocations, and forthcoming work by MacDonald P. Jackson and Pervez Rizvi suggests that continuous word sequences may be more reliable evidence. For a more detailed account of the methods used here, see Gary Taylor, 'Finding Anonymous in the Digital Archives: The Problem of *Arden of Faversham*', *Digital Scholarship in the Humanities* (2019), doi:10.1093/llc/fqy075.
22. Totals given in this chapter are 'maximalist' totals; they count only the n-gram that contains the largest number of words. The Appendix also records 'formalist' counts, which count a unique bigram or trigram as a separate parallel, even if

it is part of a unique quadgram that is also counted. 'Formalist' counts would give one extra parallel to four playwrights (Shakespeare, Greene, Heywood and Middleton). But none of those five extra parallels is also unique in the *EEBO-TCP* database.

23. On the authorship of *Edward IV*, see Martin Wiggins, *British Drama 1533–1642: A Catalogue, Volume IV, 1598–1602* (Oxford: Oxford University Press, 2014), 124, 129.
24. For my youthful endorsement of old conjectures about the influence of a lost play allegedly by Kyd, see Stanley Wells et al., *William Shakespeare: A Textual Companion* (Oxford: Clarendon, 1987), 398.
25. This phrase was first identified as unique because of the quadgram 'take my leave with', which does not occur in any other dramatic text first performed in the fifty-year period tested in *Literature Online*. The preceding first person pronoun and the following 'thousand' make it unique even when tested against the larger *EEBO* database.
26. Dekker, Drayton and Heywood have one certain link each; one of them probably has two links (if one of them is responsible for the unique n-gram match in *Edward IV*).
27. For a convenient summary of scholarship, see Stuart Gillespie, *Shakespeare's Books: A Dictionary of Shakespeare Sources* (London: Bloomsbury, 2016), 202–204 (Grafton), 404–406 (Painter), 32–36 (Bandello).
28. *Titus Andronicus*, Sc. 12/5.3.45–65, in *The New Oxford Shakespeare: Complete Works: Modern Critical Edition*, gen. ed. Gary Taylor, John Jowett, Terri Bourus and Gabriel Egan (Oxford: Oxford University Press, 2016), 245–246.
29. Stanley Wells, 'The Integration of Violent Action in *Titus Andronicus*' (1997), in *Shakespeare on Stage and Page: Selected Essays* (Oxford: Oxford University Press, 2016), 74–85, here 75–76.
30. For a succinct account of the late Latin origins of this myth, see Walter Goffart, 'Jordanes's *Getica* and the Disputed Authenticity of Gothic Origins from Scandinavia', *Speculum* 80, no. 2 (2005), 379–398.
31. Robert Fabyan, *Fabyans Cronycle newly prynted* (London, 1533: STC 10660), sig. CVII^v. For Fabyan's influence on *Henry VI* and *Richard III*, see Gillespie, *Shakespeare's Books*, 165–167.
32. Pietro Martire d'Anghiera ('Peter Martyr'), *The History of Travayle*, trans. Richard Eden (London, 1577: STC 649), 288.
33. Anglicus Bartolomeus, *Batman upon Bartholme*, trans. John Trevisa, rev. Stephen Batman (London, 1582: STC 1538), sig. ¶ii^v, p. 223.
34. Lucas Waghenaer, *The Mariners Mirror*, trans. Anthony Ashley (London, 1588: STC 24931), 167.
35. Stanley Wells, 'The Failure of *The Two Gentlemen of Verona*' (1964), in *Shakespeare on Page and Stage*, 49–57, here 49.
36. Elizabeth Montagu, *Essay on the Writings and Genius of Shakespear* (London, 1769), 147; Anne Radcliffe, *The Mysteries of Udolfo* (London, 1794), epigraph to chapter 18 in volume 4.
37. Montagu, *Essay*, 143, 141 (my italics).
38. Julia Kristeva, *Pouvoirs de l'horreur: Essai sur l'abjection* (Paris: Seuil, 1980), translated as *Powers of Horror: An Essay on Abjection*, trans. Leon S. Roudiez (New York: Columbia University Press, 1982).

39. Gary Taylor, 'Gender, Hunger, Horror: The History and Significance of *The Bloody Banquet*', *Journal of Early Modern Cultural Studies* 1 (2001), 1–45, here 23–24.
40. See the essays in Bronfen and Neumeier, eds, *Gothic Renaissance*, and in two other collections: John Drakakis and Dale Townshend, eds, *Gothic Shakespeares* (London: Routledge, 2008) and Christy Desmet and Anne Williams, eds, *Shakespearean Gothic* (Cardiff: University of Wales Press, 2009).
41. *Texts of 1603 and 1623*, ed. Thompson and Taylor, 1.34 (p. 47, commentary note). Q2 has 'horrowes'; F has 'harrowes' (1.1.43). Q2 could result from a misreading of the form in Q1 or the form in F. F's verb here also occurs in all texts of Sc. 5 (Q1 5.11, F 1.5.16). In theories of memorial reconstruction, such duplications are routinely taken as signs of corruption, in which case 'harrowes' in Sc. 1 would be the erroneous duplication.
42. Gary Taylor, '*Praestat Difficilior Lectio*: *All's Well that Ends Well* and *Richard III*', *Renaissance Studies* 2 (1988), 27–46.
43. Thomas Heywood, *A True Discourse of the Two Infamous Upstart Prophets* (London, 1636: STC 13369), 13.
44. Edward Dering, *A Collection of Speeches* (London, 1642), 85.
45. *Conversations with William Gibson*, ed. Patrick A. Smith (Jackson: University Press of Mississippi, 2014), 193.
46. Madeleine Hammond, *The Misericords of Holy Trinity Church: Stratford-upon-Avon*, illus. John F. Cheal (Stratford-upon-Avon[?]: C.J. Hammond, 2013). Many of the carvings can also be found online.
47. For the engraving of the interior, and Thomas Girtin's watercolour of the exterior, see https://www.shakespeare.org.uk/explore-shakespeare/blogs/shakespeare-100-objects-charnel-house/.

Chapter 2
The Hybrid *Hamlet*
Player Tested, Shakespeare Approved

Christopher Marino

In 2015, I directed a production of *Hamlet* for the Department of Theatre at the University of North Carolina Wilmington, where I am an assistant professor. I was new to UNCW, but I had a year to train students in the requisite text and verse work needed to approach a Shakespeare play. In the season selection process, it was suggested to produce *Hamlet* and *Rosencrantz and Guildenstern Are Dead* in one season. I always wanted to use the 'first quarto' in a production. I appreciated the text's brevity and forward momentum. I also felt that for student actors it might be a more playable version. Initially I wanted to direct the first quarto in its entirety, but I worried that a university audience might feel a little confused as to why they were being given this version, which removes some of the greatest textual hits from the play. I decided the best option might be to use the first quarto as a framework. I could then modify the text to bring some of the textual touchstones more in line with what the audience knows

Notes for this section begin on page 53.

and expects. I enlisted the help of colleague Dr Charles Grimes to collaborate on an entirely new version of the text. We would pick and choose what we wanted from the three known versions: the Folio (F1), the first quarto (Q1) and the second quarto (Q2). The amalgamation was a much faster process than I initially thought, as Q1 in the textual matchups became the preferred choice.

Are you going to do it period?

As a director, I get asked this question all the time. First by the actors and the designers, then by the press who want to know what time period, or what conceptual idea I have about the play. I have to be very careful in my answers to all sides. The question always seems to come out of a misconception about what 'period' in Shakespeare's plays means. It's very reminiscent of when I started to work in classical theatre years ago. When people would ask me what I did for a living, I would say I was an actor. After the inevitable 'what would I know you from?' question, I would explain that I work primarily in Shakespeare and classical material. Their excited response was usually some form of personal connection to Renaissance fairs and festivals. As I did not want to dash their excitement, I very delicately explained that it's not quite what I meant. So, when I am asked the question about setting and period, our dialogue generally goes something like this:

Me: So now I have to ask you a few questions. When you say 'time period', do you mean am I doing it in the period of the play's historical source or setting? In the case of *Hamlet*, this would be somewhere around the early thirteenth century in Scandinavia.

Reporter: (*Perplexed look*) No, the period Shakespeare did it.

Me: (*Carefully*) So now I have to ask you another question. Do you mean am I doing it in the period the play was first produced? Or are you asking if I am doing it how Shakespeare did it? (*An awkward silence follows*) Because if we are following what Shakespeare did, we would need either some very rich patrons, or a very large budget. In the case of these rich patrons, we would want them to donate their couture fashion cast-offs for costumes. Something in the neighbourhood of last year's Valentino or Dior. If not that, we would need funding that would give us the ability to build contemporary designer clothing with tailoring reflective of wealth and status in our modern age.

I then go on to explain that Shakespeare was really working in contemporary dress, and if we were to follow what he did, we would do the same.

So, what did we do?

In conversation with Mark Sorenson (resident faculty designer at UNCW), we discovered the students needed the experience of building Elizabethan period costumes. To be perfectly honest, I am not a huge fan of Elizabethan settings for Shakespeare. Looking backward neither serves the play, nor is this what Shakespeare would have done. My disposition with costuming is not to recreate an exact copy of period clothing. Unless you are doing 'original practices' as seen in the Mark Rylance/Tim Carroll collaborations of *Richard II* (2003), *Richard III* (2012) and *Twelfth Night* (2003 and 2012) productions at the Globe, you will create a pale representation of Elizabethan dress. A production populated with costumes rife with stiff upholstery fabric, 'SCA boots' and repurposed doublets. This is also territory that can run the risk of turning into cliché very easily. Something akin to what Peter Brook wrote about in his chapter 'The Deadly Theatre' from *The Empty Space*:

> Of course nowhere does the Deadly Theatre install itself so securely, so comfortably and so slyly as in the works of William Shakespeare. The Deadly Theatre takes easily to Shakespeare. We see his plays done by good actors in what seems like the proper way – they look lively and colourful, there is music, and everyone is all dressed up, just as they are supposed to be in the best of classical theatres.[1]

We ensured our production most definitely had some hallmarks of Elizabethan clothing but did not mire itself in fetishising the period while never creating anything that actually resembles the period. Mark created clothing that suited the actors' bodies because it wasn't stuck in an idea of period. If one were to see this production, the costumes all fit within the same world but definitely had a modern flair to them. (I do wish to qualify that by saying this was not an 'every period and no period' production, which I think is one of the biggest clichés in modern Shakespeare.)

Figure 1. Set for *Hamlet*, UNCW Department of Theatre, 2015 (note galleries on sides). Hamlet (Luke Robbins) and Laertes (Sean Owens). Courtesy Photo/2015 © University North Carolina Wilmington.

'No, you can't use the black box'

I'm going to admit something slightly controversial: the proscenium stage has hastened the death march of modern theatre. I cannot think of a deadlier configuration to watch an art form that is so alive, so immediate and vital. Even sport understands this concept and seats its audience on as many sides as they can fit. The proscenium is a deadly space; I usually do everything in my power to not direct in one. When *Hamlet* was suggested, I wanted to use our black box theatre, where we could construct a three-quarter round space. This was not feasible because of the limited number of seats. Without another option, we were left to work with our main stage proscenium space. Still desiring to have some sort of thrust, I approached colleague and technical director Max Lydy. I explained to Max that at least if we have a thrust, Hamlet might be able to communicate with the audience in a much more visceral way. As if to say, 'I am with you'. Unfortunately, fire regulations meant that there was no such luck. A thrust was impossible.

Figure 2. Hamlet (Luke Robbins) and the Ghost (Kaleb Edward Edley), UNCW Department of Theatre, 2015. Courtesy Photo/2015 © University North Carolina Wilmington.

No thrust but another way

I approached our set designer Rand Enlow with the idea of constructing something that looked a little bit like an indoor version of the Globe Theatre. A space that had galleries on either side, but in this case they were moveable. Due to budget restrictions when the theatre building was constructed, our stage does not have a trap, nor is there any way we could have one. Ideally, I wanted the Ghost to rise up out of the earth, as was most likely the case in the original productions. This entrance representing something like a passage into the Catholic notion of purgatory.

I suggested to Rand that we instead create a very long central passageway made up of archways that seem to go on forever. The idea is to achieve the look and feel of a passage to oblivion. These arches became places from where characters could emerge and hide. On a subconscious level, the arches serve as a place where the physical and metaphysical worlds meet. This deep discovery-like passage allowed actors to make very long entrances from the upstage position.

The court all emerge from this space in a procession during the marriage/funeral at the beginning of the play. This procession foreshadowed the eventuality that many of these characters will soon cross into the metaphysical world. It was, metaphorically, a procession of corpses. When the Ghost appeared, he emerged from a space that was neither Heaven nor Hell and moved through to the physical world. The galleries were used as a playing space, and a place to put audience for the play within the play. The gallery spaces served as a constant reminder to the audience that there is an aspect of *Hamlet* that is performative. This is not a terribly original idea, or a central theme of the production. The galleries rotated 180°, so we could load actors in the offstage position and then rotate them into view on stage.

For example, in scene 14, we rotated Horatio and Gertrude (spelled 'Gertred' in Q1) into view already kneeling side by side as if they were in a chapel. At this point in the play, it would be the only place Gertrude would not be discovered if seen with Horatio. Polonius (called 'Corambis' in Q1) was also killed in one of the galleries, and Hamlet physically rotated the gallery offstage to remove Polonius's body while speaking the following lines:[2]

> HAMLET
> It is enough. Mother, good night!
> Come, sir – I'll provide for you a grave,
> Who was in life a foolish, prating knave. (Q1, 11.101–3)

At this point we see the slow revolve of the body moving offstage. The gallery is still moving when Claudius, Rosencrantz and Guildenstern enter ('King, Rossencraft, and Gilderstone' in Q1). Q1 makes this theatrical moment possible as it does not attempt to jump time as in the other versions. The set functioned as an installation for the play to resonate and allowed the audience's imagination to travel with the play without setting it in realistically identifiable locations. This is very much what Shakespeare does with the play. The space was also very open and had easy access to the stage, allowing the momentum of the play to develop rather than creating a space that fights against it.

This openness facilitated something that I refer to as 'charging' the space. The principle is simple: the onstage actors charge the space with energy and the entering actors ride that charged energy. The idea of charging is another nod to the Elizabethan theatre, which

Figure 3. Entrance of the court, UNCW Department of Theatre, 2015. Photographs by Belinda Keller for the University of North Carolina Wilmington. Courtesy Photo/2015 © University North Carolina Wilmington.

was built as a resonating chamber for energy. Remarkably, while I did not get my three-quarter round space, the production was able to balance the impassiveness of the proscenium with an energetic life that kept the audience engaged.

The hybrid *Hamlet*

Many nights were spent at my desk with two different computer monitors and three different versions of the play trying to figure out which version had text that I would be most interested in using.[3] I used a few criteria for decisions. First, Wilmington, North Carolina does not have a long association with text-driven Shakespeare, so what language choice makes the play most alive for an audience that doesn't have a sophisticated relationship to the piece? Second, how can I make the play most accessible for the student actors? Which text will they be able to connect with? Third, length. I knew Q1 was by far the shortest and arguably the most active version, expending less time ruminating and more time in action. What I thought was

Figure 4. Luke Robbins as Hamlet, UNCW Department of Theatre, 2015. Courtesy Photo/2015 © University North Carolina Wilmington.

going to happen when I started this process was that I was going to end up using Q1 as a template for length, then draw the bulk of the text from Q2 and F. Once I saw the texts side by side, Q1 always won out as the preferred option. In my actor and director imagination, Q1 felt like a script for actors, while F1 felt like a text for lovers of literature and poetry. I do not think Heminges and Condell would argue about my assessment of the Folio; they say as much in their dedication, 'To the great variety of *readers*' (my emphasis). The more I dove into the play, the more Q2 and F1 felt static and almost over-full. Those texts feel writerly; Q1 feels actorly. While it is arguably a less artful script, it is my opinion that Q1 is the more 'true' script, and one far more connected to performance. It felt lived in, it felt organic, it felt like the actors had chewed these lines and processed them through their own humanity. The other versions in comparison feel self-consciously literary, like something that in four hundred years' time great institutions could ponder the significance of. Q1 won most of the matchups and ended up comprising about 80% of my script.

So why are you doing that version, isn't this a forgery or a bootleg?

I have nothing new to add to this conversation, and certainly nothing ground-breaking by way of observation. What I do have is some specific in-process observations about the text, and a few general ones about the playing of it. I am aware of some of the prevailing theories concerning Q1, such as memorial reconstruction errors on the part of the actors, a bootlegged or botched version which is a product of 'fast writing' transcription, or an early draft. It is my belief that most theories around memorisation or transcription errors are misguided. My examples will serve to contradict the aforementioned theories regarding errors. I will keep my examples brief because there are enough books on the subject to fill a small library, and certainly enough conjecture to fill several hundred volumes.

First, let's debunk the 'memorial' theory. Working with classical material for over twenty years, I can say with certainty that when an actor tries to memorise text and gets it wrong, they frequently speak a version that is very close to the original with a few alterations. Most of the time, if the actors are more experienced, the sense of metre will stay the same, but a few words will get substituted for synonymous ideas or terms. So, if Q1 was corrupted by memorial reconstruction errors by the actors, I would suggest that there should be very little difference between versions, with the exception of a few words and phrases here and there. Whole lines or ideas shouldn't exist in one and not the other. I found numerous examples where the difference in Q1 changes the entire trajectory of the scene. Such as the 'Nunnery' scene, where Ophelia in the traditional texts says:

> My Lord, I have remembrances of yours,
> That I have longed long to redeliver.
> I pray you now receive them. (F 3.1.93–5)

This line has a wonderfully alliterative hook, 'longed long', which most actors cement immediately. It's one of those anchoring phrases that when an actor is very rough on memorisation will almost certainly always hit. They will often enough botch and substitute 'my Lord' for 'my honoured Lord' or 'my honorable Lord' or even 'my most honoured Lord', but 'longed long' will never drop. So, I find it curious, if we are to believe that Q1's version is a memorial corruption or a misremembering of the line, that it would come up with an entirely different version for Ofelia's speech:

> My lord, I have sought opportunity, which now I have, to
> redeliver to your worthy hands a small remembrance – such
> tokens which I have received of you. (Q1 7.138–41)

This is a far cry from the other versions. Q1 treats this speech as prose, although it begins and ends with a perfect iambic pentameter; but whether prose or broken verse, it is an extremely clunky and inactive piece of text, almost mechanical. The type of text that perhaps somebody might coach someone to say in a court of law. A text so distant and devoid of point of view that it is almost impossible for anyone to take offence at it, especially perhaps a king who is overhearing it. It speaks nothing about relationship and mires itself in a sort of polysyllabic nothingness. It drips with plausible deniability. Whereas the F/Q2 'I have longed long' or 'I pray you now receive them' feels direct and desperate. To put my interpretive spin on it, I kept the Q1 opening because it is so odd and cold. Very unlike this young woman who has such an open and fragile heart. It is also rife with parenthetical interruptions, which are curiously similar to the style of a certain character who is also in the room, one who communicates like this:

> Now, to know the cause of this effect –
> Or else to say the cause of this defect
> (For this effect defective comes by cause) – (Q1 7.61–3)

Looking at these two passages compared below, one can't help but see some similarity between Corambis the commanding father (top) and Ophelia the obedient daughter (bottom):

> Now, to know the cause of this effect,
> Or else to say, the cause of this defect,
> For this effect defective comes by cause. (Q1 7.61–3)

> My lord, I have sought opportunity, which now
> I have, to redeliver to your worthy hands a small
> remembrance – such tokens which I have received
> of you. (Q1 7.138–41)

In this production, Q1 solved one of the interpretive questions of the scene: at what point does Hamlet know or suspect something is wrong? I think Q1 is clear about it. Ophelia (Ofelia in Q1) does not speak like the excerpted text above in any other part of the play, certainly not to the person that she loves. So, in Q1, Hamlet does indeed smell a 'rat' straight away. There is no asking him, 'How does your honour for this many a day?' as in Q2 and F1. In Q1, Ophelia dives straight in with a line akin to 'I'm breaking up with you'. No pleasantries as in Q2 and Folio. It's as if she just blurted out, or in the case of our production, recited a conned script given to her. There is yet another instance where Ophelia does not communicate like herself. Hamlet speaks to her in verse, a very heart-centric way of communicating. Ophelia responds in prose, which is much more a manifestation of the head or intellect. A very different moment than in Q2 or F1, and full of information. If it is a memorial error, it is an ingenious one.

My next example may seem to lend credence to the memorial reconstruction argument. I would argue, however, that the Q1 text is theatrically intelligent in a very actorly way. For instance, Q1 has a rather curious placement of 'O' in a number of lines. I view the 'O' as an indication of emotional expression. There was no great way to notate pain or frustration, therefore 'O' is a signal to the actor to let the emotion move out on a sound. In Q1 it is not always at the beginning of the verse line, and in some cases the addition of 'O' throws the line off metre. If we look at the Q2 and F1 version, we find that Hamlet's line joins perfectly with the Ghost's to form a regular verse line.

> HAMLET
> Haste, haste me to know it, that I with wings as swift
> As meditation, or the thoughts of love,
> **May sweep to my revenge.**
> GHOST
> **I find thee apt.**
>
> (F1 1.5.29–31, my emphasis)

In the line divided between Hamlet and the Ghost, Q1 has an 'O', and curiously in exactly the place that an actor might experience an expression of the character's emotional state:[4]

> May sweep to my revenge.
> GHOST
> **O, I find thee apt.**
>
> (Q1 5.25–6, my emphasis)

A poet obsessed with metrical regularity would not write an 'O' here, because it adds an extrametrical syllable. This extra sound happens quite apart from the verse norm. If it's an arbitrary memorial error, then again it just so happens to line up perfectly with an actor's organic expression of the text. So this might be what editors call 'an actor's interpolation'. But it might also be deliberate scripting by Shakespeare the actor-playwright, who often puts an extrametrical stressed syllable after a strong caesura. The strongest possible caesura is a mid-line switch from one speaker to another and, at the same time, one sentence to another.

The 'O' in Q1 might be something written by the actor-playwright, or something added later by an actor who played the Ghost, or the absence of 'O' from Q2/F might be the result of a scribe or compositor, at some stage in the play's transmission, omitting that single letter, either accidentally or as a deliberate 'improvement' of the metre. It's impossible to tell which of these historical conjectures is right. But what I can say with confidence is that the 'O' reflects a theatrical understanding of what an actor needs at that moment. Q1 uses the 'O' as a guide for emotional expression, and then continues with the completion of the verse line. I can't help but think that if this were the standard, we would have less melodrama attached to the dreaded 'O'.

There is also in Q1 more use of what I would call reflective repetitions. Actors love to add emotionally declamatory language: the addition of 'O', or the repeat of a line for effect, seem very actor-driven, something more akin to a method actor repeating words or phrases to get a feel for the emotional value of the moment. Reflective repetitions seem very in the moment and allow the actor to 'new coin' the next thought. We can clearly see this in the examples below.

> Than fly to others that we know not of?
> Thus conscience does make cowards of us all (F1 3.1.82–3)

These verse lines in Q2/F are wonderfully regular, but Q1 has something extra (and extrametrical):

> Than fly to others that we know not of?
> Ay, **that – O**, this conscience makes cowards of us all.
> (Q1 7.135–6, my emphasis)

This 'yes that' phrase is something an actor might add to drive the weight of the thought. He even adds an 'O' to the mix for added value. It of course completely throws the metre off, and would not be great poetry, but it certainly makes for a very human moment in the playing. As if to say, 'yes that, that's the exact thing that makes us all cowards'. It allows Hamlet to discover the significance of the thought in the moment just after he uttered it and share it with the audience. The audience really responded to this Q1 version of the line in performance.

Another example of reflective repetition can be found in the 'players scene'. The following is the familiar version:

> POLONIUS
> Look where he has not turned his colour, and has tears in's eyes. – Pray you, no more!
> HAMLET
> 'Tis well. I'll have thee speak out the rest soon. Good my lord, will you see the players well bestowed? Do ye hear, let them be well used, for they are the abstract and brief chronicles of the time. After your death you were better have a bad epitaph than their ill report while you live.
> POLONIUS
> My lord, I will use them according to their desert.
> HAMLET
> God's bodikins, man, better! Use every man after his desert and who should 'scape whipping? Use them after your own honour and dignity – the less they deserve, the more merit is in your bounty. Take them in.
> POLONIUS
> Come, sirs.
> HAMLET
> Follow him, friends. We'll hear a play tomorrow.
> (F1 2.2.515–532)

We see a Hamlet watching the players and stopping them at an opportune time in order to get Polonius out of the room. It feels like this plan has been in existence for much of the scene. Hamlet knows he is going to ask them to play the 'Murder of Gonzago'. Q1 does something interesting, and again very actor-driven. It adds a repetition, ''tis very well', onto the ''Tis well'. I call this an 'introspective turn' and we see them in Q1 quite often. In this case the sense of the scene is that Corambis (Polonius in Q2 and F1) is moved by the actors: in Q1 but not the other texts, he repeats 'no more'. Hamlet then observes that this very politic figure of his uncle's administration can be moved by a play. Corambis may not have much of a conscience, but the play has touched him.

CORAMBIS
Look, my lord, if he hath not chang'd his colour and
hath tears in his eyes. **No more, good heart, no more!**
HAMLET
'Tis well, **'tis very well**. I pray, my lord, will you see the
players well bestowed? I tell you they are the chronicles
and brief abstracts of the time. After your death, I can
tell you, you were better have a bad epithet than their ill
report while you live.
(Q1 7.376–383, my emphasis)

Hamlet says ''tis well' in his response to 'no more'. Taking in Corambis's emotional reaction then has an introspective turn, so the thought is something like this:

'Tis well that you can be moved, **'tis** very well in fact.

In this moment of recognising just how good it is, Hamlet has the idea. If this can work on one heartless man (Corambis), it can work on another one (the King) – thus giving birth to the 'mousetrap' idea onstage and in the moment. This is even clearer if we place this exchange in its larger Q1 context.

CORAMBIS
Look, my lord, if he hath not chang'd his color, and
hath tears in his eyes. No more, good heart, no more.
HAMLET
'Tis well, 'tis very well. I pray, my lord, will you see the
players well bestowed? I tell you they are the chronicles
and brief abstracts of the time. After your death, I can
tell you, you were better have a bad epitaph than their
ill report while you live.
CORAMBIS
My lord, I will use them according to their deserts.
HAMLET
O, far better, man – use every man after his deserts,
then who should scape whipping? Use them after your
own honour and dignity – the less they deserve the
greater credit's yours.
CORAMBIS
Welcome, my good fellows! [*Exit.*]
HAMLET
Come hither, masters. **Can you not play *The Murder of Gonzago*?**
PLAYERS
Yes, my lord. (Q1 7.376–93, my emphasis)

Q2/F1 really leaves no room for coming up with the idea onstage. The ''Tis well' indicates how well the players have done as actors, but certainly gives no time for Hamlet to create the idea. So at the end of the Q2/F1 version, Hamlet simply says that an unspecified 'we' will 'hear a play'. By contrast, by the end of this passage in Q1, Hamlet knows which play he wants them to perform.

Q1 also gives us a wonderfully strange repetition:

> **I tell you** they are the chronicles and brief abstracts
> of the time. After your death, **I can tell you**, you were
> better have a bad epithet than their ill report while
> you live.

These few lines are not very artful, and I believe purposely so. Hamlet speaks definitive repetitions when he gets excited and has to evade the truth. The same thing happens earlier, in 5.98:

> HAMLET
> **Right, you are in the right**, and therefore
> I hold it meet, without more circumstance at all,
> We shake hands and part, you as your business
> And desires shall lead you – for look you, every man
> Hath business and desires, such as it is –
> And, for my own poor part, I'll go pray.
> HORATIO
> These are but wild and whirling words, my lord.
> HAMLET
> I am sorry they offend you. Heartily,
> Yes, faith, heartily.
> HORATIO
> There's no offense, my lord.
> HAMLET
> Yes, by Saint Patrick, but there is, Horatio,
> And much offense too. Touching this vision,
> It is an honest ghost – that let me tell you.
> For your desires to know what is between us,
> O'ermaster it as you may. And now, kind friends,
> As you are friends, scholars and gentlemen,
> Grant me one poor request. (Q1, 5.97–113, my emphasis)

While the text is not substantively different than the Q2/F1 versions, Q1 shows us a less settled and more impulsive Hamlet. Very much a Hamlet who is thinking in the moment, improvising, as he does when he says ''Tis well, 'tis very well' in the aforementioned players scene.

Figure 5. Hamlet (Luke Robbins) considering killing Claudius (Phil Antonino). Courtesy Photo/2015 © University North Carolina Wilmington.

What Gertrude knows and how it changes the ending

The final example against memorial reconstruction by actors or memory-assisted note-taking by auditors is the simple fact that scene 14 exists. Any theory that does not plausibly explain this scene cannot be valid. Only Q1 contains the following text.

> *Enter HORATIO and the QUEEN.*
> HORATIO
> Madam, your son is safe arriv'd in Denmark.
> This letter I e'en now receiv'd of him,
> Wherein he writes how he escap'd the danger
> And subtle treason that the King had plotted.
> Being crossed by the contention of the winds,
> He found the packet sent to the King of England,
> Wherein he saw himself betray'd to death
> As, at his next conversing with your grace,
> He will relate the circumstance at full.
> QUEEN
> Then I perceive there's treason in his looks
> That seem'd to sugar o'er his villany.
> But I will soothe and please him for a time,
> (For murderous minds are always jealous).
> But know not you, Horatio, where he is?

HORATIO
Yes, madam; and he hath appointed me
To meet him on the east side of the city
Tomorrow morning.
QUEEN
O, fail not, good Horatio,
And withal commend me a mother's care to him –
Bid him awhile be wary of his presence,
Lest that he fail in that he goes about.
HORATIO
Madam, never make doubt of that. I think by this
The news be come to court he is arriv'd.
Observe the King, and you shall quickly find,
Hamlet being here, things fall not to his mind.
QUEEN
But what became of Guildenstern and Rosencrantz?[5]
HORATIO
He being set ashore, they went for England.
And in the packet there writ down that doom
To be perform'd on them 'pointed for him.
And, by great chance, he had his father's seal –
So all was done without discovery.
QUEEN
Thanks be to heaven for blessing of the Prince!
Horatio, once again I take my leave,
With thousand mother's blessings to my son.
HORATIO
Madam, adieu. [*Exeunt.*] (Q1 14.1–34)

We understand some interesting information here that differs from Q2 and F1. Gertrude knows that Claudius has indeed conspired to kill young Hamlet.

Gertrude will soothe and please the King for a time until Hamlet can act. This clarifies the trajectory for the choice of images and delivery in Gertrude's 'drowned' speech. She makes the choice to tell the story of Ophelia's drowning in a setting of great beauty.

QUEEN
O, my lord, the young Ophelia,
Having made a garland of sundry sorts of flowers,
Sitting upon a willow by a brook,
The envious sprig broke. Into the brook she fell
And for a while her clothes, spread wide abroad,
Bore the young lady up and there she sat,
Smiling, even mermaid-like, 'twixt heaven and earth,

> Chanting old, sundry tunes, uncapable,
> As it were, of her distress. But long it could not be
> Till that her clothes, being heavy with their drink,
> Dragg'd the sweet wretch to death. (Q1 15.40–50)

Taking our cue from the previous scene, we know that Gertrude is concerned Hamlet may be discovered before executing 'that he goes about'. Considering Laertes is already enraged by the death of his father and the fractured mental state of his sister, it would be best to give bad news in the least fatal way possible. Perhaps one might even set the scene as if you were there at the time of Ophelia's death. The sound structure of the verse (in lines like 'Having made a garland of sundry sorts of flowers' or 'Smiling, even mermaid-like, 'twixt heaven and earth') is almost devoid of any hard consonants and it often ends in continuant sounds ('ers' and 'rth'). The lines ease you into death, rather than abruptly offering it. The imagery itself is of a beautiful scene by a river, contrary to a brutal drowning.

The Queen's circumstances going into the final scene are unique in Q1. We know that she is really waiting to see what Hamlet is going to do ('goes about') with the King. She plays the 'soothing' the King role well. In fact, so well that she says nothing for most of the scene. Her death line in Q1 is fascinating:

> QUEEN
> O, the drink, the drink! Hamlet, the drink!
> [*She dies.*]
> HAMLET
> Treason, ho! Keep the gates! (Q1 17.86–7)

The Queen is warning her son; in Q1 there is no doubt who is responsible, and she is warning Hamlet that it is a trap. Hamlet responds in kind with a definitive 'treason'. In Q2/F1 it can only be a surprise to Gertrude; nothing indicates that she knows that this is dangerous for Hamlet, or that her husband is the villain that he is. The 'poison'd' in the later version is coming from a very confused and distressed woman as she dies. The tragedy here may be that she dies never fully knowing the truth.

> GERTRUDE
> No, no, the drink, the drink – O my dear Hamlet –
> The drink, the drink – I am poison'd.   *Dies*
> HAMLET
> O villainy! Ho! let the door be lock'd.
> Treachery! Seek it out. (F1 5.2.264–7)

I also appreciate the brevity of Q1; the deaths come fast and furious, no hanging about shouting exclamations. Q2 and F1 always must wrestle a bit with the slightly extended deaths turning towards melodrama. As an actor, I will take Q1 all day long.

Reception

The UNCW production ran for a total of nine performances over two weekends, counting preview. Most of the overwhelmingly positive feedback centred on the clarity of the text, as well as a number of the student performers. A colleague who teaches courses in Shakespeare remarked that out of all the productions he has seen of the play, the student playing Ophelia was the best he had seen. Audiences were also pleasantly surprised by the humour of this version. This was a Hamlet that made you connect with him via humour, and while there were moments of self-reflection and tragedy, they were not over-full. The production played to mostly sold-out houses and to date is the top ticket seller in departmental history, even beating the musical *Pippin*. The production won 'Best Director' at the Star News Wilmington Theatre Awards. Luke Robbins as Hamlet was nominated for 'Best Actor'; Julia Ormond who played Ophelia was awarded 'Best Newcomer' for her performances in *Hamlet* and *'Tis Pity She's a Whore*. Randall Enlow was nominated for 'Best Lighting'. All of the accolades are wonderful, but the best ones came from two five-year-olds and an eight-year-old (two of whom happen to be my daughters). They stayed through the entire performance, quoting lines while walking out. My five-year-old asked the question, 'Why did Hamlet hate the water-fly?' She was directly quoting from Horatio's line, 'but you mark yon water-fly' (Q1 17.5). If this version compelled a pre-schooler to listen, and ask a precise and intelligent question, after more than two hours of a four-hundred-year-old play, I believe there is something special in it. The first quarto, or 'bad quarto', or what you will, works. I owe much of the success of this production to this wonderful, organic and unique text. It works, and I believe if companies embraced this version more, they would also see its muscular, unfussy beauty.

Christopher Marino has a career that spans over twenty-five years in regional theatre. He is a founding member of the Helen Hayes-award-winning Taffety Punk Theatre (Washington D.C.), former Artistic Director of the Baltimore Shakespeare Festival, and current Producing Artistic Director of Alchemical Theatre of Wilmington. On faculty at UNCW, Christopher has taught at numerous universities and theatres throughout the US and England. He is a guest lecturer at Rose Bruford College in the UK. He holds an MFA from the Academy for Classical Acting at George Washington/Shakespeare Theatre Company DC. He also trained at the Webber Douglas Academy of Dramatic Art (Graduate), London, and holds a BA in Drama/Dance from Bard College.

Notes

1. Peter Brook, *The Empty Space* (New York: Atheneum, 1968). Print.
2. In this essay, I reference the line numbering of Q1 and F1 from *Hamlet: The Texts of 1603 and 1623*, ed. Ann Thompson and Neil Taylor (London: Arden Shakespeare, 2006). I sometimes modify the Arden punctuation, which seems to me more academic than theatrical.
3. In preparing the script used in my production I worked from David Bevington's transcriptions of Q1, Q2, and F1 on the Internet Shakespeare website, http://internetshakespeare.uvic.ca/Library/Texts/Ham/
4. Taylor and Thompson align these two speeches differently in their edition.
5. Q1 has 'Gilderstone and Rossencraft'; in my production I substituted the usual forms of the names. It does not seem to me that the variants in the names, between the early editions, has any significance.

Chapter 3
Ofelia's Interruption of Ophelia in *Hamlet*

Michael M. Wagoner

    BARNARDO   Last night of all,
                     When yonder star that's westward from the pole
                     Had made his course to illumine that part of heaven
                     Where now it burns, the bell then tolling one –
                            Enter Ghost.
    MARCELLUS   Break off your talk, see where it comes again!
                     (*Hamlet* Q1, 1.26–29)[1]

Hamlet is a play of interruptions. From entering ghosts to disrupted performances, the play's ideas, actions and statements often never reach their expected conclusions. This chapter considers these interruptions as formal structures. When a character invades the speaking rights of another character or when an expectation is unfulfilled, that is an interruption. Interruptions comprise three parts: premise, rupture and continuation. The premise is a statement or action that possesses the expectation of completion. A rupture is when a character speaks out of turn or an action occurs that stops the premise from reaching its expected conclusion. The continuation is the subsequent outcome: the premise can reassert itself, the rupture can dominate, or the two may combine into a synthetic new outcome.[2] For example, Barnardo's story quoted above is a premise, the Ghost's entrance is a rupture, and Marcellus's response is a continuation. In this interruption, the rupture dominates the premise as Marcellus instructs Barnardo to stop talking and pay attention. I use this terminology as I consider the interruptions in the first quarto (Q1) of *Hamlet*.

Interruptions, despite being quotidian occurrences, demand attention because they highlight dynamic power structures. Using the example above, Barnardo initially possesses the moment's power through the attention that Horatio gives him and because the audience needs the exposition that he delivers. He first describes the setting, indicating placement of stars in the night sky to situate the characters not only locally but also temporally. His use of 'yonder' and 'Where now it burns' potentially builds an expectation of the Ghost's arrival.[3] The Ghost's entrance ruptures the story as Barnardo's line is grammatically left unfinished. This rupture represents the emergence of theatricality into the space. While Barnardo prepares to give a descriptive narrative of the previous night's encounter, the audience instead experiences the same encounter in the present moment: an expositional shift from telling to showing. The Ghost wrests the power of the scene away from Barnardo's long-winded descriptions. Marcellus's line too emphasises the dominance of the performative as he tells Barnardo to stop talking and to look. The continuation gives power to action over telling, playing over narrating. The moment then encodes the power shift away from telling an audience about the occurrences and towards the acting out of them on the stage, emphasising performance. The Ghost's entrance privileges and gives power to performance over narrative, befitting the text's genre. As this analysis demonstrates, attending to interruptions means attending to the power structures within a text. Ruptures are power grabs, but the continuation indicates whether that grab is successful or not.

The textual history of *Hamlet* since the nineteenth-century discovery of Q1 is itself one of interruption. As Zachary Lesser has argued, Q1's appearance has created an 'uncanny' understanding of the texts as occurring both before and after the two more canonical versions.[4] The arrival of Q1 into critical discourse was itself a textual interruption: it was a rupture that broke the premise and revealed much about how readers understand what 'is' *Hamlet*. When critics degrade Q1 as a 'memorial reconstruction' or 'pirated text', they reassert the power of the premise (namely the authority of the second quarto [Q2] and the First Folio [F]).[5] Conversely, when scholars consider that the text could represent an early draft, they allow the rupture to dominate.[6] Either view reifies the text as interruption within the critical discourse. Q1 is an interruption without conclusion, a continuation that continues to reassess and reassert the problems of its ruptured relationships.

One of the key features that scholars consider in debating the ruptured relationships of the text of Q1 is its theatricality. Lukas Erne in *Shakespeare as Literary Dramatist* argues for the theatricality of Q1 via Ong's theory of orality and literacy.[7] His argument asserts that the shorter text represents an oral stage version, while the longer Q2 text is a reading, literary one.[8] Paul Menzer rejects the theatricality of Q1, stating that it is the '*least* theatrical of the three texts'.[9] In fact, he argues that Q1 was created strictly for publication, making it 'the most *literary* of the early *Hamlets*'.[10] Neither scholar, however, offers a definition of what they mean by theatrical. In both analyses, the term is simply oppositional, setting Q1 against another text by alleging that one or the other has some proximity to the theatre. I argue that the Q1 text is theatrical, in the sense developed by Richard Schechner, and that it contrasts not with a 'literary' text but rather with a 'dramatic' one. Schechner explains that 'theatre is the response of the performers to the drama ... theatre is the domain of the performers', while drama is the 'domain of the author, composer, scenarist, shaman'.[11] While Schechner sees the script as conduit between the drama/author and the theatre/performer, I argue that the interruptions within the text of Q1 *Hamlet* illustrate its greater relationship to performers than to the writer. The necessity of the performer to the text of Q1 makes it theatrical in Schechner's terminology, while the directed and clarified relationships in the Q2 text make it dramatic. Developing Schechner's sense of theatre is Henry S. Turner's definition of 'theatricality' as that which 'gathers the singularity [of performance] into the reiterated, enduring conventions for representing actions, objects, and ideas on stage'.[12] He adds that theatricality 'examines how the symbolic action of everyday life has been further concentrated by translation into a specific mode of art'.[13] Therefore, the quotidian nature of the interruption becomes an aesthetic intervention that highlights the performers' role in this text.

To explore this text's specific theatricality, I focus on the Nunnery scene (Q1: scene 7, Q2: scene 8), which offers interruptive possibilities unique to Q1.[14] Interruptions highlight dynamic systems of power, which the shorter, snappier, earlier version of the play uses not only to delineate Hamlet's relationship to his lover but also to deliver a more engaged and powerful Ofelia. Deanne Williams in her analysis of Ofelia's lute playing argues that Q1 allows Ofelia 'greater agency and greater respect'.[15] My analysis of Ofelia's interruptions supports Williams' conclusions. Q1 Ofelia demands a space of power and agency that her counterpart in Q2 abdicates in favour of the central male character. Whereas Q2 minimalises the interruptive impact and solidifies power within the male character, Q1's interruptions reveal an aggressive and uncertain power struggle between lovers who approach each other on equal ground.[16] Specifically, through a comparison of present and absent language, I argue that Q2's language and structure create a dramatic, meaning directed by the playwright, encounter while Q1's openness and ambiguity demand a theatrical, meaning directed by the performer, encounter.[17]

At the beginning of Hamlet and Ophelia's exchange, Q2 shifts power away from the young woman and towards the more powerful male character.[18] After Hamlet has been musing upon mortality, upon being and not being, he encounters Ophelia:

> With this regard their currents turn awry,
> And lose the name of action. Soft you now:
> The fair Ophelia. – Nymph, in thy orisons
> Be all my sins remembered. (*Hamlet* Q2, 8.89–91)[19]

To the audience, Hamlet's change – from soliloquy to Ophelia – is not an interruption because no alteration in premise has occurred. The King has already explained his intention to set up this scenario so that Hamlet might 'as 'twere by accident' come upon Ophelia (*Hamlet* Q2, 8.32). Therefore, when Hamlet sees Ophelia and engages her, it completes an expectation based upon the King's plan. However, from the vantage of the character/actor of Hamlet, this moment is significantly interruptive. His speech gives no indication that he initially sees Ophelia, and his self-instruction – 'Soft you now' – suggests a need to change his speech upon realising her presence. In this sense, these lines denote self-interruption. The premise is Hamlet's speaking by himself, considering either suicide or killing the King.[20] The rupture is his noting her presence, which his self-directive to speak more quietly points to, and the continuation is his plea for her to pray for his sins. The *New Oxford Shakespeare* provides a performance note: 'Ophelia comes forward, or re-enters; or Hamlet only now notices her' (*Hamlet* Q2, 8.89–90n). This note lays out the two potential ruptures within this action: either Hamlet notices Ophelia or she gets his attention. The performance choices within these possibilities are myriad; however, the decision determines the power dynamic, because the person who ruptures is the person who possesses power. If Ophelia performs the rupture, she becomes a powerful lady who stops Hamlet's meditations, a woman who insists upon her presence. If Hamlet ruptures, he retains the power of the scene as he controls the audience's gaze over Ophelia, allowing her to be part of the scene once he has taken her in.

While Q2 contains both possibilities, Hamlet's line – 'Soft you now: / The fair Ophelia' – guides the interpretation and reception of the interruption. In voicing the rupture, he retains the power of the scene through directing the acknowledgement of her presence. She does not exist in the scene until he notices her. Furthermore, even if she is the source of the rupture, her rupture must be somewhat distant as his line, with its self-direction and third person identification, suggests distance.[21] Her re-entrance, while allowing her control of the rupture, stages the same dynamic by physically removing her from the scene and permitting her re-entry when Hamlet allows. This control further reduces Ophelia as a character, keeping her within the strictures of Hamlet's control both visually and vocally. His word 'Nymph' further subjugates her through emphasising femininity and sexuality.[22] The interruption highlights his acknowledgement of her presence, his own determination for her not to hear him, and his diminution of her as a character through a potentially derogatory epithet. The Q2 text, therefore, creates an interruption that is realised *through* Hamlet. From the self-direction to the epithet, the interruption is one where he retains power in the continuation. This reading highlights how this text is dramatic in its methodology of control. Even if Ophelia ruptures Hamlet's speech and challenges the power dynamic, the text resists that interpretation through its presentation, placing power solely with Hamlet.

The Q1 version of this scene begins with an interruptive play between the two characters that leaves the nature of the exchange theatrically open, allowing Ofelia agency. In the earlier text, Hamlet states:

> Which makes us rather bear those evils we have
> Than fly to others that we know not of?
> Ay, that – O, this conscience makes cowards of us all.
> – Lady, in thy orisons be all my sins remembered.
> (*Hamlet* Q1, 7.136–137)

In the grammatical rupture between 'all' and 'Lady', Ofelia engages the scene. While the 1603 printed text uses a comma, Thompson and Taylor use a dash because it is the most common piece of modern punctuation to indicate interruption.[23] What the modern dash represents is Ofelia's intrusion into the moment that ruptures Hamlet's speechifying. This text, however, does not suggest how that initial interaction occurs. Thompson and Taylor provide a note, stating 'Hamlet sees Ofelia here' (*Hamlet* Q1, 7.137n), which gives Hamlet, in subject position, the power of the scene. The two lines in the text offer no such clear reading; Thompson and Taylor's note continues a bias derived from the Q2 text where Hamlet's comment on the rupture keeps himself in the power position. The lacuna that Thompson and Taylor's dash fills is a theatrical moment that the performers construct. Considering this moment as an interruption helps to lay out its possibilities. As before, the premise is Hamlet's speech, the rupture is Hamlet reacting to Ofelia's presence, and the continuation is his acknowledgement of her presence with his plea to have her pray for him. What is striking about this interruption is that the rupture is not clear in the written text. The two lines represent premise and continuation but the rupture lives between the end of one type line and the beginning of the next. While Q2 fills the rupture with Hamlet's 'Soft you now: / The fair Ophelia', Q1 instead demarcates a space for possibility. These possibilities are, as before, essentially of two varieties: either Hamlet notices Ofelia or Ofelia gets Hamlet's attention.[24] The problem with Thompson and Taylor's note is that it offers readers only one end of a spectrum in which Hamlet controls the vision of the audience. This ignores the theatricality by subsuming it within a dramatic necessity, meaning that the textual apparatus's insistence on giving Hamlet control eradicates the text's theatrical possibilities, a control that Q1 does not require or enforce.

The openness of the rupture provides Ofelia with a greater chance to engage in the power dynamic of the scene. She can establish her presence outside of Hamlet's control. Whatever the rupture, Hamlet immediately reacts. Furthermore, he calls her 'Lady' not 'Nymph'; he uses a word that powerfully denotes her aristocratic status. By referring to her with a title befitting her station and not a potentially sexualised allusion, he concretises her as the person before him and allows her an equality of agency. He does not dismiss her as something not of his world, but he situates her within a political and social reality. In Q1, Hamlet deals with a person who possesses agency in a scene that explores the struggle over who has dominance. In Q2, Hamlet deals with a lesser person whom he diminishes and continues to control.

This differentiation further plays out in Ofelia's response to Hamlet's continuation of the rupture. In all texts, Hamlet concludes the interruption with a continuation in which he attempts to move back to the premise, meaning he tries to return to his solitude. He acknowledges her, but hardly opens up for a conversation. This continuation ends the conversation and would end the scene if he exited, but Ofelia responds. Her response, interrupting his implied exit, keeps Hamlet in the scene and further demonstrates the differentiation between a less powerful Ophelia and a more equal Ofelia. In Q2, Ophelia asks, 'Good my lord, / How does your honour for this many a day?' (*Hamlet* Q2, 8.91–92). She keeps him in the scene by engaging him with a question about himself. As with his own self-focus in noticing Ophelia, here too the text keeps the audience fixated on Hamlet through Ophelia's concern for him. Her question opens dialogue whereas his first response had cut it off. She interrupts Hamlet's ending of the scene by asking him a question about himself, with which he engages. Her question ruptures his premise of leaving, and he responds, which continues her rupture. While her interruption is a power move to keep Hamlet in the scene, she relinquishes the power she gains by turning the focus solely on him.

Q1 Ofelia also interrupts Hamlet's attempt to make her continue praying, but she makes that interruption about herself. Instead of asking how he is doing, she assertively explains, 'My lord, I have sought opportunity, which now I have, to redeliver to your worthy hands a small remembrance – such tokens which I have received of you' (*Hamlet* Q1, 7.138–141). Unlike her Q2 counterpart, Ofelia interrupts and asserts her agency in describing her desire to return Hamlet's gifts. She is the subject of her own sentence. Her parenthetical 'which now I have' even further asserts her sense of self and agency by emphasising the present moment which she occupies alongside Hamlet.[25] Ofelia's move to emphasise self underscores how this text supports her as a character more equal in power to Hamlet. She does not demurely ask about his well-being, but asserts the point of her meeting him, the successful culmination of a history of seeking. A similar line appears later in Q2, but there she pleads, 'My lord, I have remembrances of yours / That I have longèd long to redeliver. / I pray you now receive them' (*Hamlet* Q2, 8.94–96). Unlike the direct assertion in Q1, Q2 Ophelia develops an image of pining through her repetition of 'long' and shows supplication in her redelivery by asking him to take them back. Q2 Ophelia is demure questions and fawning; Q1 Ofelia is assertive and direct.

Through this characterisation, the scenes develop a dichotomy in respect to the power relationship between Hamlet and Ofelia. Q2 produces a duo where power is clearly situated in the prince, and the young woman struggles as he wields his power throughout the conversation. Q1, however, offers a relationship that is more equal in its power struggle as Ofelia defies becoming Hamlet's object and assumes agency. This dynamic in Q1 becomes clear as Hamlet ruptures Ofelia's attempt to give back her 'tokens'. Hamlet's response to the returned remembrances in Q1 is the non-sequitur, 'Are you fair?' (*Hamlet* Q1, 7.142). Instead of acknowledging her request, or even denying it as in Q2, he ruptures the conversation by changing it entirely. Such an interruption is Hamlet's reassertion of power. He refuses her attempt to control the conversation by controlling the conversation himself. In this moment of leading the conversation aside, Hamlet acknowledges how Ofelia has grabbed power by wresting it back. In Q2, he responds with laughter before his question (*Hamlet* Q2, 8.104). The self-assuredness of Hamlet's responses to Ophelia's requests in Q2 clashes with his abrupt shifts in Q1, but not because Q1 is a corrupted text. Rather, Q1 offers theatrical interruptions that demonstrate an Ofelia that is almost equal in power to Hamlet, forcing him to fight for control.

Hamlet's tirade about the nunnery and Ophelia's responses reveal a similar bifurcation. In Q2, Ophelia has four speeches in this section:

> At home, my lord. (*Hamlet* Q2, 8.128)
> O help him, you sweet heavens. (*Hamlet* Q2, 8.131)
> Heavenly powers restore him! (*Hamlet* Q2, 8.137)
> O what a noble mind is here o'erthrown! ... (*Hamlet* Q2, 8.144)

The first speech is a response to Hamlet's question, and the final speech, which has eleven more lines, is her only soliloquy, delivered after Hamlet exits. Neither of these are interruptions. The two other speeches, however, are interjections that have the shape of an interruption. They break up Hamlet's rant. Neither has incomplete grammar, commentary from the speakers, or punctuation (in any early or modern edition) to signal an interruption. Two aspects of the exchange, though, suggest that these moments are interruptive: the cue structure of the exchange and Hamlet's responses.

The cue structure of this moment indicates that Ophelia's part has one repeated cue, which creates an interruption in performance.[26] Ophelia's part for this section would have looked like this:

> .... [Where's] [your] father?
> At home, my lord.
> .... [own] [house.] Farewell.
> O help him, you sweet heavens.
> .... [quickly] [too.] Farewell.
> Heavenly powers restore him!
> .... [a] [nunn'ry,] go.
> O what a noble mind is here o'erthrown!

Hamlet notably cues both of the interjecting speeches with 'Farewell' (*Hamlet* Q2, 8.130, 136), which means that the actor playing Ophelia would be listening for that word of dismissal to deliver those lines. The actor might have the two words before the Farewell, but the word itself would be a sufficient cue to deliver her pleas to heaven. Importantly though, if the young boy actor is listening for a second 'Farewell' after delivering, 'O help him, you sweet heavens', he would in the middle of Hamlet's speech hear a repeated cue:

> HAMLET   If thou dost marry, I'll give thee this plague for thy dowry: be thou as chaste as ice, as pure as snow, thou shalt not escape calumny. Get thee to a nunn'ry, **farewell**. Or if thou wilt needs marry, marry a fool; for wise men know well enough what monsters you make of them. To a nunn'ry, go, and quickly too. Farewell. (*Hamlet* Q2, 8.132–136, emphasis added)

The mid-speech 'farewell' might prompt Ophelia to begin delivering her next interjection. If she does speak, then the repeated cue creates an interruption in which both characters interrupt each other. Ophelia will begin her next line before Hamlet has finished, and he will stop her from continuing that line to complete his own. A performance or a rehearsal would easily eliminate the spontaneity of this repeated cue (as with all repeated cues), but whether the actors clarify the exchange or use it, the text offers it as a dramatic possibility. Furthermore, it establishes and colours the way that the other interjections work both within the power dynamic and the interruptive structure. As I have argued, Q2 renders Ophelia firmly within the control of Hamlet as central character, and this moment places her further within that structure. If she tries to begin speaking and he does not allow her to, because of the repeated cue, then we see a Hamlet who interrupts Ophelia's attempt to pray for him, precisely the act that he enjoins her to at the top of their scene. This Hamlet relinquishes control by dismissing her only to grab it back by continuing to speak and not allowing her to complete her thought. She only asserts her own mind in her final speech once Hamlet has left the stage.

While the repeated cue gives Ophelia one moment of interruption, Hamlet's wresting the speaking rights back illustrates how Ophelia is not the interrupter: Hamlet is. Both of her interjections, as noted, respond to Hamlet's saying goodbye to her. In saying 'Farewell', Hamlet opens a space for Ophelia to respond as he should leave. He has concluded the scene. Instead of allowing her to deliver a speech, which she eventually does, he stops her interjections by continuing to speak over her. He re-engages the scene after he has ended it. In terms of interruptions, he ruptures the premise of the end of the scene by insisting on its continuance, and the continuation is a further rant that once more reaches a conclusion and is once more continued. Hamlet crafts his power through assertive ruptures and continuations that rupture his own proposed premise, meaning that he is the one trying to end the scene, yet cannot do it. In this way, Ophelia's brief interjections are passive interruptions that do not alter the course of Hamlet's tirade. His speech here becomes more self-interruption than dialogic. In fact, we might posit an edition that ends both of Ophelia's interjections with dashes:

OPHELIA	O help him, you sweet heavens –
HAMLET	If thou dost marry, I'll give thee this plague for thy dowry: ... To a nunn'ry, go, and quickly too. Farewell.
OPHELIA	Heavenly powers restore him –
HAMLET	I have heard of your paintings well enough ...

In this presentation, a reader may perceive Hamlet's interruptive moves, even imagining that Ophelia has more to say, which she eventually does.

Ofelia too has a series of interjections in the Q1 text; however, her series demonstrates a character vying for power. Her intensity of response demands an intensity of response from Hamlet, raising the emotional game for both characters. Ofelia's part in Q1 in this section is greater than her counterpart. In fact, examining the section from Hamlet's first acknowledgement of Ophelia/Ofelia to the first line of her soliloquy reveals that, in both texts, she speaks about 26% of the words in that section. However, during the nunnery tirade, Ofelia speaks 11% while Ophelia only speaks 8%.[27] Once more, the change in texts reduces Ophelia's ability to engage with the power dynamic of the scene. This reduction accords with the alteration in characterisation, reducing her interruptive and aggressive theatricality.

As explored above, Ophelia's interjections are mostly not interruptive as they stem from Hamlet's goodbye. Q1's Ofelia, however, vies for power against a Hamlet who tries to dismiss her, but is repeatedly ignored. Like Q2, the cue structure of the exchange reveals these aspects of the power dynamic.[28] Ofelia's part would look like this:

```
............................................. [a] [nunnery,] go!
O heavens secure him!
............................................. [Where's] [thy] father?
At home, my lord.
............................................. [a] [nunnery,] go!
Help him, good God.
............................................. [a] [nunnery,] go!
Alas, what change is this?
............................................. [a] [nunnery,] go!
Pray God restore him.
............................................. [a] [nunnery,] go!
Great God of heaven, what a quick change is this?
```

Five of her cues are 'a nunnery, go', making Ofelia's memorisation of cues a bit easier, even if slightly confusing. The boy actor would speak the next line whenever he heard that phrase. Perhaps the repetition becomes almost a mnemonic aid, allowing a young boy actor a crutch. However, the phrase 'a nunnery, go' is repeated in non-cue position three other times during the exchange. Hamlet's first speech about the nunnery contains two of those mid-speech iterations:

> HAMLET   O, thou shouldst not ha' believed me! Go to **a nunnery, go**. Why shouldst thou be a breeder of sinners? I am myself indifferent honest, but I could accuse myself of such crimes it had been better my mother had ne'er born me. O, I am very proud, ambitious, disdainful, with more sins at my beck than I have thoughts to put them in. What should such fellows as I do, crawling between heaven and earth? To **a nunnery, go**. We are arrant knaves all. Believe none of us. To a nunnery, go.
> (*Hamlet* Q1, 7.162–171)

Unlike Q2 Ophelia whose repeated cue occurs after her first interjection, Ofelia here immediately reacts to Hamlet's suggestion that she enter a nunnery. His command to her elicits an attempted response, which he quickly closes off in order to keep speaking. She tries to interrupt him, but he overrides her interruption. The same reaction occurs at the end of the speech as well, building the dynamic between the characters, until Ofelia finally delivers her line in full. Her first iteration significantly is 'O heavens secure him!'. As Thompson and Taylor note, 'secure' means 'save, protect' (*Hamlet* Q1, 7.172n), which accords with her following verbs of 'help' and 'restore'. However, unlike those later lines, this iteration is unique in that it prompts a specific response from Hamlet. To her request that he be secured, Hamlet asks, 'Where's thy father?' (*Hamlet* Q1, 7.173). Her line requesting his security signals Hamlet's awareness that something might be not right and that Corambis may be involved. One theatrical potential is that Ofelia calls out not to heaven in general but to her father and the King specifically for help. While the meaning of 'secure' as to fasten or to confine is not recorded in the *Oxford English Dictionary* until the early seventeenth century, this line leads towards that sense of the verb as she requests protection for him, but also potentially *from* him in his erratic behaviour.[29] Her line interrupts his twice, trying to get the attention of her father and the King, who do not help her. She remains locked in the battle with Hamlet, but unlike Ophelia, Ofelia continues to contend with him.

After the repeated cue at the beginning and the request for securing Hamlet, Ofelia has three more interjections, two of which are almost exactly repeated in Q2 (though the more direct 'God' in Q1 is changed to the milder 'heavens' in Q2).[30] The third line occurs between those two and is another moment of Ofelia's unique interruptive and theatrical power. In Q1, Ofelia breaks up Hamlet's commentary on marriage with the interjection, 'Alas, what a change is this!' (*Hamlet* Q1, 7.182). Like the others in Q1, this interjection is cued by 'a nunnery, go', which is a command for her to leave. Unlike Hamlet's cue of 'Farewell' in Q2 (which renders the interruption Hamlet's), his command and her disregard of it in Q1 makes the interruption hers. She ruptures his premise by ignoring the command and taking power back, attempting to remind him of what has previously been. She rejects his callous discussion of marriage, by highlighting the newness of these views. Before she can continue, though, Hamlet is back on the attack, further deprecating her. Notably, the single repeated cue in Q2 occurs at this moment where Ofelia comments on Hamlet's change. Even when Q2 gives Ophelia the chance to rupture and grab power through a repeated cue, her power is less than what the Q1 text permits, as Ofelia directly confronts Hamlet with his change in attitude. The completed vocalisation from Ofelia denotes a successful grab for power, even if Hamlet immediately takes it back, whereas Q2's repeated cue gives an ineffectual interruption. Therefore, Q2's one repeated cue loses its interruptive power in light of Q1's complete and direct confrontation. While Q1 has several repeated cues, which call for Ofelia to try but fail to grab power, their greater amount coupled with their placement disrupts an audience's ability to adjudge who possesses power in the scene. The power brokers become the performers as they hash out Ofelia's many interruptions, both successful and not.

While the repeated cues in Q1 may make the scene messy, that messiness charges the power dynamic between the characters as they interrupt each other. Considering that Hamlet's last line is a repeated 'To a nunnery, go. To a nunnery, go!' (*Hamlet* Q1, 7.194), we might notice how Hamlet loses his battle with Ofelia. He has repeatedly insisted upon her leaving, but she has refused his commands and instead has attempted to communicate with him. Therefore, her final speech begins potentially with exasperation – 'Great God of heaven, what a quick change is this!' (*Hamlet* Q1, 7.195) – as she first tries to talk with him, but he leaves. His leaving the fight gives up the power to Ofelia in an almost childish storming off, while she maintains her ground and expresses her anger and annoyance over his behaviour, which she characterises violently as 'dashed and splintered thence!' (*Hamlet* Q1, 7.197). As a comparison, the later Ophelia, once alone, shifts immediately to consideration of Hamlet's 'noble mind' that is 'o'erthrown' (Q2 8.144) and recolours the violence of Q1 in the softened phrase, 'quite, quite down' (*Hamlet* Q2, 8.148). Once more, the end of the scene illustrates the disparity between the two characters, where Q2 renders Ophelia a passive object and Q1 gives Ofelia an assertive agency.

Q1's nunnery scene contains interruptions that are theatrical in nature. They open up opportunities for performers to explore the dynamics of the characters, but they also illustrate characters that are in a more equal and dynamic relationship, perhaps because in Q1 the two characters seem to be about the same age, both teenagers.[31] Q2 removes the interruptions between the characters and enhances the sense of self-interruption for Hamlet, placing the power firmly within his grasp and objectifying Ophelia. If Q1 represents a young Burbage in his first big role, then his scene with a boy actor here is one of equals, perhaps because he too not long before might have been playing such roles.[32] It is not the patriarchal dynamic within Q2 where an older Burbage would have been working with a much younger apprentice.[33] Q1 and its interruptive schema represents a young and vital text with an Ofelia who is assertive and aggressive, able to contend with the prince of Denmark not as a weepy girl but as a powerful young woman.

Michael M. Wagoner is Assistant Professor of English at the United States Naval Academy. His book *Interruptions in Early Modern English Drama* is forthcoming from Arden Shakespeare/Bloomsbury.

Notes

1. A note about texts: quotations from the first quarto (Q1) are from *Hamlet: The Texts of 1603 and 1623*, ed. Ann Thompson and Neil Taylor (London: Bloomsbury Arden Shakespeare, 2006). Quotations from the second quarto (Q2) are from *Hamlet*, ed. John Jowett, in *The New Oxford Shakespeare: Complete Works: Modern Critical Edition*, ed. Gary Taylor et al. (Oxford: Oxford University Press, 2016), 1993–2099.
2. I present these as discrete outcomes, but they exist on a spectrum with asymptotic limits on either side. Once a rupture has occurred, the premise can never fully recover its power; so too, as a rupture invades the space of the premise, that premise will colour the rupture's dominance.
3. Expecting the interruption does negate some of its power; however, as I argue elsewhere, this is typical of Shakespearean interruptions, which broadly speaking embrace dramatic irony, meaning the interruption occurs for the characters though not necessarily for an audience member. See Michael M. Wagoner, 'Defining Dramatic and Theatrical Interruptions: Shakespeare, Jonson, Fletcher' (PhD diss, Florida State University, 2018).
4. Zachary Lesser, *Hamlet After Q1: An Uncanny History of the Shakespearean Text* (Philadelphia: University of Pennsylvania Press, 2015), 10–11.
5. While memorial reconstruction has been mostly abandoned, Tiffany Stern advocates for the theory that Q1 is a pirated text made by note-takers in the audience. This is a modification of the mostly abandoned 'shorthand' theory, but like shorthand and memorial reconstruction, Stern's theory insists that Q1 is a 'bad quarto'. See Tiffany Stern, 'Sermons, Plays, and Note Takers: *Hamlet* Q1 as a "Noted" Text', in *Shakespeare Survey* 66, ed. Peter Holland (Cambridge: Cambridge University Press, 2013), 1–23.
6. The leading voice for this hypothesis is Terri Bourus, who argues that Q1 represents the so-called Ur-*Hamlet* from the late 1580s and was written by Shakespeare as his first draft of the play. See Terri Bourus, *Young Shakespeare's Young Hamlet* (New York: Palgrave Macmillan, 2014), passim, but especially 209–212. Gary Taylor and Rory Loughnane also consider Shakespeare's authorship of the Ur-*Hamlet* in their examination of the date of the play. See Gary Taylor and Rory Loughnane, 'The Canon and Chronology of Shakespeare's Works', in *The New Oxford Shakespeare: Authorship Companion*, ed. Gary Taylor and Gabriel Egan (Oxford: Oxford University Press, 2017), 417–601, here 542–548.
7. Lukas Erne, *Shakespeare as Literary Dramatist* (Cambridge: Cambridge University Press, 2003), 244.
8. For a thorough consideration of the problems that Erne encounters in arguing Q1 as a theatrical but also bad text, see Bourus, *Young Shakespeare's Young Hamlet*, 95–98.
9. Paul Menzer, *The Hamlets: Cues, Qs, and Remembered Texts* (Newark: University of Delaware Press, 2008), 64–65.
10. Ibid., 21. Zachary Lesser and Peter Stallybrass also advocate for seeing the text as a literary one because of its commonplacing quotation marks. See Zachary Lesser and Peter Stallybrass, 'The First Literary *Hamlet* and the Commonplacing of Professional Plays', *Shakespeare Quarterly* 59, no. 4 (2008), 371–420, here 379–380. It bears mentioning, however, that Lesser and Stallybrass specifically examine the

text as presented in the printing of Q1, noting, 'We do not want to deny that Q1 testifies in some way to a version of the play as produced on the early modern stage (as do Q2 and F)' (379). This caveat to their analysis makes it not fully at odds with Bourus's hypothesis, nor does it advocate for Menzer's theory of literary assemblage.
11. Richard Schechner, 'Drama, Script, Theatre, and Performance', *TDR* 17, no. 3 (1973), 5–36, here 8.
12. Henry S. Turner, 'Generalization', in *Early Modern Theatricality: Oxford Twenty-First Century Approaches to Literature*, ed. Henry S. Turner (Oxford: Oxford University Press, 2013), 1–23, here 6.
13. Ibid., 6.
14. For the rest of the chapter, I focus on the differences between Q1 and Q2. I exclusively use Q2 in this analysis for simplicity, and not because the F does something different. Importantly, both texts (Q2 and F) present Ophelia and her interruptions in the Nunnery scene in the same manner.
15. Deanne Williams, 'Enter Ofelia Playing on a Lute', in *The Afterlife of Ophelia*, ed. Kaara L. Peterson and Deanne Williams (New York: Palgrave Macmillan, 2012), 119–136, here 132.
16. If Q1 is indeed by Shakespeare, this reading then prompts a consideration of his altering conception and creation of female characters for the early modern stage.
17. Many of my observations about the theatrical interactions in the Q1 text derive from my work co-directing a production with Terri Bourus at Florida State University in the autumn of 2017. I could not have conceived of the theatrical power of this exchange were it not for the great work of our actors: Blair Graff as Ofelia and Bradley Johnson as Hamlet. That said, because I examine the text throughout and not the choices of Graff or Johnson, I often engage dramatic qualities of Q1. However, the various lacunae that performers like Graff and Johnson must fill engenders the productively interruptive nature of this text and asserts its theatrical identity.
18. I begin with Q2 because that is what most readers and critics will recognise. Therefore, I intend to establish an understanding based upon received knowledge before examining the less well-known Q1 text. While this may 'reiterate the anachronistic vector that has governed all readings of the 1603 text since it was rediscovered in 1823' (Bourus, *Young Shakespeare's Young Hamlet*, 97), my reading of Q1 as a critical interruption supports such a vector. We must first understand the expectation before it can be ruptured. To this end, I explore the critical expectation as established in Q2 before analysing the radical rupture found in Q1.
19. The best indicators of interruptions within a text are grammatical incompletion, comments by the speakers, and punctuation. Punctuation is the most contentious of the three because the earliest texts do not follow clear standards: see John Jowett, 'Full Pricks and Great P's: Spelling, Punctuation, Accidentals', in *Shakespeare and Textual Studies*, ed. Margaret Jane Kidnie and Sonia Massai (Cambridge: Cambridge University Press, 2015), 317–331, especially 319. Therefore, modern editors often feel at liberty to punctuate a speech to fit their conception of the character or scene. For the impact of an editor on punctuation, see Stanley Wells, 'Modernizing Shakespeare's Spelling', in *Modernizing Shakespeare's Spelling with Three Studies in the Text of Henry V*, by Stanley Wells and Gary Taylor (Oxford: Oxford University Press, 1979), 3–36, here 31–34.

20. For an overview of the scholarship of this speech in both texts, see Lesser, *Hamlet After Q1*, 157–206.
21. We might think of a humorous alternative, but the humour would be a choice of a production and still would underserve Ophelia as his acknowledgement of her becomes an awkward joke and not a serious consideration.
22. See 'nymph, n.1', *OED Online* (accessed June 2017), Oxford University Press, www.oed.com/view/Entry/129400. Definition 2a notes that the word could mean prostitute, which accords with the resonance of 'nunnery' with brothel.
23. Dashes were rare pieces of punctuation in the period and became significant in printed drama later in the seventeenth century through their usage in the works of Ben Jonson. See David Bevington, Martin Butler and Ian Donaldson, 'General Introduction', in *The Cambridge Edition of the Works of Ben Jonson*, Vol. 1 (Cambridge: Cambridge University Press, 2012), lx–lxxxvi, here lxxxi; and H.R. Woudhuysen, 'The Foundations of Shakespeare's Text', in *Proceedings of the British Academy: 2003 Lectures*, Vol. 125 (Oxford: Oxford University Press, 2004), 69–100, here 90. A convention of twentieth/twenty-first-century editions of early modern drama is to add a dash whenever a speaker changes addressee. Not all of these are interruptions, though some are. Jowett's dash in his edition of Q2 seems only to indicate the change in addressee as the rupture has already occurred when Hamlet says 'Soft you now'. But the dash in Thompson and Taylor's edition of Q1 is both interruption and change of addressee.
24. During a recent workshop that I conducted, one student offered that Ofelia might interrupt Hamlet by kissing him, which would prompt his mentioning of 'sin'. This delightful interpretation not only makes sense of his response, it establishes the characters' back story and theatrically represents their relationship. Ultimately, Q1's openness allows for such theatrical innovation, whereas a kiss would be unclear and awkward in the middle of Q2's 'Soft you now'.
25. We might even consider this parenthetical as a self-interruption. Self-interruptions, as I argue, hint at interiority and subjectivity for a character as it presupposes a mind that can change in the moment through its hidden rupture. See Wagoner '"Close-Dilations, Working from the Heart": Self-Interruptions', in 'Defining Dramatic and Theatrical Interruptions'.
26. For more on repeated cues and interruptions, see Simon Palfrey and Tiffany Stern, *Shakespeare in Parts* (Oxford: Oxford University Press, 2007), especially 157–164. Their analysis concludes that while repeated cues can create interrupted dialogue, they should not be seen as demanding an automatic response from an actor; they would be negotiated by both actors (163). As I demonstrate here, this moment is an important usage of a repeated cue, even if the actor playing Ophelia knows that her cue is later. As I indicate below with square brackets, cues are generally of one to three words in length (21).
27. *Hamlet* Q1, scene 7, lines 162–195 is made of 283 words, divided into thirty-four lines and twelve speeches (six each). I am only counting the first line of Ofelia/Ophelia's soliloquy and not the entirety. I do not count the whole because Q2 significantly amps up that speech (adding fifty-nine words), which would overweight Ophelia's participation in the scene. I do not omit it entirely because Q1's early cue in Hamlet's final line makes the first part of Ofelia's final speech part of the exchange. *Hamlet* Q2, scene 8, lines 120–144 is made of 274 words, divided into twenty-five lines and eight speeches (four each). In both texts, Hamlet speaks 252

words, which means that his part does not significantly change in size between the two. The main difference is a reduction in Ofelia's part: she goes from 11% of the exchange down to 8%. Therefore, while in Q1 she has more to say in the nunnery exchange, in Q2 she speaks more in the earlier half of their interaction. The reduction is in the number of interruptive interjections that she has during Hamlet's rant: for Q1, four of Ofelia's six speeches are such interjections, while only two of her four speeches in Q2 perform the same function.

28. This passage is a central example for Paul Menzer's demonstration that Q1 is not a theatrical text. He argues that the cues here make the scene 'virtually unplayable' and concludes: 'Commentators who automatically assume Q1 to be a theatrical text do not attend closely enough to processes of textual dissemination in the early English theater' (65). I disagree. As my analysis demonstrates, the repeated cue structure and messiness that it produces reveal the complicated power dynamics of the Q1 text between Hamlet and Ofelia and provide a specifically theatrical text, though perhaps not a dramatic one. See Menzer, *The Hamlets*, 59–70.
29. See 'secure, v.'. *OED Online* (accessed June 2017), Oxford University Press, www.oed.com/view/Entry/174648, especially meanings 5a and 6. Jonathan Hope has argued that we cannot equate the first recorded entry in the *OED* with the first usage. As he explains, 'citations [in the *OED*] are exemplary not evidential' (23). This usage of 'secure' might be a site where Shakespeare is 'respond[ing] to and reflect[ing] the rapid changes going on in the vocabulary of English at the time' (45). See Jonathan Hope, 'Who Invented "Gloomy"? Lies People Want to Believe about Shakespeare', *Memoria di Shakespeare: The Shape of Language* 3 (2016), 21–45.
30. Thompson and Taylor add the stage direction '[*aside*]' to all three of her iterations except for 'Alas what a change is this'. I disagree with these emendations as they remove the dynamic between the characters. The usage of asides accords better with Q2 Ophelia who has little or no power in the scene, whereas Q1 Ofelia actively engages Hamlet. Like their other notes, too often Thompson and Taylor edit Q1 in light of Q2, trying to make the texts the same when they are clearly different.
31. For more on the age of Hamlet, see Terri Bourus, 'Enter Shakespeare's Young Hamlet, 1589', *Actes des congrès de la Société française Shakespeare* 34 (2016), paragraphs 1–36, here paragraph 35, doi:10.4000/shakespeare.3736.
32. Bourus explores the idea that Q1 Hamlet was Burbage's first major role and collaboration with Shakespeare. See Bourus, *Young Shakespeare's Young Hamlet*, 156.
33. For more on the idea of Burbage as a boy actor playing female characters, see Terri Bourus, 'Performance and Attribution: *Arden of Faversham*, Richard Burbage, and the Early Shakespeare Canon', in *Early Shakespeare*, ed. Rory Loughnane and Andrew Power (Cambridge: Cambridge University Press, forthcoming).

Chapter 4
Beautified Q1 *Hamlet*

Douglas Bruster

Whatever its origins, moment or moments of composition, performance history or subsequent reception, Q1 *Hamlet* participated – perhaps even more consequentially than other imprints of 1603 – in the representation market of its time.[1] As a playbook issued in the busy print marketplace of early modern London, it was evaluated alongside a host of options for entertainment and edification that year, and would soon be joined by, and doubtless measured against, Q2 *Hamlet*. For this reason, *what* Q1 was, and is, can be better grasped by examining more closely *how* it looked to contemporary readers. Such is one lesson of Zachary Lesser and Peter Stallybrass's groundbreaking essay on Q1 *Hamlet* (hereafter 'Q1'), which deepens our understanding of this puzzling text in part by revisiting elements of the playbook's physical presentation.[2] The quotation marks applied to Corambis's wise saws in Q1, for example, demonstrate its links to the culture of commonplacing and to the larger literary domain with which that culture was associated. What is often

Notes for this section begin on page 87.

received as a performance text therefore takes on additional meaning when examined in the contexts of the London book trade.[3] Building on such recent attention to Q1's material text, we could investigate an often overlooked aspect of this playbook's makeup: the dominance of typographic verse in its pages. It is important to qualify the word 'verse' this way, as *typographic verse*, for a curious and still unexplained feature of this playbook is its representation of various prose speeches as blank verse.

Before addressing this feature of Q1, however, we need to locate it in the pages of today's editions. This is easier said than done, for Q1's predominance of verse – its typographic representation of prose as verse – is downplayed, if not entirely erased, in the most recent and authoritative version of the text. Like several earlier versions, the Arden 3 edition of Ann Thompson and Neil Taylor beautifies Q1 for the modern eye and ear by manufacturing prose for it – or, as they describe the process, 'setting the text as prose'.[4] It will be worth returning to the significance of this adjustment, as well as to its unacknowledged irony. First, though, some basics. Q1 *Hamlet* has 2,220 lines, most of them (2,155) dialogue.[5] Of these dialogue lines, only fifteen, or less than 1% of the text, are right justified serially in the blocks that would confirm dramatic prose to the eye of an early modern bookbuyer. And of these fifteen, only eleven, or just over half of 1% of the text, seem unmistakably to be prose at a glance. Visually, the *Hamlet* of 1603 is largely a verse drama. To the ear, however, more than a little of this verse lacks the rhythm of iambic pentameter. Thus, a passage such as the following from Q1:

> Pronounce me this speech trippingly a the tongue as I taught thee,
> Mary and you mouth it, as a many of your players do
> I'de rather heare a towne bull bellow,
> Then such a fellow speake my lines.
> Nor do not saw the aire thus with your hands,
> But giue euery thing his action with temperance.
> O it offends mee to the soule, to heare a rebustious periwig fellow,
> To teare a passion in totters, into very ragges,
> To split the eares of the ignoraut, who for the
> Most parte are capable of nothing but dumbe shewes and noises,
> I would haue such a fellow whipt, for o're doing, tarmagant
> It out, Herodes Herod. (F2r)

is represented in the following way in Thompson and Taylor's New Arden edition:

> Pronounce me this speech tripplingly o'the
> tongue as I taught thee. Marry, an you mouth it, as a
> many of your players do, I'd rather hear a town-bull
> bellow than such a fellow speak my lines. Nor do not
> saw the air thus with your hands but give everything his
> action with temperance. O, it offends me to the soul to
> hear a robustious periwig fellow to tear a passion in
> tatters, into very rags, to split the ears of the ignorant –
> who for the most part are capable of nothing but dumb-
> shows and noises – I would have such a fellow whipped
> for o'erdoing Termagant: it out-Herods Herod! (9.1–11; 3.2)

Few would deny that Hamlet's Advice to the Players is much more plausibly set as prose than verse. Yet Q1 did the opposite, here and elsewhere, and with that decision (and other decisions) left a dilemma for every subsequent editor of this text: whether to fix verse that seems really to be prose. And, if this is done, how to rationalise this action – to justify right justification – alongside an argument concerning Q1's worth and authority as a text.

Thompson and Taylor tell us that they relineate their text only 'after considerable reflection'.[6] And across such editions, the verbal gymnastics that explain such relineation are as instructive as they are amusing. For instance, Thompson and Taylor's sober 'Policy on Q1 metre and lineation', in which they address the 'verse layout' of Q1 and intimate misgivings about compositorial habits, comes only a few pages before they announce that 'we begin with the working assumption that the copy-text accurately reflects the compositor's copy', and that they 'attribute authority to the compositor's copy'.[7] Somewhere among compositor's copy, compositor, early text and the New Arden edition, then, 'authority' seems to have become decidedly less authoritative, for the text Thompson and Taylor print diverges radically in layout from Q1. Equally contradictory but more stentorian was Albert Weiner, an earlier editor, when he declared that, 'Save for the fact that I have ... attempted to regularize, whenever possible, the lineation, I have reproduced Q1 exactly'.[8] We might notice that, in his sentence, Weiner puts the resonant 'exactly' as far as possible from the words ('Save for the fact that') that contradict it. In this same vein, when Kathleen Irace relates that 'because the differences between Q1 and the longer, more familiar versions (Q2 and F) are especially intriguing, this edition preserves as many of those differences as possible', her sentence asks us to believe that it was not merely difficult but indeed nearly impossible for her to reproduce, in a modern edition, the lineation of Q1.[9] Like the editions of Weiner, and Thompson and Taylor, Irace's edition sets much of Q1's typographic verse as prose.

For a modern edition to replicate Q1's lineation may well be undesirable, and from many standpoints, but it is far from impossible. This is confirmed by, among others, Graham Holderness and Bryan Loughrey's edition in the 'Shakespearean Originals' series.[10] There Holderness and Loughrey preserve most of Q1's lineation. Thus, Hamlet's speech to the Players, reproduced above, is identical to the 1603 quarto save for two 'turned' or 'tucked' lines (the words 'fellow' and 'noises', respectively), which their edition chooses to carry over and print on separate, subsequent lines.[11] Q1 prints them above their respective lines, preceded, as was customary, by an open paren in each instance.

If it is indeed possible to print a diplomatic Q1, doing so runs the risk of alienating modern readers, who might expect words printed as verse to scan like verse. Indeed, Thompson and Taylor may give away the game when they admit that, were a modern edition to accept Q1's lineation, 'the resulting lines are so clearly non-standard that the result might be to make Q1 appear an even stranger (and "worse" text) than it already is'.[12] We might linger over Thompson and Taylor's phrasing here, though not primarily for the scare quotes around 'worse'. Indeed, more to the point is the odd repetition of the word 'result' (both in 'resulting lines' and 'the result might be'), which seems to betray an anxiety over what Q1 would have looked like had they printed it 'as is'. We could represent the reasoning as follows: 'Because X is undesirable, let us do something to get not-X and set our policy accordingly'. As so often in editing, product precedes policy; the process is shaped strongly, even primarily, by the appearance of the book that is to be sold and evaluated.

And why not? There is no compelling reason, after all, to begrudge Weiner, Irace or Thompson and Taylor their noticeably bilingual Q1s.[13] Nothing about verse and prose is easy, not least confidently distinguishing them. So, when these media come to us apparently jumbled, as in Q1, editors' solutions are bound to create some problems even as they solve others. Following tradition, many editors change their texts' lineation to produce the maximum fit between visual cues (the arrangement of words on the page) and rhythmical reality (in the case of verse, the susceptibility of syllables to metrical interpretation). The editors of these mixed, verse/prose

Q1s have every reason to make their editions less strange than they would be were they to be printed with the 1603 text's lineation. With an apparently new Shakespeare text, being commercially viable means bringing pleasure to readers. In this case, such means acknowledging the *Hamlet* with which readers are familiar (Q2, F1, or a composite thereof) by making an unfamiliar text (Q1) look more familiar, formally, than it does in its original state. In today's textbook market, this paradox is inescapable.

Our investigation of Q1 might therefore take this lesson to heart, and proceed from the likelihood that the desire to produce an attractive, marketable book was as strong then as it is now. That said, we would eventually need to account for the *kinds* of things that made for a marketable text in or before 1602, when the idea for publishing a *Hamlet* quarto had certainly occurred to James Roberts and probably others. As part of this endeavour, we should also speculate as to what may have constituted an attractive *Shakespeare* text at the time. As we will see, answering these questions will help us understand the strange nature of verse and prose in Q1 *Hamlet* – and what, in part, Q1 is.

We saw that of Q1's 2,155 dialogue lines, only fifteen, or less than 1%, are right justified serially in blocks, and that of these fifteen, only eleven, or just over 0.5%, seem at first glance to be prose. Perhaps significantly, these eleven lines come on consecutive pages, I1r–I1v, quite late in the quarto, in the apparently unforgettable apostrophe to 'Yoricke'. There, in blocks of seven and four lines, respectively, are clear instances of prose set *as* prose in Q1. Of course, as so often with verse and prose, the grey space between these modes (at once linguistic and typographical) is larger than one suspects.[14] Throughout Q1, for instance, are thirty-odd lines that, continuing syntactically from previous lines, begin with lower-case letters – a typical signal of prose. And among these are four instances of paired prose lines – consecutive lines, that is, whose words run to the right margin: Hamlet ('Haste me to knowe it', C4r; 'Who I, your onlie jig-maker', F4r), Ofelia ('My Lord, I haue sought opportunitie', E1r) and the Clowne ('Prety agen, the gallowes', H4r) have short speeches recognisable as prose in the text. Yet it is only late in Q1 that the eleven lines of Hamlet's 'Yoricke' speech assert themselves plainly to the eye *as* prose.

Contrasted with prose-heavy plays of the era, in fact, Q1 looks like a dramatic poem, a document made up almost entirely of verse dialogue. In this, it is closer to *The Tragedie of King Richard the second* (1597; STC 22307) and *The Tragedy of King Richard the third* (1597; STC 22314), both printed, of course, by Valentine Simmes, the same man responsible for Q1 *Hamlet*. Alan Craven has argued that a single individual – 'Compositor A' – set most of Simmes's playbooks, including, in addition to Q1 *Hamlet*, *Richard II* and twelve sheets of the 1597 *Richard III*, *The First Part of the Contention* (*2 Henry VI*), *2 Henry IV* and *Much Ado About Nothing*.[15] Non-Shakespearean playbooks to which Compositor A appears to have contributed include *A Warning for Fair Women* (1599), *The Shoemakers' Holiday* (1600), *The Malcontent* (Q1 & Q3, 1604), and *Doctor Faustus* (1604). Calling him 'a compositor of unusual importance', Craven identifies various of Compositor A's habits, including preferences of spelling, punctuation and typography, and the italicising of proper names in the play's dialogue.[16] The collocation of such habits in Q1, Craven argues, 'strongly support[s] the ascription of the entire quarto to one workman, Compositor A'.[17]

What was the nature of the copy that came to Compositor A? We can assume that, acting independently or at the behest of his superiors (that is, Simmes and/or Ling and Trundell), Compositor A made programmatic adjustments to the text he received: like all manuscripts, handwritten plays routinely went through substantial modification to fit the demands of print.[18] Q1 displays a number of these modifications, and some particular ones as well: for instance, in addition to (1) the commonplace marks that Stallybrass and Lesser have examined, Q1 is notable for (2) the extent of italics it employs for characters' names and other proper names and (3) the verse template it offers readers. Together, these three aspects of Q1's typography could be seen as prestige ornamentation, a marker of what Paul Yachnin might call the 'populuxe' *Hamlet*.[19] As we will see, it seems likely – though not certain – that each of these features originated at least partly as a result of the publishing process.

Whose idea was the superflux of verse in Q1? The recorder(s)'? The publishers'? Simmes's? Compositor A's? Some combination of these? Table 1 may help us work through this question; it lists, respectively, the number of turned lines and prose lines on each page of the quarto. Because the aforementioned 'Yoricke' lines on the final sheet (sheet I) seem exceptional, they have been asterisked, and the figures for prose have been tabulated both with and without them.

Table 1. Turned lines and prose lines in Q1, by sheet and page.

Sheet / feature	1r (1)	1v (2)	2r (3)	2v (4)	3r (5)	3v (6)	4r (7)	4v (8)	Total
B prose	0	4	0	2	0	0	2	0	8
B turned lines	0	0	0	0	0	0	0	0	0
C prose	0	0	0	0	0	0	1	0	1
C turned lines	0	0	0	0	0	0	1	0	1
D prose	1	1	0	0	0	0	0	0	2
D turned lines	0	0	0	0	0	0	0	0	0
E prose	**2**	**0**	**1**	**0**	**0**	**0**	**0**	**1**	**4**
E turned lines	**0**	**0**	**0**	**0**	**3**	**1**	**1**	**0**	**5**
F prose	**0**	**0**	**2**	**0**	**2**	**2**	**3**	**0**	**9**
F turned lines	**0**	**2**	**2**	**1**	**2**	**0**	**2**	**2**	**11**
G prose	0	0	1	1	0	1	2	0	5
G turned lines	1	1	1	0	1	0	0	0	4
H prose	0	0	0	0	0	0	3	0	3
H turned lines	0	0	0	1	0	0	1	1	3
I prose	8*	4*	0	0	1	0	0	n/a	13
I turned lines	0	0	0	0	0	0	1	n/a	1
Total per page	12	12	7	5	9	4	17	4	
Total turned lines	1	3	3	2	6	1	**6**	4	
Total prose	11*	9*	3	6	3	3	**11**	1	
Prose w/o 'Yoricke'	3	4	3	4	2	3	11	1	

Several things have been bolded in the table in order to call attention to them. First, we will notice that sheets E and F feature a significant number of prose lines and turned lines. Not coincidentally, these are the two sheets that, according to modern editions that relineate some of Q1's verse as prose, have the most mislineated verse and prose to begin with. (These sheets involve the arrival of the Players, and Hamlet's discursus on acting.) Leaving this one conjunction aside for a moment, we might notice still another, for turned lines (there are sixteen on these two sheets alone) seem strongly related to prose on these sheets, and are arguably the best predictor for 'hidden' prose throughout Q1.

Bolded towards the bottom of the table are the total number of turned lines and prose lines on 4r pages. These are particularly remarkable when the 'Yoricke' prose is removed from the tabulation, for they reveal that the 4r pages – typically set last in each forme – contain the greatest number of turned lines and prose lines: eleven, which is over half as much as the rest of this total (twenty) put together. What might this suggest? Here we should recall relevant scholarship on inaccurate casting off (that is, the estimation of how much manuscript text could be set into print using a specific number of pages) and its knock-on effects in the printing process. For what can be read, from one perspective, as creative and intellectually inspired revision may have had a material prompt as the type was imposed. Both Eric Rasmussen, analysing Q2 *Hamlet*, and Anne Meyer, examining apparent space-saving in the 1608 quarto of *King Lear*, show how erroneous casting off could have led a compositor, rather than author, to adjust the text he set from copy.[20] It is possible that the 4r pages of Q1 reveal the same phenomenon.

These sets of figures may therefore lead us to conclude that turned lines and many prose lines in Q1 may not have been two different things in the manuscript pages from which Compositor A worked. That is, the concentration of such lines in the 4r pages in Q1 likely comes from a single feature of the manuscript pages: longish lines rendered, alternately, as turned lines and (shorter) prose lines on the Q1 page. Thus, Compositor A dealt with the real or imagined surplus in lines roughly equivalent in length, like

> there need no Ghost come from the graue to tell you this.

and

> Ile prophecie to you, hee comes to tell mee a the Players,

by setting the extra words either in the form of a turned line (as with 'Players', on E3r) or as what we could call a 'turned prose-line' (as with 'you this'. on D1r). The assumption, again, is that these lines came from the same kind of raw material – single long lines across a manuscript page – and were treated differently by Compositor A owing to contingencies of page, plot and speaker. If we were to scan these two lines independently of Q1, in fact, we would be likely to call the first one 'verse' and the second one 'prose', even though Q1 sets them precisely the opposite way.

How did these and other lines come to be set as they were? It is probable that Compositor A cast off his copy by forme, counting vertically on the manuscript pages before him. (Whether Compositor A did the casting off, or someone else in the printing house did so, the result could be the same.) These manuscript pages most likely featured lines of various lengths, most if not all of them probably uncapitalised, as we will see. When Compositor A got to the 4r pages (the seventh in the quire and eighth – out of eight – in the forme), the variation of these lines from the length of a standard pentameter caught up with him, forcing him to 'turn' them. The presence of some of the prose on these pages may be accounted for by space-saving as well. For example, on pages like C4r and F4r the prose lines seem a function of space-saving. That the figures in the table above also reveal a concentration of prose and turned lines in sheets E and F – parts of Q1, as we have seen, that represent material heavily in prose in Q2 and F – suggests that the compositor's text for Q1 represented these speeches as more in keeping with conventional prose than verse. It would have done so by running some of its dialogue further to the right margin in a manner that signalled prose to Compositor A, who set them accordingly.

Although there is great variety among the dramatic manuscripts that have survived from the era, we might surmise the following about the compositor's text for Q1 *Hamlet*. If, like other manuscripts of the time, it featured approximately twenty-five lines of dialogue per page, its text would have taken up about eighty-nine sides of manuscript paper, justified along an imaginary line indented from the left side with enough room for speech prefixes. (In some cases, these seem to have been appended later, with the help of ruled lines inserted between the lines of dialogue.) Save for the beginning of sentences and the pronoun 'I', it was common to begin verse lines with minuscules – as is evident in manuscripts like those for *John of Bordeaux*, *Sir Thomas More* and *Woodstock*, from which the preceding estimates have been derived. Even Munday's autograph *John a Kent*, which, of all these surviving manuscripts through the early Jacobean era, makes the most concerted effort to capitalise the beginnings of its verse lines, does not do so regularly. And if manuscript roles testify to anything about a reporter's or reporters' text, the small letters beginning most lines in the Alleyn role for *Orlando* confirm a convention that may have influenced the copy for Q1.[21]

Judging from the length of Q1's twenty-six turned lines – that is, the total length of lines turned both above and below the main line, by means of open parens – we can estimate that the manuscript copy and penmanship afforded room for the scribe to record approximately sixty-nine alphabetic characters (including spaces) per line of dialogue. This figure excludes speech headings (which, again, were probably appended by rule in the left margin), and is derived by calculating the total number of spaces required for the twenty-six turned lines (that is, the 'turned' portions, minus their open parens) added to the lines they complete. These lines range from a low of fifty-four to a high of sixty-nine ens, with the average at approximately sixty-two spaces. This figure squares with evidence from other surviving dramatic manuscripts; for instance, in the *Sir Thomas More* manuscript, the longest lines in the Hand D portions take up sixty-six to sixty-seven spaces, with most being much shorter than that.

As we have seen, prose and turned lines cluster in the E and F sheets in Q1, and turned lines seem associated with prose in this text. With the exception of the 'Yoricke' speech, turned lines and prose are often found together. This would seem to imply that the compositor's text for Q1 came already 'versified', as it were, by presenting much of the play's pentameter-approximate dialogue as shorter units of speech that were readily tabulated as separate lines when the text was cast off. For if the compositor's copy had not presented its lines in such a manner as to encourage a simple counting of manuscript lines, it is unlikely that he would have needed to employ so many turned lines for sheets E and F. What seems more plausible is that whoever recorded Q1 wrote down most of the dialogue in grammatical units that could be mistaken for verse. Some dialogue was written out to the right margin, although the preponderance was not. This led Compositor A to miscalculate the number of lines needed to impose the type on various sheets, producing an underestimate of the space needed on sheets E and F. Because prose and turned lines in sheets E and F imply an error in the casting off there, it is unlikely that Q1's compositor took a fully bilingual text – that is, a text alternating prose and verse in the manner of many other dramatic texts from the era – and sophisticated its verbal structures by arranging prose as pseudo-verse. What seems likelier is that, for whatever reason, the compositor's text presented much of its dialogue in shorter units that were either (1) recalled imperfectly as verse or (2) meant to be taken as verse by a recorder or recorders. Possible too are scenarios in which the compositor interpreted the dialogue as verse (3) by accident or (4) for a specific reason or reasons.

Even if we grant that his manuscript copy text featured a number of pentameter-approximate lines, we still need to explain why Compositor A set so many of them as verse when they do not scan adequately as metre to the modern eye and ear. By this point in his work as a compositor in Simmes's shop, Compositor A had set a great deal of prose – and of Shakespeare's prose, in particular – in plays like *Much Ado About Nothing* and *2 Henry IV*. *Much Ado* has 15,020 words in prose of a total of 20,768, for 72% of the whole. For its part, *2 Henry IV* has 13,318 words in prose of 25,706 total words, for nearly 52% of its whole.[22] Compositor A's deep familiarity with dramatic verse is clear from some of the playbooks mentioned earlier: 1597's *The Tragedie of King Richard the second*, for instance, comes from Shakespeare's 'lyrical' period; all of its 21,809 words are in verse. Having set both *Richard II* and *Much Ado*, Compositor A was arguably as familiar as anyone in early modern London with the difference between these two linguistic media as Shakespeare used them. So it is unlikely that a lack of experience contributed to the jumble of the two in Q1. More likely is scenario (4), in which the decision to take the majority of these over-long lines as verse rather than prose was influenced not only by his manuscript text, but by various contingencies of London's market in representations.

What influence might the market for representation have had on the typographical layout of Q1 *Hamlet*? Any examination of Q1's status in 1603 should begin by acknowledging that Shakespeare had been the king of the literary marketplace at the turn of the new century. In the year 1600, he was the best-selling author in England, with more new titles printed that year than any other author, living or dead.[23] In the wake of that year, of what we could call 'peak Shakespeare', a *Hamlet* text by Shakespeare – a play performed widely, as Q1's unprecedented title page boasts – would have been an attractive proposition for the London publishing community, albeit one that would compete with an extensive backlist.

As a literary 'king', Shakespeare seems to have depended on a notable but narrow source of authority. By 1602/3, that is, it would have been apparent to those who followed the market in representations closely that Shakespeare was strongest at verse: his majority prose works had not seen a second edition (and in fact would not do so during his lifetime). What *had* sold well, in contrast, were poems like *Venus and Adonis* and *The Rape of Lucrece*, and plays like *Richard II* and *Richard III*. The prose-heavy *Much Ado About Nothing* was never republished; *As You Like It* was entered but not printed; and, perhaps not coincidentally, when *The Merry Wives of Windsor* saw print in the bad quarto of 1602, much of its prose was set as pentameter. It was in this context that Q1 *Hamlet* was printed as a drama largely in verse.

To more deeply explore Q1's representational context, let us imagine a back-story for it that captures more than authors, scribes, printers, publishers and imprints. That is, a trajectory that would supplement a traditional stemma that centres on paper and traces out relationships among specific texts and specific agents of transmission. In addition to these things, let us picture a series of stages and features in the representation market, something that encompasses the formal economy from which Q1 emerged. This is not to downplay the important roles that such individuals as Nicholas Ling, John Trundell, James Roberts and many others played in bringing us the *Hamlet* texts. It is instead to add a formal dimension to the narrative we commonly tell ourselves about the genesis of these playbooks. Following the design of a new model for Shakespearean stemmata recently proposed by Pervez Rizvi, we might adduce at least eight contextual factors and stages behind Q1 *Hamlet*.[24]

Figure 6 begins with two prominent generic resources for the *Hamlet* plays: the tragedies of Seneca and Belleforest's Hamlet narrative. These clearly influenced the genre of revenge tragedy as it appeared in Kyd's *Spanish Tragedy* and in an early play on the Hamlet story (whether by Kyd or by Shakespeare), here represented in the second row. It will be helpful to note that the arrows in this stemma indicate formal, sometimes material influence, while the lines without arrows imply resemblance: thus, Seneca resembles Belleforest, and vice versa; both constituted a generic resource for later *Hamlet* texts, earning an arrow indicating influence. (Obviously, such resources could be multiplied; the stemma aims merely to collocate some of the more influential agents and agencies behind Q1.) The third and next row indexes Shakespearean verse from 1592 to 1596, including his two narrative poems, *Venus* and *Lucrece*, and two examples of verse-only drama, *Richard II* and *King John*. Although *John* would not see print until the First Folio in 1623, the narrative poems and *Richard II* were published frequently during the 1590s and early 1600s, establishing Shakespeare as one of London's pre-eminent poets. Indeed, these works' deployment of iambic pentameter helps explain the next row of the stemma, which features two quartos

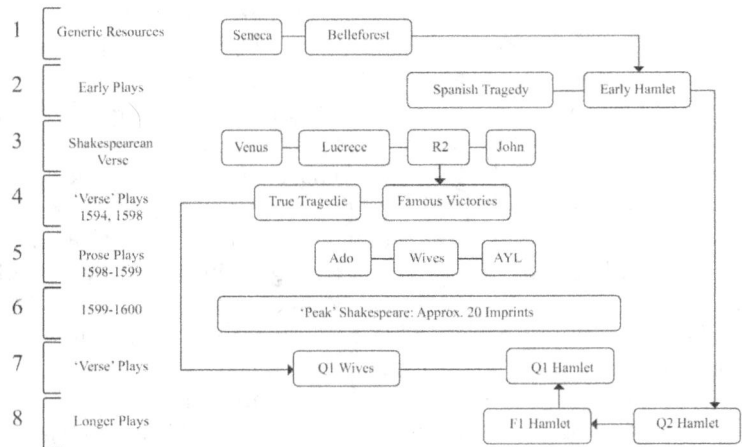

Figure 6. A formal stemma for Q1 *Hamlet*. Figure created by Madeleine Bruster, used with permission.

published by Thomas Creede, *The True Tragedy of Richard III* and *The Famous Victories of Henry V*. The former was published in 1594; while the latter's first surviving edition is dated 1598, the fact that Creede had entered it for publication in 1594 suggests the possibility of an earlier printing.

It is worth a digression here to point out that each of these Creede quartos features what Scott McMillin and Sally-Beth MacLean call a 'puzzle':

> page after page of prose set as verse. In *True Tragedy of Richard III* such mislineation begins on A4r and continues seriatim through B4v, over nine pages. Another burst of over a page runs from the final 21 lines on F3v through F4r, and there is another complete page on G1a. *The Famous Victories of Henry V* is written entirely in prose, but the quarto has 34 pages set as verse, running in two segments: A2v through A4v, and C4v through G2v. Mislineation is the leading characteristic of these two Queen's Men's texts, and the puzzling form of mislineation turns prose into verse for long stretches at a time – to the advantage, it would seem, of no one. How could this have happened?[25]

McMillin and MacLean believe they answer their own question by suggesting 'dictation in the playhouse, with actors reciting their parts after they had memorised them, and with a scribe recording those recitations in order to have a temporary copy of a revised play'.[26] Yet we could note that their turn to the playhouse leaves out the printing house, and also something crucial about the playbooks they are describing. That is, with the exception of a single line on the first page of *The Famous Victories* (line 10: 'part of me to rob my fathers Receivers'), both of these playbooks offer themselves as verse plays to a reader who begins with their first pages. (McMillin and MacLean miss the mislineation on A2r, the first page, of *Famous Victories*.) It is therefore worth considering whether the question of the 'advantage' that McMillin and MacLean raise, only to neglect as rhetorical, might be related to a publisher who hoped to sell a playbook with a more sophisticated appearance.

Following these two playbooks, our stemma has two rows, the fifth and six, which are not connected to others. This is meant to imply influence of a different nature. In both cases, this involves a possible context for the later decisions relating to Q1 and Q2 *Hamlet*. Row 5 reflects Shakespeare's turn to prose in such plays as *Much Ado*, the *Henry IV* plays and *As You Like It*, and row 6 the profusion of Shakespeare publications in 1599–1600 labelled '"Peak" Shakespeare'. These rows point to developments in the Shakespearean brand by featuring both a divergence from that brand (in his prose plays' turning away from iambic pentameter) and the potential saturation of the market for Shakespeare books in the closing years of the sixteenth century. It is precisely this saturation that may have led the publishers of Q1 *Merry Wives* and Q1 *Hamlet* to hedge their bets on these Shakespeare texts by amplifying their apparent percentages of verse – long the gold standard of the Shakespearean brand. Thus, Q1 *Merry Wives* and Q1 *Hamlet* replicated the feature of two quartos in the fourth row here, *True Tragedie* and *Famous Victories*, which presented their opening pages to readers as iambic pentameter. The final row of the stemma is speculative, suggesting that material that would later be published as Q2 *Hamlet* preceded the version that would be published as F1 *Hamlet*, and that Q1 *Hamlet* is a version of F1 *Hamlet*, perhaps from a report, dictation or otherwise imperfect transmission. While traditional stemmata would emphasise the specifics of the relations of these three texts – which came first, second and third, and how each related to the other – the stemma offered here seeks to adduce other agencies and contexts for our understanding of Q1. Iambic pentameter is clearly key to this formal economy.

Earlier in this chapter we noted that modern editions' reversal of Q1's prose-to-verse adjustment offers an unanticipated irony. We might unpack that irony as follows: the same impulse that leads modern editors to shape their text in one way for marketability may have been what led the publishers or printers or recorders of Q1 to shape *their* text in exactly the opposite way. Whether Ophelia/Ofelia is *'most beautified'* (Q2; E4r, 2.2.110–111), *'most beautiful'* (F1; TLN 1137–1138) or merely *'beautiful'* (Q1; D4r, 794), the Hamlet of 1603 was beautified with the appearance of verse, and various Q1 *Hamlets* of the last century have been beautified by the transformation of this apparent verse to prose. The definition of marketability shifts depending on the market. Modern editors inherit a 'worse' text that they sophisticate through the ornamentation of prose – which is attractive to the modern eye precisely because of the success of such texts as Q2 and F1 *Hamlet*. These editors' beautification of Q1 for modern readers ironically erases its textual history. In performing such an erasure, a true text for our time is asked to become a false witness of its own.

Douglas Bruster teaches at the University of Texas, where he is Mody C. Boatright Regents Professor of American and English Literature and Distinguished Teaching Professor. His research focuses on Shakespeare and early modern drama in England.

Notes

The author would like to thank Eric Rasmussen for his comments on an earlier version of this essay, and Madeleine Bruster for the illustration of Figure 1.

1. On London's market in representations, see Douglas Bruster, 'The Representation Market of Early Modern England', *Renaissance Drama* 41, no. 1–2 (2013), 1–23. For a recent interpretation of Shakespeare's relation to the verbal economy of his day, see Jonathan Lamb, *Shakespeare in the Marketplace of Words* (Cambridge: Cambridge University Press, 2017).
2. See Zachary Lesser and Peter Stallybrass, 'The First Literary *Hamlet* and the Commonplacing of Professional Plays', *Shakespeare Quarterly* 59 (2008), 371–420. Lesser examines the typographical identities of various dramatic texts of the era in *Renaissance Drama and the Politics of Publication: Readings in the English Book Trade* (Cambridge: Cambridge University Press, 2007).
3. Recent years have witnessed valuable explorations of Q1 by such scholars as, among others, Terri Bourus, Margrethe Jolly and Christy Desmet. The playbook's linguistic and literary style receives particular attention in Bourus, *Young*

Shakespeare's Young Hamlet: Print, Piracy, and Performance (New York: Palgrave Macmillan, 2014), 170–179; Jolly, *The First Two Quartos of 'Hamlet': A New View of the Origins and Relationship of the Texts* (Jefferson, NC: McFarland, 2014), 102–141; and Desmet, 'Text, Style, and Author in Hamlet Q1', *Journal of Early Modern Studies* 5 (2016), 135–156. In addition to these recent studies, this chapter has benefitted from Charles Adams Kelly's synoptic *Hamlet*. See Charles Adams Kelly, Cara MacBride and Sarah Mandlebaum, eds, *The 'Hamlet' 3x2 Text Research Toolset*, 2nd ed. (Detroit: The Triple Anvil Press, 2009). I am also grateful to Kelly for sharing this research with me, as well as to Kelly and Dayna Leigh Plehn-Peavyhouse for sharing their chapter on Q1 in this issue.

4. See Ann Thompson and Neil Taylor, eds, *'Hamlet': The Texts of 1603 and 1623*, Arden Shakespeare, 3rd series (London: Thomson Learning, 2006).
5. Figures here from Laurie E. Maguire, *Shakespearean Suspect Texts: The 'Bad' Quartos and Their Contexts* (Cambridge: Cambridge University Press, 1996), 255.
6. Thompson and Taylor, *'Hamlet'*, 6.
7. Ibid., 5–7, 11.
8. Albert B. Weiner, ed., *'Hamlet': The First Quarto 1603* (Great Neck, NY: Barron's Educational Series, 1962), 61.
9. Kathleen O. Irace, ed., *The First Quarto of 'Hamlet'*, The New Cambridge Shakespeare: The Early Quartos (Cambridge: Cambridge University Press, 1998), 28.
10. See Graham Holderness and Bryan Loughrey, eds, *The Tragicall Historie of Hamlet Prince of Denmarke*, Shakespearean Originals: First Editions (Lanham, MD: Barnes & Noble Books, 1992).
11. Ibid., 71.
12. Thompson and Taylor, *'Hamlet'*, 6.
13. On what I am calling the bilingual system of verse and prose in early modern drama, see Douglas Bruster, 'Christopher Marlowe and the Verse/Prose Bilingual System', *Marlowe Studies* 1 (2011), 141–165.
14. It is not unusual to feel iambic rhythm in early modern dramatic prose, making prose and verse in plays of the era sometimes difficult to untangle. Early on, John Dover Wilson offered a theory of 'verse fossils' to explain iambic rhythms in the prose of *Much Ado About Nothing*, which he saw as a prose version of an earlier verse play. See Arthur Quiller-Couch and John Dover Wilson, eds, *Much Ado About Nothing*, New Shakespeare (Cambridge: Cambridge University Press, 1923). However, Dover Wilson soon found such fossils in a variety of other plays, and enhanced his examples to strengthen his argument – which ultimately discredited his theory. For a critique, see Milton Crane, *Shakespeare's Prose* (Chicago, IL: University of Chicago Press, 1951), Appendix II: 'A Note on the Text of *As You Like It*', 203–209. It is unfortunate that Dover Wilson took his argument to such an extreme, for the discrediting of his theory has made it awkward to discuss the overlap of these two linguistic media in early modern plays.
15. Alan Craven, 'Simmes' Compositor A and Five Shakespeare Quartos', *Studies in Bibliography* 26 (1973), 37–60. It should be noted that Pervez Rizvi has recently offered a critique of traditional scholarship's 'unintentional confirmation bias' when it comes to identifying compositors this way. See Rizvi, 'Use of Spellings for Compositor Attribution in the First Folio', *The Papers of the Bibliographical Society of America* 110 (2016), 1–53, here 20. Rizvi notes that 'compositors in Shakespeare's era did not always have discernible preferences ...' (23). If Rizvi's

scepticism applies to Simmes's shop, 'Compositor A' in this chapter should perhaps be understood as a convenient label rather than a discrete historical actor.
16. Craven, 'Simmes' Compositor A', 48.
17. Ibid., 40.
18. Two recent studies offer valuable introductions to the business of playbook publication in early modern London by means of case studies. See John Jowett, *Shakespeare and Text*, Oxford Shakespeare Topics (Oxford: Oxford University Press, 2007), which examines the printing of Q1 and Folio *Troilus and Cressida*; and David L. Gants, 'Mine of Debt: William White and the Printing of the 1602 *Spanish Tragedy ... with new additions*', in *The New Oxford Shakespeare Authorship Companion*, ed. Gary Taylor and Gabriel Egan (Oxford: Oxford University Press, 2017), 231–240.
19. See Yachnin in Anthony B. Dawson and Paul Yachnin, *The Culture of Playgoing in Shakespeare's England: A Collaborative Debate* (Cambridge: Cambridge University Press, 2001), esp. 9, 38 ff.
20. See Eric Rasmussen, 'The Relevance of Cast-off Copy in Determining the Nature of Omissions: Q2 *Hamlet*', *Studies in Bibliography* 39 (1986), 133–135; and Ann R. Meyer, 'Shakespeare's Art and the Texts of *King Lear*', *Studies in Bibliography* 47 (1994): 128–146.
21. For the Alleyn role from *Orlando Furioso*, see the digital image in the Henslowe-Alleyn Digitisation Project online, MSS 1, Article 138, 08 recto: http://www.henslowe-alleyn.org.uk/images/MSS-1/Article-138/08r.html (accessed 24 November 2018).
22. All figures here from Marvin Spevack, ed., *Complete and Systematic Concordance to the Works of Shakespeare*, 9 vols (Hildesheim: Georg Olms, 1968–1980).
23. Here and subsequently I draw on research published in Douglas Bruster, 'Shakespeare the Stationer', in *Shakespeare's Stationers: Studies in Cultural Bibliography*, ed. Marta Straznicky (Philadelphia: University of Pennsylvania Press, 2013), 112–131.
24. See Pervez Rizvi, 'Stemmata for Shakespeare Texts: A Suggested New Form', *The Papers of the Bibliographical Society of America* 108, no. 1 (2014), 97–106. I should point out that the formal categories of this chapter's stemma are not part of Rizvi's suggested design.
25. See Scott McMillin and Sally-Beth MacLean, *The Queen's Men and Their Plays*, rev. ed. (Cambridge: Cambridge University Press, 2006), 113.
26. Ibid., 114.

Chapter 5
The Good Enough Quarto
Hamlet as a Material Object

Terri Bourus

We owe to the great librarian and bibliographer Alfred W. Pollard the distinction between what he called 'bad quartos' and what he called 'good quartos'. Most people interested in *Hamlet* do not even know, or care, what a 'quarto' is, and they may be forgiven for assuming that Pollard's distinction does not matter to anyone outside the tiny technical fields of bibliography and textual criticism. But in fact Pollard's claim has governed almost all scholarly and critical thinking about the first quarto of *Hamlet* for more than a century; in innumerable ways it has shaped what students read and critics do. I want to demonstrate that there is, indeed, a real, material, verifiable distinction between some quartos, which can properly be called good, and other quartos, which can properly be called bad. But the material distinction I am making fundamentally differs from the distinction Pollard made.

Notes for this section begin on page 105.

Pollard articulated and named the categories of good and bad quartos in 1909, in his book *Shakespeare Folios and Quartos: A Study in the Bibliography of Shakespeare's Plays 1594–1685*.[1] He later expanded that argument in *Shakespeare's Fight with the Pirates*. In the new introduction he added to the second edition of *Shakespeare's Fight*, looking back a decade, he declared: 'When I wrote *Shakespeare Folios and Quartos*, I wrote as a bibliographer and a lover of logical economy impatient of hypotheses disproportionately large compared with the facts they were framed to explain'.[2] There are two claims here: the first about bibliography, the second about the economy and scale of hypotheses. These two claims need to be separated.

As a bibliographer

Pollard was one of the two main compilers and editors of the *Short-Title Catalogue*, the foundation for almost a century of bibliographical scholarship.[3] No one can question Pollard's credentials 'as a bibliographer' (and, specifically, as a descriptive bibliographer). Those bibliographical skills are evident in *Shakespeare Folios and Quartos*, where he for the first time identified the unnamed printer of the 1603 first edition of *Hamlet*. That edition was, like most printed editions of individual plays in the sixteenth and seventeenth centuries, a 'quarto'. On the basis of the ornament and the typeface, Pollard attributed the printing of the first quarto ('Q1') to Valentine Simmes.[4] Pollard's claim depends on a very technical, specialist kind of bibliographical analysis, and although many people can see the distinctions between different typefaces once they are pointed out, very few are able to identify the typeface used in an anonymously printed book. But W. Craig Ferguson is one of those few; he wrote the book, literally, on pica roman type in English texts printed between 1553 and 1610.[5] Pollard's claim about the typeface of Q1 *Hamlet* was confirmed in the 1960s by Ferguson's systematic examination of all Simmes's books.[6]

The identification of Simmes as the agent responsible for manufacturing Q1 *Hamlet* can be proven because it is based on material evidence. The typeface used by a printer leaves its marks on every page of every book he or she produces, and by precise description and measurement one printer's typeface can be distinguished from another. Pollard, in 1909, 'writing as a bibliographer', made an empirical, material, verifiable distinction between two categories of early modern printed books: those printed by Simmes, and those printed by everyone else. Between 1597 and 1611, Simmes printed no fewer than twenty-seven quarto editions of plays, including five by Shakespeare.[7] There is a real distinction between Simmes-play quartos and not-Simmes play quartos, and Pollard's 1909 book for the first time placed Q1 *Hamlet* in the category of Simmes quartos.

The fact that Simmes printed the 1603 quarto significantly contributes to our understanding of *Hamlet*'s place in the early modern book trade. It situates that book within the long-standing relationship between the printer Simmes and the bookseller Nicholas Ling, who published both the first and second quartos of *Hamlet*. Ling and Simmes had almost certainly met as young men, because they had both been apprenticed in the same shop; Ling was the publisher with whom the printer Simmes most often worked. So there is nothing suspect about their collaborative work on Q1. Nor is there anything suspicious about the second quarto of *Hamlet* being manufactured by a different printer than the first: Valentine Simmes (who printed the first) and James Roberts (who printed the second) were Ling's two favourite printers, and Ling elsewhere switched back and forth between them in editions of the same title.[8] John Payne Collier, the editor and forger who originated the theory that Q1 represents a text of the play taken down by shorthand, dismissed the quarto as the work of 'some inferior and nameless printer, who was not so scrupulous'.[9] But that is not an accurate description of either Ling or Simmes. Like his master and mentor Henry Bynneman, Simmes was a skilled and careful craftsman, particularly sensitive to the visual appearance of his books. According to Ferguson, Simmes had 'a good eye for detail and layout'; 'he generally used good paper and careful inking to avoid the show-through that makes many books of the period unreadable. He was thus a printer whose work was certainly at or above the standard of the day'.[10]

Pollard, who first identified Simmes as the printer of Q1, did so on the basis of personal examination of thousands of books in the British Library and other archives. But scholars and students can now access images of Q1 *Hamlet* (and all the later quartos of the play printed from 1604 to 1637) on the British Library webpage 'Shakespeare in Quarto'.[11] All books printed by Simmes (including Q1) are visible in the digital database *Early English Books Online* (*EEBO*), available to scholars and students in all British universities (and in many American ones). If you want to get a sense of what Q1 looked like when it went on sale in 1603, you can examine online photographs of an opening (sig. D2v–D3) in a copy previously owned by the Duke of Devonshire, which is now at the Huntington Library in California; this was the copy first rediscovered in the early 1820s, and photographs of its pages are available on *EEBO*. Using the same database, you can look at a different opening (sig. G3v–G4) in the copy now in the British Library, rediscovered in the 1850s. At the bottom left and right corners of the online images of the British Library copy you will see solid black ovals: the fingertips of someone holding the book open so that the opening can be photographed. The fingers are a reminder of the modern users and technologies responsible for the creation and dissemination of these images. But these pages are (with the exception of the tell-tale fingers) pristine, containing no handwritten marginalia or other evidence of wear and tear. I've chosen openings in the middle of the book because the outer pages of the quarto were the most susceptible to damage over time. Like other early play quartos, this one was almost certainly originally sold stitched together but not bound, meaning that the outside pages were not protected from wear and tear. It is therefore not surprising that, for instance, all that remains of the first edition of what we now call *Henry the Fourth, Part One* (STC 22279a, 'The Hystorie of Henrie the fourth') are four leaves from the interior of that quarto (signature C). The British Library copy of Q1 *Hamlet* is missing the first leaf, containing the title page, and the Huntington Library copy is missing the final leaf, containing the end of the play.

As these facts about the two existing copies of the 1603 quarto remind us, even when we are talking about a 'material book' printed in 1603, we have to acknowledge that there are significantly different material forms of that book. First, we have to acknowledge the material differences between different copies of the same edition, originally manufactured in a single-proprietor printing shop in London, but soon dispersed to metropolitan and provincial bookshops, and now scattered around the world. Secondly, we have to acknowledge the material difference between any particular physical specimen as it existed in 1603 and as it exists now. The material Q1 *Hamlet* has been distributed, and altered, across space and time.

Those spacetime distinctions have larger implications, but for the moment their significance is that they explain why I have called attention to two particular openings from two different copies of Q1 *Hamlet*. First, because we can view images of both openings online, anyone who is interested can put them side by side and compare them. We can thereby overcome the geographical distance that now separates the paper objects, restoring something similar to their shared origin in one small shop. Secondly, any viewer can see that the two openings are well printed. They illustrate and support Craig Ferguson's description of the quality of Simmes's craftsmanship. As originally printed, Q1 *Hamlet* was, as a material object, a solid, professional, well-made, good-looking piece of work.

Not all early modern play quartos were so well crafted. Some elements of the craftsmanship of a book are not readily discernible from online photographic images. For instance, David L. Gants has remarked on 'the uniformly poor quality of the paper supplied by the publishers' for the books printed by William White in 1601–1603, including the 1602 quarto of *The Spanish Tragedy*, the first edition to contain the 'Additions' that are now attributed in whole or part to Shakespeare.[12] But *EEBO* doesn't give you a good sense of the quality of the paper; Gants had to actually hold and examine the surviving books, and compare the quality of their paper with the quality of the paper of the thousands of other books from the period that he has personally examined, including in particular the 1616 edition of Ben Jonson's *Works*. Evaluating the quality of the paper requires what we might call 'Close Encounters of the Nerd Kind'. And on the basis of such encounters, Ferguson could conclude that Simmes generally used 'good paper'. Not the best paper available in London in the early seventeenth century; not as good as the paper for the 1616 edition of Jonson's *Works*, or the 1632 edition of Shakespeare's *Comedies, Histories, & Tragedies*. But good enough, as Ferguson observed, 'to avoid the show-through that makes many books of the period unreadable'. And better than the paper used for the 1602 and 1603 quartos of *The Spanish Tragedy* and most of the other texts printed by William White in those years.

Some material deficiencies in early modern books *are* visible on *EEBO*. In his edition of *The Old Law* for the Oxford Middleton, Jeffrey Masten described the first printing of that play, published in 1656, as 'poorly manufactured'. Masten was describing 'in the most literal way' the book 'as a material artifact: the letters of the type have been inadequately (or sometimes *excessively*) inked, and the result is a text in which some letters ... do not register on the page'.[13] That sloppiness is visible even in the photographs of a single opening (B3v–B4) of a single copy of the book on *EEBO*. In the long speech by Creon on the middle of B4 (the right side of the opening), the unevenness of the inking makes some words very difficult to read; not as conspicuous but just as problematic, there's a similar unevenness at the bottom of B3v (the left-hand side of the opening).

From the perspective of the material book, by the standards of craftsmanship in the hand-press period, the 1656 edition of *The Old Law*, printed in the shop of Jane Bell, is a 'bad quarto'; for a different reason, so is the 1602 edition of *The Spanish Tragedy*. By contrast, both the 1603 and the 1604 editions of *Hamlet* are, materially, from the perspective of the bookmaker's craft, good quartos. If we are, like Pollard, writing 'as a bibliographer', as a specialist in the early modern material book, we can objectively distinguish between well-printed books and badly printed books, just as objectively as we can distinguish between a quarto and a folio, just as objectively as we can distinguish between a quarto printed by Valentine Simmes and a quarto printed by James Roberts.

Hypotheses disproportionately large

But of course my distinction between good and bad quartos is not the distinction that Pollard made in 1909. Unlike his identification of Simmes as the printer of Q1 *Hamlet*, Pollard's categories of good and bad were not based on a response to the materiality of any of the books to which he applied those adjectives. Pollard's nomenclature paradoxically, and incoherently, combines a bibliographical and material category, 'quarto', with an ethical category, 'good/bad'. The power of that combination, and its longevity in Shakespeare studies, depends on the electric spark that leaps between those two words: the material, objective, empirical category 'quarto' lends an apparently material, objective, empirical authority to the ethical category 'bad'.

But the seemingly scientific authority of Pollard's ethical claim is, of course, bogus. 'Good and Bad pertains to literary taste', Randall McLeod reminds us, 'not properly to literary objects'.[14] Pollard's good-bad binary hides a bibliographical and ethical sleight of hand. The ethical question about quartos ('is this a good or a bad quarto?') obscures the ethical foundation of Pollard's argument. Pollard does not even admit the possibility of a binary distinction between 'good and bad folios'. However, his argument actually begins with a quotation from the preliminaries to the 1623 Shakespeare Folio, and a defence of the accuracy of that Folio's claim about 'diuers stolne, and surreptitious copies, maimed, and deformed by the frauds and stealthes of iniurious impostors'.[15] Pollard's category 'bad quartos' is thus essentially an attempt to prove that the 1623 *Comedies, Histories, & Tragedies* is *not* a 'bad folio'. If by 'bad' we mean 'textually derivative', or 'without independent substantive textual authority', then there can indeed be bad folios. The fifteenth- and sixteenth-century printed editions of Chaucer's works were, by such criteria, bad folios, as we can see if we compare them to surviving fifteenth-century manuscripts of the same works. And parts of the 1623 Shakespeare Folio are, as has long been recognised, textually derivative, being essentially reprints of earlier quartos. The 1623 folio is uneven, rather like the inking of the 1656 quarto of *Old Law*; but the unevenness in 1623 is not a matter of ink, but of what an editor or textual scholar would consider 'stemmatic authority'. A textual stemma represents a genealogy, usually an imagined or theorised genealogy.[16] It is clear that the Folio texts of *Love's Labours Lost, Much Ado about Nothing, The Merchant of Venice, A Midsummer Night's Dream, Richard II, 1 Henry IV, Richard III, Romeo and Juliet* and *Titus Andronicus* are, to a greater or lesser degree, reprints of earlier quartos, and for most of those plays the Folio is based not on the original quarto but on a subsequent, less accurate reprint. The farther down the genealogical line a particular text is, the less stemmatic authority it has, and for approximately a quarter of its texts the Folio has less stemmatic authority than an extant quarto. Acknowledging that Shakespeare's First Folio is 'partly derivative', or 'partly bad' points out the clumsiness of the Pollard binary. In terms of stemmatic authority, as in material terms, there is a spectrum of quality, not a simple either-or.

For Pollard, a text is bad if it is 'pirated', and the 1623 Folio cannot be accused of having been pirated (at least, not in its entirety). Pollard's interpretation of the significance of the Stationers' Register and his claims that certain texts were pirated have been demolished by a succession of bibliographers, who have challenged his interpretation of the historical documents. But we should also recognise that the original claim was logically incoherent. Piracy is a legal and moral category, but it does not refer to the material object itself. Pirates have, after all, no interest in stealing something that is worthless, and what they steal does not become worthless once it is stolen by a pirate; indeed, the pirate's ability to make a profit from what has been stolen depends upon the fact that the stolen material object retains its material value, whoever possesses it. So good quartos could be stolen by bad men, and they would still be good. The good or bad workmanship that produces a particular quarto tells us nothing about that material object's relationship to the legal procedures of a particular time and place – and nothing about the possible stemmatic relationship between one textual witness and another.

So if we are writing or thinking 'as a bibliographer' about material objects, what we can literally see and confidently claim is that Q1 *Hamlet* belongs to the categories of Simmes quartos, Ling quartos and well-made quartos. We can also say – as Zachary Lesser and Peter Stallybrass demonstrated in 2008 – that it belongs to the material category of literary quartos. It is 'the first play of Shakespeare's to be printed with what was rapidly becoming a distinguishing feature of plays for the learned or scholarly reader – a feature central to early seventeenth-century attempts to forge a culture of literary drama and poesy in the vernacular: sententiae or commonplaces that are pointed out to the reader … by commas or inverted commas at the beginning of each line'. This emphasis on the elite literary nature of the play can also be seen on the title page of Q1, which is unique in its invocation of 'the two Vniuersities of Cambridge and Oxford'. Q1 *Hamlet* is 'the only professional play in the entire period that claims on its title page to have been performed at a university' – at even one university, let alone two.[17] This material evidence that the 1603 edition of *Hamlet* is a literary quarto of course contradicts the assumption by Pollard, and the editorial tradition in general, from John Payne Collier (1843) to Martin Wiggins (2014), that Q1 is a fundamentally and systematically corrupt text derived in some way from theatrical performance.[18]

Zachary Lesser followed up his collaborative essay on Q1 as a literary text with an entire book, *Hamlet After Q1*. This is a pioneering and important reception history of Q1, which I have praised elsewhere.[19] Because Lesser's book traces reactions to Q1 in the nineteenth and twentieth centuries, it naturally pays relatively little attention to analysis of Q1 as a material object manufactured in 1603, but Lesser does devote two pages to a comparison of the title pages of Q1 and Q2 (which he also reproduces photographically).[20] For the most part, those two pages in Lesser's book repeat material from the 2008 article, but in 2014 Lesser provides more bibliographical evidence for his claims. He points out that the 'hanging indent' – between the attribution to Shakespeare, above, and the woodcut ornament, below – is rare in early modern secular books, that Simmes used it 'far more frequently than other printers did: one in five of his editions (forty out of 198) used the format for something other than a biblical verse'.[21] This design feature provides further evidence that Q1 is, as a material object, a book crafted by Simmes. And that unusual feature is duplicated on the title page of Q2, which was printed by James Roberts. The *content* of the title page, and of the hanging indent in particular, has changed, but the *form* has not. And because the form is *not* characteristic of Roberts, Lesser takes this as evidence that Roberts in printing Q2 was directly influenced by the Simmes design of the Q1 title page. He makes the valid point that, 'Ever since Malone, critics have focused on the part of Q2's title page that most *distinguishes* it from Q1'. Lesser, instead, argues that 'the title pages of the two editions do far more to align than to distinguish them'.[22]

So far, so good. But, like Pollard, Lesser wants to make a valid, material, bibliographical argument the foundation for a much larger hypothesis. He claims that 'the title pages of Q1 and Q2 themselves suggest, subtly, that Q1 had not sold out and that copies of the [first] edition were still available in bookshops'.[23] The similarity between the two title pages was what first sparked my own interest in Q1, and in bibliography, when I was a graduate student; Lesser's hypothesis, that Q1 had not sold out when Q2 was published, is one that I made myself in my doctoral dissertation, almost twenty years ago, so I can't blame Lesser for jumping to the same conclusion.[24] But I am now more sceptical about the significance of the very real similarities.

Lesser begins by focusing on the woodcut ornament on both title pages, which is a typically elaborate design that incorporates a visual pun on the fish called a 'ling', flanked by the initials 'N.' and 'L.'. Ling's device, Lesser observes, 'dominates the page in both' [title pages].[25] That is not surprising; in fact, it is inevitable. The device is printed from a single block, and therefore it is always the same size wherever it is printed, and consequently it will always take up the same amount of space on a normal quarto page. If a title page has been severely cropped (as is the only surviving copy of the Q1 title page), it will appear to take up more space – and it therefore seems to take up more space in modern photographic reproductions of the two title pages (which generally do not reproduce the actual size of the original pages). The only way to overcome this photographic illusion is to examine, and measure, the actual material Q1 title page and an actual material Q2 title page.

Lesser's observation about the device dominating the two title pages is correct, but meaningless. To give it meaning, Lesser appends the clause 'unusually for a publisher who was not a printer'. If the visual emphasis on the device is unusual, it may be significant. However, the prominence of the publisher's device was *not* unusual for Ling; indeed, for Ling it was absolutely normal. He began using this device in 1595, on the title page of a reprint of Nashe's *Pierce Penniless* (STC 18375). By 1599 it was appearing on almost all his title pages. The occasional exceptions are religious books, or those with a woodcut specific to that book, like Michael's Drayton's *The Owl* (1604).[26] Between 1604 and Ling's death in 1607, only one other book he published or co-published does *not* include his device on the title page: an octavo, which instead puts Ling's device on the back of that title page.[27] Demonstrably, there is nothing at all unusual about the fact that Ling's device appears on the title page of the second quarto of *Hamlet*, published late in 1604. Lesser is therefore mistaken to claim that 'the use of Ling's device on [Q2] as well seems like a deliberate effort to mirror Q1'.[28] No: it's just a deliberate effort to mirror almost all of Ling's other books.

Ling's trademark device on the title page reminds us that Q1 is not only a Simmes quarto, but also a Ling quarto. Ling was at the very least a collaborator when it came to the design and the contents of the title pages of Q1 *Hamlet*, Q2 *Hamlet* and all the other books he published. There is consequently nothing surprising, or suspicious, about 'the similarity between the two title pages' – which, Lesser concludes, 'was a deliberate decision on Ling's part'.[29] Of course it was deliberate. But this still leaves two questions. How great is the similarity? And what was the motive behind that similarity?

Both title pages attribute the play to Shakespeare, and both place the attribution just below the title, in much smaller type. The placement, relative size and formula are all normal for Ling's title pages. There are small differences: Q1's 'By William Shake-speare' is indented right, whereas Q2 centres 'By William Shakespeare'. It is significant that both quartos attribute the text to Shakespeare, but it is hardly surprising that Ling would repeat the author's name: books with Shakespeare's name on them had sold exceptionally well.[30] However, if Ling had wanted the two title pages to look identical, the changes in alignment and hyphenation must be mistakes. 'The plays' titles are', Lesser also notes, 'identical'.[31] But, as with the attribution, the shared information ('The Tragicall Historie of Hamlet') is not really surprising: presumably the play's title, as advertised by the acting company, had not changed between 1603 and 1604.

More dubiously, in the same sentence Lesser claims that the titles are 'virtually identically set'. Much virtue in 'virtually'. It is true that the words of the play's title are, in both quartos, spread across three lines, and spelled the same way. However, before the end of the sentence Lesser concedes that 'Roberts's xylographic *"THE"* in Q2' disrupts the visual similarity. The word 'xylographic' may, for readers more familiar with the vocabulary of critical theory than technical terms invented by Victorian bibliographers, obscure the issue here. In Q1, the word 'THE' is printed using three single metal types, one for each letter; in Q2 the same word is printed 'xylographically', meaning that Roberts used a single engraved wood block, containing all three letters. Roberts undoubtedly possessed enough metal types to set the word exactly as Simmes had done, if he had wanted to emphasise the similarity between the two title pages. More important than the technical difference in the way the word was printed is the fact that the word is in *ITALIC* upper-case in Q2, and in ROMAN upper-case in Q1. The article monopolises the top line of both title pages; since we read from the top down, that difference between the two title pages is probably the first thing anyone would notice, especially if their attention was primarily visual.

In both quartos the word 'HAMLET' has a line to itself, all in upper case; it's arguably the most important word on the title page, and certainly the one that distinguishes these two Ling quartos from anything else in print or for sale in London bookshops from 1603 to 1605. But that proper name is much larger in Q2 (where it is ten millimetres high and 82 wide) than in Q1 (where it is only seven millimetres high and 57 wide).[32] The proper name occupies just 399 square millimetres in Q1, but 820 in Q2. So the largest and most distinctive word on the Q2 title page is more than twice as large as the same word in Q1 – even without counting the large superfluous comma that follows the name in Q2. Of the three lines of the play's title, only the second is visually similar.

Both title pages do have a 'hanging indent' between the author's name and the publisher's device, but Q1 fills all three lines of the indented material, whereas in Q2 the third line is mostly blank, containing only the single word 'Coppie'. Even an inattentive customer, uninterested in the fact that the *words* of the hanging indent are all different, would notice the very different visual text-block. Below the hanging indent, the printer's device is, of course, always the same, but beneath it, Q2 has four lines of type, each distinct from the others verbally and typographically, and full of information, where Q1 has just one full line and then a second containing only the date '1603'.

To sum up: the only things identically set on the two title pages are an indent, the printer's device (always the same size, and normally placed in this same position in Ling's books) and the line 'Tragicall Historie of'.

I stress these visual differences because Lesser's hypothesis about Q1 depends on the claim that a 'casual browser ... might miss the distinction' between the two editions 'altogether, giving Ling a chance to sell off copies of Q1' that were still unsold after Q2 was published.[33] This claim is implausible on many levels. 'Casual browsers' in a bookshop are, by definition, readers, and Lesser seems to be imagining that (Ling imagined that) people would buy one of these books without reading the title page. Is the idea that Ling has copies of both editions in his shop, mixed randomly together, hoping that readers would not notice the difference? If the two books are both in the same shop, then their proximity calls attention to the differences between them.

But the real objection to this hypothesis is that we can easily find similar patterns in other Ling books, where no one imagines that the first edition was in any way illegitimate, or that the prior edition had sold poorly and was still hanging around in the shop. For instance, Ling sold five separate quarto editions of Drayton's *English Heroical Epistles*. Drayton was one of Ling's favourite authors; the publisher and the poet clearly had a personal relationship. But the title pages of successive editions of Drayton's collection look just as similar as Q1 and Q2 *Hamlet*.[34] As anyone can now see in *EEBO*, the 1597 and 1598 editions (STC 7193 and 7194) are, visually, identical for the bottom two-thirds of the title page; the top third is very similar. Likewise, the 1599 quarto (STC 7195) is in visual terms 'virtually identical' to the 1598 edition. The 1599 title page is even more similar to the title page of the 1600 quarto (STC 7196). That 1600 title page is very hard to distinguish at a glance from the 1602 quarto (STC 7197). Quickly browsing these titles, the careless customer imagined by Lesser might not notice the distinction between 'Newly enlarged' (1598, 1599) and 'Newly corrected' (1600, 1602). They might ignore the change in location of Ling's bookshop (from St Paul's to St Dunstan's). If you read the title pages of the five Drayton quartos carefully, as readers usually do before they buy one, you would notice these important differences. But the pages are not conspicuously different, visually, to a casual browser – certainly no more conspicuous than the differences between Ling's first and second edition of *Hamlet*.

Such material similarities arise naturally from the routines of book production. The title page of a previous edition serves as a template for the new edition; the old title page, marked up by the publisher with handwritten additions or alterations, could efficiently serve as the printer's copy for a new title page. In 1604, Ling did not need to change the play's title, or its attribution to Shakespeare, or the placement of his device. He *did* want to emphasise that the new edition was 'enlarged to almost as much againe as it was', because that enlargement made it necessary to use much more paper, which in turn would have allowed Ling to charge more for the book. Since Q2 makes no reference to *Hamlet* in performance, Ling need not have been constrained by the usual price of sixpence for a 'play quarto', and could instead price the book on the basis of the actual number of sheets it contained. If a casual browser, not paying much attention to the title page, picked up a copy of the second quarto, he would have seen, or felt, the difference emphasised by the title page: it is a significantly thicker, and consequently heavier, quarto, with 104 pages instead of only sixty-four. This material difference would have been especially obvious because such quartos would normally have been sold unbound; the hardcover binding is the heaviest part of a small book, and if neither quarto was bound, the difference in size and weight would have depended entirely on the paper itself. It would not have been obscured by the size and weight of a shared hard binding.

When a new edition is published, we generally assume that the old edition has sold out. There is no reason to doubt that Q1 had sold out before Q2 was printed. Since the publisher owned what we would now call the copyright, he did not need to finance a second edition until he had unloaded the first. And most of the copies of the first edition would have been sold or traded, at wholesale prices, to other booksellers. Those retailers had also invested their limited private capital in copies of the first edition. With unsold stock on their hands, they would be most unlikely to purchase from Ling any copies of the new edition. They would also, understandably, be annoyed with him. Ling was a publisher, not a printer; as a publisher, Ling could not afford to alienate those other retailers, on whom the long-term health of his business depended.

For readers who are not bibliographers or book historians, I may seem to be nitpicking about a mere three paragraphs of Lesser's book. But those three paragraphs, which misrepresent the two title-pages as material objects, also misrepresent the material practices of early modern printing and publishing. The misrepresentations in those three paragraphs lay the foundation for Lesser's following four pages, and those four pages conclude the first chapter of his book, setting out his own hypothesis about the origins of Q1 and its differences from Q2. The three paragraphs thus lead directly to the final sentence of his first chapter, which asserts that the distinctions between the two title-pages 'emerged out of Ling's publishing strategy and not ... out of Shakespeare's biography.'[35] On the basis of a purportedly scientific (but actually inaccurate) bibliographical analysis of material objects, Lesser, like Pollard before him, builds 'hypotheses disproportionately large'.

The good-enough quarto

Materially, bibliographically, the 1603 edition of *Hamlet* is a good quarto, a well-made quarto, printed and sold by ethical, reliable professionals. It is not the best-made early Shakespeare quarto: Richard Field's 1593 first edition of *Venus and Adonis* is, as an artisanal object, more elegantly made. But even Field's *Venus and Adonis* was not perfectly made. All early modern forms of textual transmission were error-prone, and no early Shakespeare text is error-free.[36] Even the most conservative modern editions of Shakespeare's works emend some of the words, punctuation and lineation found in the earliest texts; some of those early texts require more emendation than others. What we face, as editors and theatre artists, is not a comfortingly simple choice between 'good' and 'bad' quartos, but repeated wrestling and negotiation with texts that are not perfect, texts that we might call 'good enough'.

When I call Q1 *Hamlet* a 'good-enough quarto', I am of course invoking Donald Winnicott's concept of 'the good enough mother'.[37] Winnicott was reacting against an idealisation of the mother that resulted, in practice, in constant debilitating criticism of actual mothers, who did not live up to that fantasy standard. Like actual mothers, actual Shakespeare quartos are never ideal. And if my analogy between mothers and quartos seems bizarre, it is worth remembering that Winnicott's initial invocation of 'the good enough mother' occurred in the context of an analysis of *material objects*. A 'transitional object' is something that a human infant could recognise as 'not-me'; such transitional objects were, Winnicott argued, fundamental to human imagination, affection and disillusion. The 'good enough quarto' is, for those who read and perform Shakespeare's plays, also a transitional object: something not-me, which comes from an increasingly alien time and place, which nevertheless makes possible an imaginative and emotional transition into another world.

For most Shakespeare scholars, Q1 *Hamlet* is not good enough, not worthy of our idealised Bard. Consequently, most Shakespeare scholars *want* to believe that Q1 *Hamlet* sold poorly, because they assume – and I also initially assumed – that early buyers of these material objects *must* have disdained the first edition, just as we do. But the material evidence does not support that assumption. Lesser's history of the reception of Q1 skips from 1604 to 1823, giving the impression that, after publication of the second quarto, Q1 simply disappeared. But it did not. An anonymous eighteenth-century owner juxtaposed it with pages from a 1718 acting edition and a 1733 scholarly edition.[38] That owner certainly read it anachronistically and comparatively, but s/he read it attentively, and devoted considerable time and labour to it. Henry Oxinden, a landowning Kentish gentleman and minor poet who had been educated at Oxford University and Gray's Inn, recorded his ownership of a copy in 1647.[39] In 1623, the poet William Basse quoted, and attributed to Shakespeare, five lines from Horatio's speech in the play's first scene ('Some say for ever 'gainst that season comes ...'); on the only four occasions in those lines where Q1's wording differs from Q2 and the Folio, Basse prefers Q1.[40] The obvious explanation is that he had read the speech in Q1, and was quoting it twenty years after Q1 was published – meaning that he had not bothered to replace Q1 with the expanded Q2 or Q3. Basse was the author of an enormously popular elegy on Shakespeare, so his familiarity with *Hamlet* is hardly surprising. But for the poet Basse, as for the poet Oxinden, Q1 *Hamlet* was good enough. In other cases, we simply assume that, when Shakespeare's contemporaries referred to *Hamlet,* they *must* have read the Q2 version, when they might just as easily have been reading and praising Q1.

But we do not have to rely on conjectures about who was reading which quarto. The 1603 edition apparently sold out within no more than eighteen months – and possibly as little as twelve months. By contrast, the 'enlarged' 1604 edition took seven years to sell out; it was not reprinted until 1611, four years after Ling's death. We may celebrate the expanded *Hamlet* for other reasons; we may regard it as a greater literary achievement, and/or as a better play. But those are aesthetic judgements. As a material object, in the early English book trade, the 'enlarged' Q2 *Hamlet* was not nearly as successful as the first enlarged edition of *The Spanish Tragedy* (which was reprinted one year later). Q2 *Hamlet* was even less successful if measured against Ling's 1598 edition of Drayton's 'enlarged' *English Heroical Epistles*, which was reprinted the next year, and then again two years later: three editions in just four years, instead of two editions in seven years. From a purely materialist perspective, Ling did not make a mistake in publishing Q1; his mistake was to publish Q2.

Terri Bourus is Professor of English and Professor of Theatre at Florida State University, where she teaches English and Irish drama in performance and on the page. She is one of the General Editors of the *New Oxford Shakespeare Complete Works* (2016–2017) and *Complete Alternative Versions* (forthcoming), in print and online. Her monograph, *Young Shakespeare's Young Hamlet* (2014), delves into the textual and staging quandaries of the first quarto of *Hamlet*. She has written essays on stage directions, the performance of religious conversion, Shakespeare and Fletcher's *Cardenio*, the role of Alice in *Arden of Faversham*, and Middleton's female roles. Bourus is an equity actor, and has directed two very different productions of *Hamlet* both based on Q1.

Notes

1. Alfred W. Pollard, *Shakespeare Folios and Quartos: A Study in the Bibliography of Shakespeare's Plays 1594–1685* (London: Methuen, 1909).
2. A.W. Pollard, *Shakespeare's Fight with the Pirates and the Problems of the Transmission of his Text*, 2nd ed. (Cambridge: Cambridge University Press, 1920), xxi.

3. *A Short-Title Catalogue of Books Printed in England, Scotland, & Ireland and of English Books Printed Abroad, 1475–1640*, comp. A.W. Pollard, G.R. Redgrave et al. (London: Quaritch, 1926). I refer to specific early modern books with an abbreviated citation to this catalogue; for instance, Q1 *Hamlet* is 'STC 22275'.
4. Pollard, *Shakespeare Folios and Quartos*, 52.
5. W. Craig Ferguson, *Pica Roman Type in Elizabethan England* (Aldershot: Scolar Press, 1989). For a substantive examination and critique of this book by another specialist in font identification, see the review by Adrian Weiss, *PBSA* 83, no. 4 (1989), 539–546. Because descriptive bibliography is an empirical discipline, the application of new techniques can discredit or improve old hypotheses. But Pollard's attribution of Q1 *Hamlet* to Simmes has remained unchallenged for more than a century.
6. W. Craig Ferguson, *Valentine Simmes* (Charlottesville: Bibliographical Society of the University of Virginia, 1968), 14.
7. Alan Craven, 'Proofreading in the Shop of Valentine Simmes', *PBSA* 68 (1974), 361–372.
8. For a fuller consideration of the working relationships between Ling, Simmes and Roberts, based on new documentary evidence, see Terri Bourus, *Young Shakespeare's Young Hamlet: Print, Piracy, and Performance* (New York: Palgrave Macmillan, 2014), 11–33.
9. J. Payne Collier, ed., *The Works of William Shakespeare: The Text Formed from an Entirely New Collation of the Old Editions*, 8 vols (London: Whittaker), VII (1843): 191.
10. Ferguson, *Valentine Simmes*, 246, 248.
11. British Library, 'Shakespeare in Quarto', https://www.bl.uk/treasures/shakespeare/homepage.html (accessed 30 May 2018).
12. David L. Gants, 'Mine of Debt: William White and the Printing of the 1602 *Spanish Tragedy … with new additions*', in *The New Oxford Shakespeare: Authorship Companion*, ed. Gary Taylor and Gabriel Egan (Oxford: Oxford University Press, 2017), 231–240, here 235. For a summary of the evidence for Shakespeare's authorship of at least one of the 1602 additions, see Gary Taylor and Rory Loughnane, 'The Canon and Chronology of Shakespeare's Works', in Taylor and Egan, *Authorship Companion*, 417–602, here 528–531.
13. Jeffrey Masten, 'An/The Old Law', in *Thomas Middleton and Early Modern Textual Culture*, ed. Gary Taylor and John Lavagnino (Oxford: Clarendon Press, 2007), 1123.
14. For the best (and wittiest) analysis of the prejudicial ethical terminology, see Random Cloud (= Randall McLeod), 'The Marriage of Good and Bad Quartos', *Shakespeare Quarterly* 33 (1982), 421–431, here 431. He focuses on the 'bad quarto' of *Romeo and Juliet*, but the critique is equally relevant to claims about Q1 *Hamlet*.
15. John Heminge and Henry Condell, 'To the Great Variety of Readers', in *Mr. William Shakespeares Comedies, Histories, & Tragedies* (London: Jaggard and Blount, 1623), A3.
16. The best up-to-date introduction to stemmatics I have read is at http://phylonetworks.blogspot.com/2017/05/on-stemmatics-and-phylogenetic-methods.html (accessed 28 December 2018).
17. Zachary Lesser and Peter Stallybrass, 'The First Literary Hamlet and the Commonplacing of Professional Plays', *Shakespeare Quarterly* 59, no. 4 (2008), 371–420.

18. Martin Wiggins, *British Drama 1533–1642: A Catalogue*, Vol. 4 (Oxford: Oxford University Press, 2014), 241–251. Wiggins's volume went to press before my critique of the 'bad quarto' hypothesis (*Young Shakespeare's Young Hamlet*) was published.
19. Terri Bourus, 'Enter Shakespeare's Young Hamlet, 1589', *Actes des Congrès de la Société Française Shakespeare* 34 (1 March 2016), para. 8, 15, 35, http://journals.openedition.org/shakespeare/3736, doi:10.4000/shakespeare.3736.
20. Zachary Lesser, *Hamlet After Q1* (Philadelphia: University of Pennsylvania Press, 2014), 66–67.
21. Ibid, 66.
22. Ibid, 66.
23. Ibid, 66.
24. Theresa Anne Bourus, 'Shrouded Behind the Arras: The Shadow of Shakespeare in the First Quarto of *Hamlet*' (PhD diss., Northern Illinois University, 2000), 126–127; Terri Bourus, 'Shakespeare and the London Publishing Environment: The Publisher and Printers of Q1 and Q2 *Hamlet*', *Analytical and Enumerative Bibliography* 12 (2001), 206–228.
25. Lesser, *Hamlet After Q1*, 66.
26. Michael Drayton, *The Owle* (London: E. White and N. Ling, 1604), STC 7213. The co-publication might be relevant to the absence of Ling's device.
27. William Smith, *THE Black-Smith* (London: Nicholas Ling, 1606), STC 22881.5. There is not room for Ling's device on the octavo title page, because of the space taken up by the subtitle and attribution: 'A / SERMON PREACHED / at *White-Hall* before the Kings most / excellent Majestie, the young / *Prince, the Councell, &c. On Loe- / Sunday,* 1606, *and by com- / mandment put to / print.* / By / *W.S.* Doct. in Diuinitie, Chaplaine to / his Majestie'. This information is clearly fundamental to marketing the sermon. However, Ling's device is instead printed on the recto of the title page (A1v), which contains nothing else, and faces Smith's epistle to King James.
28. Lesser, *Hamlet After Q1*, 66.
29. Ibid, 67.
30. For Shakespeare's popularity in print, see Lukas Erne, *Shakespeare and the Book Trade* (Cambridge: Cambridge University Press, 2013).
31. Lesser, *Hamlet After Q1*, 66.
32. I am grateful to Stephen Tabor, curator of rare books at the Huntington Library, for personally measuring the only surviving title page of Q1, and to Maddy Smith, curator of British Heritage Collections 1601–1900 at the British Library, for personally measuring that library's exemplar of the Q2 title page. Digital images and printed photographs cannot be relied upon to reproduce the actual size of books; the images of the title pages in Lesser's book (pp. 2, 7) do not replicate size differences between the two material objects.
33. Lesser, *Hamlet After Q1*, 67.
34. In all these comparisons of title pages, I ignore subsequent handwriting, damage or cropping in the particular copies that are photographically reproduced in *EEBO*.
35. Lesser, *Hamlet After Q1*, 71.
36. See John Jowett, 'Shakespeare and the Kingdom of Error', in *The New Oxford Shakespeare: The Complete Works: Critical Reference Edition*, ed. Gary Taylor et al., 2 vols (Oxford: Oxford University Press, 2017), xlix–lxiv.

37. D.W. Winnicott, 'Transitional Objects and Transitional Phenomena: A Study of the First Not-Me Possession', *International Journal of Psychoanalysis* 34 (1953), 89–97, here 94.
38. Arthur Freeman and J.I. Freeman, 'Did Halliwell Steal and Mutilate the First Quarto of Hamlet?' *Library*, VII: 2, no. 4 (2001), 349–363. The interleaving (which I have personally examined) is now bound separately with the shelf mark C.34.K.1.*
39. For Oxinden's books, see W.W. Greg, *A Bibliography of English Printed Drama to the Restoration*, 4 vols (London: Bibliographical Society, 1939–1959), 3: 189–193; for his life, Sheila Hingley, 'Oxinden, Henry', in *Oxford Dictionary of National Biography* (Oxford: Oxford University Press, 2004), https://doi-org.proxy.lib.fsu.edu/10.1093/ref:odnb/21053, accessed June 2018.
40. William Basse, *A Helpe to Discourse* (London: Becket, 1623), STC 1549.5, 250. This passage, attributed to "*W. Shaks.*", was cited in Tiffany Stern, 'Sermons, Plays and Note-Takers: *Hamlet* Q1 as a "Noted" Text', *Shakespeare Survey* 66 (2013), 1–23. In order to support her conjecture that the text of Q1 was produced by rapid note-taking by several members of the audience at several times, Stern also conjectured that Basse's own quotation results from him taking notes in the theatre. But it is more economical to assume that Basse was remembering Q1 itself, which has 'say' (instead of 'says'), 'dare' (instead of 'can'), 'walk' (instead of 'sturre') and 'and so hallowed' (instead of 'and so gratious'). Posters advertising plays did not name their authors, so the attribution of this passage to Shakespeare is also more likely to come from a book than a performance. For other problems with Stern's theory, see Bourus, *Young Shakespeare's Young Hamlet*, 69–94.

Chapter 6
Harvey's 1593 *'To Be* and *Not To Be'*
The Authorship and Date of the First Quarto of *Hamlet*

Dennis McCarthy

Shakespearean researchers have always faced the obstacle of concentrating on an era when biographers were few and modern-day newspapers non-existent, forcing them to piece together information about the Stratford dramatist from numerous indirect and extraneous sources – legal documents, snippets in diaries and commonplace books, Shakespeare's dedications and so on. One important source of contemporaneous commentary on the literary scene – the late Elizabethan and early Jacobean satires by theatrical insiders Gabriel Harvey, Thomas Nashe, Henry Chettle, Thomas Dekker, John Marston and Ben Jonson – has offered some important nuggets of information on Shakespeare, but these works have yet to be fully excavated. Certainly, editors and scholars are familiar with the 'upstart crow' comment on 'Shakes-Scene' in *Greene's*

Notes for this section begin on page 123.

Groatsworth of Wit (1592) and Nashe's allusion to an early *Hamlet* in his preface to Greene's *Menaphon* (1589). But we have yet to uncover, let alone fully understand and assimilate, all the literary and theatrical allusions in the Nashe-Harvey pamphlet wars or the later 'war of the theatres'.

With his *Shakespeare and the Poets' War*, James P. Bednarz has led the most important recent expedition in this direction, revealing valuable information about the literary quarrels slyly alluded to in Shakespeare's *As You Like It*, *Troilus and Cressida*, *Twelfth Night* and other war-of-the-theatre plays by Jonson and Marston.[1] Just as a complete understanding of Arthur Miller's *The Crucible* and Elia Kazan's *On the Waterfront* would not be possible without familiarity with their McCarthy-era dispute, a full knowledge of the war of the theatres helps to expose new themes and uncover previously hidden relationships, both personal and literary.

These satires can also help us to ascertain the chronology and historical background of certain plays and are at times especially informative about who wrote what when. Nashe's preface to *Menaphon* necessarily confirms the existence by 1589 of a Senecan tragedy titled *Hamlet*, filled with many tragic monologues. *Groatsworth's* spoof of a line from *3 Henry VI* ('tiger's heart wrapped in a player's hide') in the autumn of 1592 sets the latest possible date for the English history. Moreover, as it associates the work with a player-dramatist with the nickname 'Shake-Scene', we know this is an allusion to a Shakespearean version of the play – not some earlier, now lost source play. Satirists of the era often spoofed a writer's lines as a way of both identifying the target and mocking that writer's style.

Ben Jonson would become a frequent practitioner of this device. For example, when spoofing the playwright John Marston with Crispinus in *Poetaster*, Jonson placed a number of Marston's idiosyncratic words and lines into the character's mouth. As Sean McEvoy writes: 'Horace makes Crispinus swallow a pill which causes him to vomit up the absurd Latinate vocabulary in which Marston delighted ('O – glibbery – lubrical – defunct – O – ')'.[2] Similarly, Crispinus recites a poem that ends with the line 'Of strenuous vengeance to clutch the fist' (5.3.286).[3] This is an unmistakable parody of a line in Marston's *Antonio's Revenge*: 'The fist of strenuous vengeance is clutched' (5.1.3).[4]

In *Every Man Out of His Humor* (1600), Jonson uses the character of Sogliardo, the newly wealthy, satin-clad, social-climbing rustic, to mock Shakespeare. In the character descriptions, Jonson writes that Sogliardo is 'an essential clown ... so enamoured of the name of a gentleman, that he will have it, though he buys it' (Characters, 74–76).[5] Thus, in the satire, Sogliardo aggressively pursues a higher social rank and purchases his coat of arms with the crest 'Not without mustard' (3.1.244). Similarly, Shakespeare's social aspirations were well known, and he had recently obtained a coat of arms with the crest 'Not without right'. H.N. Gibson, noting the similarity of the crests and the fact that 'Shakespeare did aspire to gentility', writes that 'there can be little doubt that Shakespeare was one of [Jonson's] victims in *Every Man Out Of His Humour*'.[6] Bednarz, likewise, agrees that Sogliardo is a caricature of Shakespeare, writing that Jonson was mocking Shakespeare's 'outlandish aspiration to gentility'.[7] And Katherine Duncan-Jones points out that it is 'impossible not to find a Shakespearean reference' in the arms, referring to it as Jonson's 'mockery' of 'Shakespeare's pursuit of gentility'.[8] Recent discoveries by Heather Wolfe of documents found in the archives of the College of Arms confirm that it was indeed Shakespeare who was pushing to acquire the coat of arms and that granting arms to such upstarts soon became the subject of controversy. As Wolfe observes in a *New York Times* article on her findings: '"It makes it abundantly clear that while Shakespeare was obtaining the arms on behalf of his father, it was really for his own status," she said'.[9]

In substituting 'Not without mustard' for 'Not without right', Jonson probably took his cue from the not-without-mustard scene in *The Taming of the Shrew*, in which Grumio, attempting to starve Katherine, refuses to serve her beef without mustard:

GRUMIO	What say you to a piece of beef and mustard?
KATHERINE	A dish that I do love to feed upon.
GRUMIO	Ay, but the mustard is too hot a little.
KATHERINE	Why then, the beef, and let the mustard rest.
GRUMIO	Nay then, I will not. You shall have the mustard, Or else you get no beef of Grumio.
KATHERINE	Then both, or one, or anything thou wilt.
GRUMIO	Why then the mustard without the beef.
KATHERINE	Go, get thee gone, thou false deluding slave. (4.3.23–31)[10]

'Not without mustard' is an effective shorthand description of this scene and perhaps one of the few Shakespearean scenes Jonson could think of to spoof the phrase 'Not without right'.[11] Grumio is also a rustic Italianate clown, just like Sogliardo.

Perhaps the satirist's most obvious jibe at Shakespeare is Sogliardo's comment, 'I'll give coats, that's my humour: but I lack a Cullisen' (1.2.146–147). The comment alludes to one of the jests mentioned by Hamlet in Q1 when he complains about the various jokes that clowns will improvise on the stage:

> ... and 'My coat wants a cullison;'
> and 'your beer is sour' and, blabbering with lips
> And thus keep in his cinquepace of jests. (9.25)[12]

The *Early English Books Online* digital database (*EEBO*) reveals no works, printed at any time, other than *Every Man Out of His Humor* and Q1, that place *coat* near *cullison* (*cullisen*). Evidently, Jonson was again using the clown Sogliardo to spoof one of the lines that Shakespeare had associated with clowns. Yet, significantly, this line does not appear in the 'authentic', longer versions of *Hamlet*, which is likely the reason that it has not yet been conventionally associated with Shakespeare. Had the unique line appeared in the second quarto or Folio versions, no doubt many scholars today would accept this as another jibe at Shakespeare – just as they do with the *tiger's heart* line in *Groatsworth*.

Moreover, Hamlet's comment in Q1 has chronological significance as we know the clown to whom Hamlet is referring. As Leah Marcus writes about the 1580s clown Richard Tarlton:

> two resembling the 'jeasts' to which Hamlet refers were eventually published in *Tarlton's jests. Drawne into these three parts* (1613). The quip about sour beer was probably based on a jest in which Tarlton played drunkard before the queen, and the line about the coat wanting a cullison appears in a jest the same clown played on a red-faced gentleman in an alehouse to make the company merry.[13]

To be clear, the line about a *coat* that *wants* or *lacks* a *cullison* does not appear in *Tarlton's Jests* – that is exclusive to Jonson and Shakespeare – but Tarlton does appear to have been involved in a jest in which he referred to the 'cullisance upon my sleeve'.[14] With that and the ale joke, it seems clear that Hamlet in Q1 is spoofing Richard Tarlton. And since Tarlton died in 1588 and as Hamlet's line appears to refer to specific moments from his life, this would seem to point to a date of origination closer to 1588 than 1603. If a dramatist wanted to break the spell of *Hamlet* and insert a topical joke the theatre audience would understand, one would think he would choose allusions less than fifteen years old.

Every Man Out of His Humor was a war-of-the-theatres play, and Jonson soon followed it with another salvo in *Cynthia's Revels* (1600) that also appears to include a knock on *Hamlet*. In the introduction, Jonson underscores a recent revival of Senecan tragedies: 'they say, the umbrae, or ghosts of some three or four plays, departed a dozen years since, have been seen walking on your stage here'.[15] Jonson here even uses *umbrae*, Seneca's Latin term for ghosts.[16] Moreover, not only was *Hamlet* well known for its ghost walking the stage, but the phrase 'departed a dozen years since' again sets a date of the original at about 1588. Finally, as Jonson here is grouping it with other Senecan revivals from that time, he is not distinguishing Shakespeare's play as a new and transformed work but a reappearance of an old play – like Thomas Kyd's *A Spanish Tragedy* (c. 1588), which was revived in the late 1590s.

Two other literary insiders, Nashe and Harvey, also appear to make blatant allusions to *Hamlet*. These references appear in their long-standing pamphlet feud, which began in 1589 with Nashe's preface to Robert Greene's *Menaphon* (1589) and continued into the 1590s. The *Menaphon* preface included the first known mention of *Hamlet*:

> yet English *Seneca* read by candlelight yields many good sentences ... and if you entreat him fair in a frosty morning, he will afford you whole *Hamlets*, I should say handfuls of tragical speeches. (Original emphasis)[17]

The allusion to *Seneca*, tragical speeches and the gratuitous stumble over *Hamlets*, which was italicised in the original, makes it clear that Nashe is referring to some version of the Danish tragedy. Typically, scholars who accept the orthodox chronology assume Nashe's preface has no relevance to Shakespeare himself and that Nashe was referring to a lost *Hamlet*, perhaps by Thomas Kyd. However, the next two allusions to *Hamlet* in the pamphlet war, which include quotations from *Hamlet*, suggest that Nashe was not referring to a lost version.

The context is important. After many scathing pamphlets, especially attacking Gabriel Harvey and his brothers, Nashe writes an apology in his foreword to *Christ's Tears Over Jerusalem* (1593), in which he retracts everything, bids a 'hundred unfortunate farewells' to such vitriol, and promises 'an unfeigned conversion'.[18]

But Harvey, perhaps doubting his rival's sincerity, would have none of it. In his very next reply, *A New Letter of Notable Contents*

(1593), Harvey seems to imply that Nashe's sudden vacillation in the quarrel appears rather Hamlet-like and uses the Danish prince to mock Nashe's sudden wavering.

> Did I never tell you of a graver man, that wore a privy coat of interchangeable colours; and for the Art of Revolting, or recanting might read a Lecture to any retrograde Planet in Heaven or Earth? ... or of sheep, as Seneca writeth, changed them from white to black, and from black to white? After a stern and ruthful *Tragedy*, solemnly acted, who deeplier plunged in sober and melancholy dumps, then some good fellows; that from a pleasant and wanton *Comedy*, finely played, return as merry as a cricket, and as light as a feather? ... What say you to a spring of rankest *Villainy* in February and a harvest of ripest *Divinity* in May? May they not surcease to wonder, that wonder how Machiavel can teach a prince *to be and not to be* religious? (Original emphasis)[19]

Harvey makes a few explicit references to Nashe, who was now *recanting* his past invective. Having first penned hateful tracts – 'his spring of rankest villainy in February' – Nashe was now apologising in his religiously oriented *Christ's Tears* – 'a harvest of ripest divinity in May'. But a number of his comments suggest that Harvey was comparing this reversal to Hamlet's notorious fluctuations. The important lines and phrases are:

1) Graver man that wore a privy coat
2) And for the art of revolting or recanting might read a lecture to [the heavens]
3) Seneca writeth ... ruthful tragedy, solemnly acted ... melancholy dumps [i.e. tragical speeches]
4) Machiavel can teach a prince *to be* and *not to be* religious [original emphasis]

'*Graver* man' would be a peculiarly apt description for Hamlet, due not only to his melancholy but also to his seemingly endless reflections on and allusions to the grave. Indeed, in one of the more memorable scenes, Hamlet visits a graveyard, talks with a grave-digger, delivers a speech to and about a skull, and even ends up jumping into the grave. As Terri Bourus notes, unlike the second quarto, Q1 includes the stage direction 'Hamlet leaps in [to the grave] after Laertes' (16.119 SD). This became a peculiarly distinctive feature of the play. Bourus also quotes a 1619 manuscript elegy of Richard Burbage that fondly refers to his role as 'young Hamlet' and then the elegist remembers: 'Oft have I seen him [Burbage] leap into the grave'.[20]

We do not know what Burbage wore on stage as Hamlet, but it is not unreasonable to think he often wore a 'privy coat', which is a kind of armoured vest, or chain mail, worn to protect against daggers. Many theatrical productions of *Hamlet* that strive for chronological authenticity do indeed include chain mail in their costuming. For example, director Vsevolod Meyerhold envisioned the ghost encounter in which both Hamlet and his father wear silver chain mail.[21] Franco Zeffirelli's 1990 film version also placed Mel Gibson's Hamlet into a privy coat for the final scene.

The next line then seems to be a direct hit: 'And for the art of revolting or recanting might read a lecture to any retrograde Planet in Heaven or Earth'. Due to the prince's ethereal philosophising on heaven and earth, the tragedy is the most peculiarly celestial in the canon. This is also true in the first quarto version in which we find a juxtaposition of *heaven* and *earth* no fewer than seven times, four of them in Hamlet's speeches. But the description of a graver man reading a lecture to the heavens seems to aim at the *to be or not to be* soliloquy in particular. In Q1, Hamlet enters this scene 'poring upon a book' (7.109) just before he launches into its version of the speech. In their introduction to *Hamlet*, editors Jonathan Bate and Eric Rasmussen stress this particular staging of the famous soliloquy: 'His famous question [*'To be or not to be'*] is asked as if in response to something in the book he is reading'.[22] W.B. Worthen even suggests that the intent may have been for Hamlet to read from parts of the book during its delivery: 'in the 1603 quarto, the King notes Hamlet "poring upon a book" (1603 quarto, 7.110) just prior to the "To be, or not to be" soliloquy, licensing the notion that Hamlet's reflections are prompted by, perhaps even read from, a book'.[23] Burbage, as Hamlet, reading a book on stage and then giving a speech to the sky would indeed provide a dramatic example of a graver man, perhaps in a privy coat, reading a lecture to the heavens.

The next lines only reinforce this interpretation. In them, Harvey gratuitously forces allusions to *Seneca, a stern and ruthful tragedy, solemnly acted*, and its actor, *deeplier plunged in sober and melancholy dumps*. The *OED* defines 'dumps' as 'a fit of abstraction or musing', and so perhaps no better phrase could be used to describe Hamlet's incessant penchant for sad reflection. Also, several times Hamlet is described as beset by melancholy, including thrice in Q1 (2.27, 6.89, 7.383). Moreover, this is a comment about Nashe, who also referred to *Seneca* in the context of *tragical speeches*, and there the allusion to *Hamlet* is undeniable.

If any doubt remains, certainly Harvey removes it at the end by quoting from the opening line of the soliloquy to which he has been hinting, indeed quoting what would become the most famous line in history. As Nashe's religious-related vacillations seem rather Hamlet-like, then he has no need to 'wonder how Machiavel can teach a prince *to be and not to be* religious' (original emphasis). Harvey's last comment hits the monologue dead centre, specifically alluding to a prince and placing *to be and not to be* in italics, confirming it is a quotation.[24] Elsewhere in the pamphlet, Harvey also puts quotations in italics.[25]

Hamlet is also a prince tussling with religious questions. As Benjamin Bertram writes, 'Religious doubt takes a number of forms in *Hamlet* ... The soliloquy [*To be or not to be*] suggests that even something so fundamental to Christianity as the afterlife could be called into question'.[26] The prince wavers on what happens to us after we die: is it just oblivion, or do we dream and so possibly suffer? He concludes that we do not know, and the unknown brings dread. But, significantly, this is a Machiavellian question. As John Roe notes in *Shakespeare and Machiavelli*:

> If Claudius is the minor Machiavel in the play, then Hamlet might qualify as the major Machiavel – or Machiavellian (to employ the more serious term). What incapacitates Hamlet for so much of the play is the very same thing that propels Richard forward: the recognition that there appears to be no moral significance to what happens in the world. Hamlet struggles with this problem at length and in his own way.[27]

This almost appears to be a paraphrase of Harvey, who also associates Machiavelli with Hamlet's wavering on religious questions. This would not be Harvey's only allusion to *Hamlet*. He also refers to the play in his marginalia of his edition of Chaucer's *Works*, printed in 1598. In summary, Harvey, who is responding to pamphlets of Nashe, the first of which necessarily refers to *Hamlet* in 1589, is essentially arguing that Nashe's reversals are like that of a 'graver' prince in a recently staged Senecan tragedy, filled with many melancholy speeches – and in one of the soliloquies, the actor playing the prince enters the stage reading a book, looks up, gives a speech to the heavens in which he wrestles with religious questions à la Machiavelli, and says *to be* and *not to be*. This would appear to establish the existence of this monologue in some form, in *Hamlet*, by 1593.

Naturally, Harvey's response infuriated Nashe, who reprinted *Christ's Tears Over Jerusalem* the next year, taking out the repentant foreword and replacing it with one that includes a response to Harvey's *Hamlet* allusion. After twice referring to *Machiavel*, Nashe stresses Harvey's recent literary attacks on the deceased, likening him to the clownish grave-digger whom Hamlet denounces for being so brutish and vile with the bones and skulls of the buried:

> Master Lyly, poor deceased Kit Marlowe, reverent Doctor Perne, with a hundred other quiet senseless carcasses before the Conquest departed, in the same work he [Harvey] hath most notoriously & vilely dealt with, and, to conclude, he hath proved himself to be the only Gabriel Grave-digger under heaven.[28]

Two sentences prior, Nashe even quotes the grave-digger scene, mocking Harvey's flourishing style: 'His vainglory (which some take to be *his gentlewoman*) he hath new *painted over an inch thick*'.[29] This repeats Hamlet's plea to Yorick's skull: 'now go to *my Ladies* chamber, and bid her *paint her self an inch thick*' (16.88–89). This was not a common phrase. A search of *EEBO* for all works that place *paint* within ten words of *inch thick* records Q1 (1603) as the earliest example – and only three non-*Hamlet*-related uses after that. Nashe's altered edition with this foreword is not yet searchable on *EEBO* or else his pamphlet would have provided the first recorded example. But the parallels linking Nashe's pamphlet to *Hamlet* include more than just that phrase. Both use similar language about a woman applying makeup (*my lady's [his gentlewoman]... paint[ed]... an inch thick*) in the context of a *grave-digger* disrespecting the bones of the deceased. Of course, no other works in *EEBO* juxtapose such disparate elements. In an article underscoring these parallels, J.W. DeMent dismisses the idea that this might be a coincidence and argues it is unlikely Shakespeare was the borrower: 'it is much easier to believe that Nashe recalled a highly dramatic scene from a current play and used it as a topical reference than that Shakespeare turned back to a single Nashe metaphor when he was constructing the scene six or seven years later'. In a footnote, he also asks reasonably: 'Is it not unlikely that Shakespeare would have introduced allusions to controversial books of eight or ten years back had he written his first version around 1600?'[30]

Moreover, we know Nashe has seen *Hamlet*, and here he is responding to a passage of Harvey's that refers to a *graver man* and then quotes the *to be/not to be* monologue in the context of a melancholy speech in a Senecan tragedy, solemnly acted and delivered by a vacillating prince, holding a book and wrestling with religious questions! Are we to believe that Harvey and Nashe, the allusive satirists, were referring to nothing at all and were gratuitously forcing in quotations and images that pertain to nothing?

Finally, Paul Menzer offered an important analysis of the title page claim of Q1, which describes the play as having been 'acted ... in the cittie of London'. He observes that 'the "Cittie of London" was not a vague phrase in Elizabethan London. Then, as now, the term referred to the 677 acres (just over one square mile) ruled by the Lord Mayor and Corporation of London, who owed their privileges to a royal charter dating from the thirteenth century'. The city had very definite boundaries, usually marked by walls, and Menzer confirmed from references at the time that there were well-known and 'sharp distinctions between within and without and between what does and does not constitute part of the City'.[31]

More importantly, the 'in the cittie' claim would seem to have chronological significance. After 1594, plays were strictly prohibited from performance within the city of London – a ban that was almost certainly the result of a compromise between the Lord Mayor of London and the all-powerful Privy Council.[32] The better-known theatre companies, and particularly the Lord Chamberlain's Men, would have to take such a ban seriously, of course, for flagrantly violating it could have incurred severe penalties.[33] And even if Shakespeare's company, for some reason, managed to perform an unadvertised play surreptitiously within the city, it would have been folly to flaunt such a violation on a title page.

Terri Bourus also stresses the title page claim and its importance in dating the play: 'the last known performances of the Lord Chamberlain's Men "in the city of London" took place in the winter of 1594–5, at the special request of their patron', referring to Lord Hunsdon's letter to the Lord Mayor asking for permission for the London performances at Cross Keys theatre. Bourus also points out that Shakespeare's company had performed a *Hamlet* in early 1594, outside the city, at Newington Butts, and that Thomas Lodge alluded to a performance of *Hamlet* at the Theatre, also outside the city, in 1596. Bourus makes the only reasonable conclusion:

The obvious explanation for this anomaly would be that the Chamberlain's Men, at the Cross Keys Inn 'in the City of London' in the winter of 1594–5, performed the same Hamlet play they had performed in Newington Butts (outside the City) earlier in 1594 and also performed at the Theatre (outside the City) in 1595 or 1596: in other words, that the Hamlet play of 1594 is the Hamlet play printed in 1603.[34]

This is indeed a very simple and reasonable explanation that accepts the straightforward declaration of the title page. Even if no permission had been granted for the Chamberlain's Men to perform that winter, it is reasonable to accept that the city performance of *Hamlet* still would have had to precede the ban.

Explaining the title page while adhering to the conventional chronology, in contrast, is problematic. Menzer, for example, provides a thorough analysis of all potential explanations consistent with a post-1600 date for Q1. First, he considers the possibility that the title page claim was just a typical advertisement for plays and not meant to be taken literally, that it was just 'standard boilerplate copy'.[35] To that end, he analysed 836 title pages collected in W.W. Greg's *Bibliography of the English Printed Drama to the Restoration*,[36] which covers the years 1512 to 1689. Menzer found that, counting Q1, only six of the 836 plays refer to performances specifically within the city of London. Moreover, he determined that the five other plays were likely performed within London – just as their title pages state. Quoting Menzer: 'In nearly every case, the designation can be read literally, for the texts can be linked to companies known to have played in the City'.[37] And in the one case where he could not confirm a city performance, he still deemed it reasonable to accept the title page claim, having found no evidence suggesting otherwise:

> The notion that Q1 included the phrase 'acted in the Cittie of London' for fashion's sake has been discounted on the grounds that such claims were not fashionable: only eight of the hundreds of extant plays published between 1512 and 1689 boast of performances in or about the City. Of the eight, only six advertise performances *within* the City, and in five cases there exists no reason to dispute those claims.[38]

The second explanation that Menzer considers is that the 'in the city' claim was not really meant to describe Q1, but an early, non-Shakespearean *Hamlet* also performed by the Chamberlain's Men prior to the ban. 'We know their repertory included a play of that name. The title page may fold those performances in with those of Shakespeare's play, maximizing its marketing reach.'[39]

Menzer also found this explanation wanting. After all, how likely is it that the printers would have advertised Shakespeare's *Hamlet* as an earlier version if those in the market for Shakespeare's work, that is, the literate Elizabethan theatregoers, would have believed this to be false? If it were known among the purchasers of dramas that Shakespeare's *Hamlet* was still a new play in 1603 and that the 1594 *Hamlet* played in London was an inferior, non-Shakespearean version of the play, then it would seem that printers would have only hurt their sales by advertising the first quarto as this older rendition. Moreover, it is somewhat unusual to suggest that title page claims are not meant to describe the work that they front.

This leaves Menzer with the last possible explanation: the Lord Chamberlain's Men ignored the ban, and companies continued to play in London in spite of it. Menzer accepts this as the most likely reason, even though he points out that it is at odds with the conventional view of late Elizabethan theatre practices, especially Andrew Gurr's conclusion that the winter of 1594–1595 would have marked 'the last occasion that the city inns were ever used for playing'.[40]

But this new case that Menzer makes to support 'fugitive inn-playing' is weak. For example, Menzer notes that 'some of the clearest evidence comes from Thomas Platter',[41] a Swiss physician whose 1590s travel journal provides detailed descriptions of Elizabethan theatrical practices. The line that captured Menzer's notice, however, does not appear in Platter's extensive discussion of English plays, but later in his diary when he alludes to the variety of entertainments available in London. Platter refers to the 'great many inns, taverns and beer-gardens scattered about the city, where much amusement may be had with eating, drinking, fiddling and the rest, as for instance in our hostelry, which was visited by *players* almost daily'.[42] The operative word in this translated passage is 'players'. Quoting Menzer:

> 'Players' here translates Platter's *spilleut*, which in sixteenth-century German more commonly meant 'play actors'. If so, Platter, lodged in Mark Lane in the middle of the City of London, describes the players' near-daily recourse to his inn during the autumn months of 1599.[43]

A more recent analysis by M.A. Katritzky challenges this interpretation and contends that *spilleut* refers to *musicians*:

> Because the regulation of theatrical performances was especially stringent within the City of London, many London theatres were located just outside the legal limits of its city walls. The performers who came almost daily to Platter's Inn are almost certainly musicians, not

'fugitive inn-playing' actors staging performances of the type officially banned within the City of London.[44]

Indeed, when explicitly discussing the English theatre, Platter uses the term *comedienspiller* for *actors*, twice.[45] In the latter passage, he is referring to *eating, drinking, fiddling and the rest*, supporting the translation of *spilleut* as *musicians*. Moreover, in another essay on the Swiss theatre enthusiast, Katritzky translates a passage in which Platter plainly distinguishes the *comedien spiller* (*players*) from *spilleut* (*musicians*) when describing a Commedia dell'arte troupe in Italy:

> Alweil ich zu Avinion gewesen, hab ich oft undt viel seltzame *Comedien spiler*. ... Auch hatten sie gute *Spilleut* under ihnen selbs, konten die Lauten, Harpfen unndt Violen gar lieblich zu ihrem eigenen gesang accommodieren, daß sich menniglich mußte dorab verwundern.

> Throughout my stay in Avignon, I often saw many unusual comedy players. ... They also had good *musicians* among their number, who could accompany their own singing so well on the lute, harp and viola that all were amazed by their skill.[46]

Finally, Platter also provides a comprehensive description of all theatres around London and explicitly places them all outside the city. For example, he notes that he 'went over the water [i.e. across the Thames] and saw in the house with the thatched roof [in dem streüwinen Dachhaus] the tragedy of the first emperor Julius Caesar'. Most scholars accept that this refers to Shakespeare's *Julius Caesar* playing at the Globe, although some suggest it may have been a non-Shakespearean play at the nearby Rose, both in the suburb of Southwark. Platter also describes another play he watched 'in the suburbs' near Bishopsgate, which some scholars suppose is the Curtain. Platter then sums up: 'And so every day at two in the afternoon in the city of London sometimes two sometimes three plays are given in different places, which compete with each other, and those which perform best have the largest number of listeners'.[47] This would appear to exclude a fourth venue within the city and especially seems to contradict the supposition of plays performed daily at his own inn. Certainly, he would have described those performances as he did the other plays he had seen and then added them to his tally of London play production.

Menzer's other examples are less compelling. He notes that in 1608, 'William Claiton, an East Smithfield victualler, [was] charged "for the suffering playes to be played in his [house in] the night season"'.[48] But this likely refers to the playing house on Nightingale Lane in East Smithfield, which is in the suburb just east of the city, near the Tower of London.[49] He refers to Philip Henslowe's record of a performance 'in fleatstreat pryuat', but again this is likely a reference to a suburban house. Fleet Street also went through the Whitefriars district, just outside of the city, and Whitefriars was associated with theatres. His other allusion to a play at 'the Maidenhead Inn, Islington, on 14 October 1618' is again a reference to the suburbs. He also discusses Henry Crosse's comment on 'nocturnall and night Playes' in *Vertues common-wealth* (1603), but there is little reason to believe Crosse refers to performances in the city.[50]

The greatest support for Bourus's conclusion may come from Menzer's own analysis of title pages. The question is whether the Q1 title page claim has chronological significance, and Menzer confirms that all the other plays that flaunt the same claim were performed within the city *prior to the 1594 ban*. The other five are *Tamberlaine* (first performed c. 1587; published 1590), *The Troublesome Reign of King John* (performed c. 1590; published 1591), *FairEm* (performed c. 1591; published 1591), *Edward the Second* (performed c. 1590–1591; published 1594) and *Mucedorus* (performed c. 1590; published 1598).[51] In other words, the five other plays were all written and performed between 1587 and 1591.

Thus, as one would suspect, printers and playwrights were extremely selective about using the London designation on title pages – and they only did so for plays written before 1594 that were performed in the city. This poses a problem for the view that Q1 was first written in the early 1600s, making it the only known play to advertise a city performance despite supposedly originating after 1594.

In summary, this chapter makes the following points:

- The title page of Q1 carries Shakespeare's name – and no one at the time objected to it.
- The title page clarifies that this is the *Hamlet* that was performed in London, which is consistent with Henslowe's reference to a *Hamlet* performance in 1594. Plays were banned in London after that – and only plays performed prior to the ban included this designation.
- Jonson, who would spoof playwrights in his satires by associating them with their own lines, places a quotation exclusive to Q1 into the mouth of his Shakespeare caricature, Sogliardo.
- Nashe and Harvey, in their back-and-forth, refer to *Hamlet* at least three times, using images and quotations from the tragedy

to mock each other. This includes a spoof on two of its most memorable moments: the grave-digger scene and the *to be or not to be* speech. Harvey even uses italics to demarcate the latter as a quotation in a lengthy passage that includes other apparent allusions to *Hamlet* and particularly the same speech.

We can now add these arguments for Shakespeare's authorship of a much earlier Q1 to other evidence discussed by Gary Taylor and Rory Loughnane,[52] and most especially the arguments gathered by Terri Bourus in her important works, *Young Shakespeare's Young Hamlet* and a subsequent article on the subject.[53] These independent lines of evidence all point to the same conclusion: there was no lost *Hamlet*; Shakespeare did indeed write Q1 just as the title page states; and he did so much earlier than previously believed.

Dennis McCarthy is an independent researcher and co-author with June Schlueter of *'A Brief Discourse of Rebellion and Rebels' by George North: A Newly Uncovered Manuscript Source for Shakespeare's Plays* (2018). The manuscript discovery made the front page of *The New York Times* and appeared in many other major newspapers around the world. He has also published articles in the flagship journals of geophysics, biogeography and literature.

Notes

1. James P. Bednarz, *Shakespeare and the Poets' War* (New York: Columbia University Press, 2001).
2. Sean McEvoy, *Ben Jonson: Renaissance Dramatist* (Edinburgh: Edinburgh University Press, 2008), 29.
3. Ben Jonson, *Poëtaster*, ed. Tom Cain (Manchester: Manchester University Press, 1996).
4. John Marston, *Antonio's Revenge*, ed. W. Reavley Gair (Manchester: Manchester University Press, 1999).
5. Ben Jonson, *Every Man Out of His Humor*, ed. Helen Ostovich (Manchester: Manchester University Press, 2001).
6. H.N. Gibson, *The Shakespeare Claimants* (New York: Routledge, 1971), 44.
7. Bednarz, *Shakespeare and the Poets' War*, 24.
8. Katherine Duncan-Jones, *Ungentle Shakespeare: Scenes from His Life* (London: Thomson Learning, 2001), 96.
9. Jennifer Schuessler, 'Shakespeare: Actor. Playwright. Social Climber', *The New York Times*, 30 June 2016, https://www.nytimes.com/2016/06/30/theater/shakespeare-coat-of-arms.html?mcubz=3.

10. William Shakespeare, 'The Taming of the Shrew', *The Riverside Shakespeare* (Boston, MA: Houghton Mifflin, 1997).
11. Some scholars suggest that Jonson's *mustard* may refer to the yellow of Shakespeare's coat of arms. But bright yellow mustard seems to be an early twentieth-century American invention, brought about by the addition of turmeric. Vinegar, verjuice, wine and horseradish were some of the main ingredients of the 'Tewkesbury mustard' that was mentioned by Falstaff and was popular in Shakespeare's England. See Alan Davidson, *The Oxford Companion to Food* (Oxford: Oxford University Press, 2014), 542.
12. William Shakespeare, *The First Quarto of Hamlet*, ed. Kathleen O. Irace (Cambridge: Cambridge University Press, 1998). Subsequent citations follow this edition and are provided in the text.
13. Leah S. Marcus, *Unediting the Renaissance: Shakespeare, Marlowe, Milton* (New York: Routledge, 1997), 173. See also Margrethe Jolly, *The First Two Quartos of 'Hamlet': A New View of the Origins and Relationship of the Texts* (Jefferson, NC: McFarland & Company, 2014), 19–20.
14. Richard Tarlton, *Tarlton's Jests* (London: John Budge, 1613), sig. Bv.
15. Ben Jonson, *Cynthia's Revels*, in *Cambridge Edition of the Works of Ben Jonson*, ed. Eric Rasmussen and Matthew Steggle (Cambridge: Cambridge University Press, 2012), Praeludium 154–156.
16. For example, 'Umbrae Creontis' appears in Lucius Seneca, *Hercules Furens*, trans. Jasper Heywood (London: Henry Sutton, 1561), sig. f2v.
17. Thomas Nashe, preface, in Robert Greene's *Menaphon: Camillas alarum to slumbering Euphues*, etc. (London: Sampson Clarke, 1589), sig. **3r.
18. Thomas Nashe, *Christs Teares Over Jerusalem* (London: Andrew Wise, 1593), sig. *3v.
19. Gabriel Harvey, *A New Letter of Notable Contents* (London: John Wolfe, 1593), sig. B2v–B3r.
20. Terri Bourus, *Young Shakespeare's Young Hamlet: Print, Piracy, and Performance* (New York: Palgrave Macmillan, 2014), 104 and references therein.
21. Mike Wilcock, *Hamlet: The Shakespearean Director* (Dublin: Carysfort Press, 2002), 30.
22. Jonathan Bate and Eric Rasmussen, eds, *Hamlet: The RSC Shakespeare* (Basingstoke, Hampshire: Macmillan, 2008), 11.
23. W.B. Worthen, *Drama: Between Poetry and Performance* (Oxford: Wiley-Blackwell, 2010), 94.
24. Jolly, *The First Two Quartos*, 148. Jolly notes the use of italics by Nashe for titles, Latin, places, apparent quotations, etc.
25. For example, just prior to this '*to be* and *not to be*' passage, Harvey again uses italics for obvious quotations: 'and who would not rather say to his Tongue, *Tongue thou art a lyer*; or to his penne, *Pen thou art a fool*...?' (original emphasis). Harvey, *A New Letter*, sig. B2v.
26. Benjamin Bertram, *The Time is Out of Joint: Skepticism in Shakespeare's England* (Newark: University of Delaware Press, 2004), 14–15.
27. John Roe, *Shakespeare and Machiavelli* (Cambridge: D.S. Brewer, 2002), 21.
28. Thomas Nashe, *Christs Teares Over Jerusalem* (London: Andrew Wise, 1594), sig. **r.
29. Ibid.

30. Joseph W. DeMent, 'A Possible 1594 Reference to *Hamlet*', *Shakespeare Quarterly* 15, no. 4 (1964), 446–447.
31. Paul Menzer, 'The Tragedians of the City? *Q1 Hamlet* and the Settlements of the 1590s', *Shakespeare Quarterly* 57, no. 2 (2006), 162–182, here 169.
32. Andrew Gurr, 'Henry Carey's Peculiar Letter', *Shakespeare Quarterly* 56, no. 1 (2005), 51–75, 52.
33. Ibid., 58.
34. Bourus, *Young Shakespeare's Young Hamlet*, 152–153.
35. Menzer, 'The Tragedians of the City', 162.
36. W.W. Greg, *A Bibliography of the English Printed Drama to the Restoration*, 4 vols. (London: Oxford University Press, 1939–59), 1:197(a).
37. Menzer, 'The Tragedians of the City', 164.
38. Ibid., 181.
39. Ibid.
40. Ibid., 175. Menzer is quoting Andrew Gurr, *Shakespearian Playing Companies* (Oxford: Clarendon Press, 1996), 66.
41. Ibid., 176.
42. Ibid. Menzer is quoting Thomas Platter, *The Journals of Two Travellers in Elizabethan and Early Stuart England: Thomas Platter and Horatio Busino*, ed. Peter Razzell (London: Caliban Books, 1995), 31–32.
43. Ibid.
44. M.A. Katritzky, *Healing, Performance and Ceremony in the Writings of Three Early Modern Physicians: Hippolytus Guarinonius and the Brothers Felix and Thomas Platter* (Farnham: Ashgate, 2012), 138.
45. For both Thomas Platter's German passage on London's suburban theatres and an English translation, see 'Thomas Platter Visits London Theaters, 1599: Documents of the Elizabethan Playhouse', in *Shakespeare's Globe Rebuilt*, ed. J.R. Mulryne and Margaret Shewring (Cambridge: Cambridge University Press, 1997), 190–191.
46. M.A. Katritzky, 'Was *Commedia dell'arte* Performed by Mountebanks? *Album amicorum* Illustrations and Thomas Platter's Description of 1598', *Theater Research International* 23, no. 2 (1998), 104–125, here 117–118, 120. Katritzky is quoting from Platter's German original: University Library, Basel, MS. A X 7 & 8, ff. 262r–265v.
47. 'Thomas Platter Visits London Theaters', 190–191.
48. Menzer, 'The Tragedians of the City', 177.
49. Glynne Wickham, *Early English Stages, 1300 to 1660, Volume Two 1576 to 1660, Part II* (London: Routledge, 2002), 138–139.
50. Menzer, 'The Tragedians of the City', 177.
51. Ibid., 163–168.
52. Gary Taylor and Rory Loughnane, 'Canon and Chronology', in *The New Oxford Shakespeare: Authorship Companion*, ed. Gary Taylor and Gabriel Egan (Oxford: Oxford University Press, 2017), 542–548.
53. Terri Bourus, 'Enter Shakespeare's Young Hamlet, 1589', *Actes de Congrès de la Société Française Shakespeare* 34 (2016), https://shakespeare.revues.org/3736.

Chapter 7
'To Be, or Not To Be'
Hamlet Q1, Q2 and Montaigne

Saul Frampton

Hamlet's soliloquy beginning 'To be, or not to be' is probably the most famous passage in English literature. According to Douglas Bruster, it is a speech that has been 'imitated, translated, venerated, and parodied' to the point of becoming a symbol of 'literature itself'.[1] But despite this degree of attention, no clear source for Shakespeare's most famous lines has emerged. Summing up centuries of commentary, the revised 2016 Arden edition makes interesting suggestions about specific images (for example that Hamlet's 'bodkin' may recall Chaucer's Monk's description of the murder of Caesar), but like most editions it offers no general inspiration for the speech as a whole.[2]

This situation is complicated by the textual history of *Hamlet*, in that the passage exists in three different versions: Q1 (1603), Q2 (1604–1605) and F (1623). The Q1 version is very different from Q2 and F, which are almost but not exactly the same. The debate

Notes for this section begin on page 139.

over the primacy of these texts need not be rehearsed here. But in this chapter, I would like to entertain the hypothesis that Q2 is an expansion of Q1 and that the title page of Q2 is therefore telling the truth: that it is 'Newly imprinted and enlarged to almost as much againe as it was, according to the true and perfect Coppie'. To be 'newly ... enlarged' it must have been enlarged from something, and that something was Q1. In other words, the publication of Q1 prompted its expansion and publication as Q2 the following year.[3]

If we entertain this hypothesis, then the addition of some twelve lines between Q1 and Q2 is more likely to bear the marks of outside influence than if they were omitted accidentally by Q1. Having to add to a play might suggest the need for literary refreshment or stimulation. Cutting (or failing to remember) lines requires none.

I would like to suggest that the outside influence that may be detected in these lines is that of Montaigne. Montaigne's essays were first published in English in 1603, in a translation carried out by John Florio. It has been claimed that Florio's translation influenced a number of Shakespeare's plays, most famously shown in Gonzalo's speech in *The Tempest* and its indebtedness to Montaigne's 'Of Cannibals'.[4] But it has also been said to have influenced *Hamlet*. In his introduction to the 1982 Arden edition, Harold Jenkins suggested that, 'of the ideas which Shakespeare so lavishly bestowed on Hamlet, a few at least were prompted by his recent reading in Florio's Montaigne'. More specifically, Walter N. King argues that *Hamlet* 'reflects and borrows from Montaigne's savage onslaught against human vanity in "An Apologie of Raymond Sebond"'.[5]

However, unlike *The Tempest*, the influence of Montaigne on *Hamlet* is complicated by the textual question. If *The Tempest* was written around 1610–1611, Shakespeare would have had ample opportunity to consult Florio's translation of Montaigne published seven years before, and the near identical wording of the two passages in question suggests that this may have been the case. But if Q1 of *Hamlet* is a 'bootleg' copy of something like Q2 performed either in 1603 or some years before, it makes consulting Florio's published translation either impossible or very tight. James Roberts recorded an entry for 'the Revenge of Hamlett' in the Stationer's Register on 26 July 1602. Florio's translation was published earlier than Elizabeth's death on 24 March 1603, as is shown by a bookplate in a copy belonging to her.[6] It is therefore possible that Q1 was published before Florio's translation. In terms of the text published in Q2, recent research has suggested that it was written after Elizabeth's death.[7] Normally critics have overcome any problems in dating Montaigne's influence by proposing that Shakespeare consulted a translation in manuscript, although as the editors of the *New Oxford Shakespeare* observe, 'scribal copies of such a large book would have been expensive, and we possess no manuscript, or other evidence that it circulated in advance of publication'.[8]

However, if Q2 is simply an enlargement of Q1, and it can be shown that Montaigne's influence is more present in Q2, then it suggests that Shakespeare may have simply consulted the published text of Florio's translation, a far more easily imagined scenario.

Obviously the first thing that is needed is a comparison of the two speeches. Here is Q1:

> To be, or not to be, I there's the point,
> To Die, to sleepe, is that all? I all:
> No, to sleepe, to dreame, I mary there it goes,
> For in that dreame of death, when wee awake,
> And borne before an euerlasting Iudge,
> From whence no passenger euer retur'nd,
> The vndiscouered country, at whose sight
> The happy smile, and the accursed damn'd.
> But for this, the ioyfull hope of this,
> Whol'd beare the scornes and flattery of the world,
> Scorned by the right rich, the rich curssed of the poore?
> The widow being oppressed, the orphan wrong'd,
> The taste of hunger, or a tirants raigne,
> And thousand more calamities be sides,
> To grunt and sweate vnder this weary life,
> When that he may his full Quietus make,
> With a bare bodkin, who would this indure,
> But for a hope of something after death?
> Which pusles the braine, and doth confound the sence,
> Which makes vs rather beare those euilles we haue,
> Than flie to others that we know not of.
> I that, O this conscience makes cowardes of vs all,
> Lady in thy orizons, be all my sinnes remembred.
> (TLN 1710–1744)[9]

If we then turn to Q2, we can identify (on this reading) the lines and phrases that are added to the text (here, in bold):

> To be, or not to be, **that is the question,**
> **Whether tis nobler in the minde to suffer**
> **The slings and arrowes of outragious fortune,**

> Or to take Armes against a sea of troubles,
> And by opposing, end them, to die to sleepe
> No more, and by a sleepe, to say we end
> The hart-ake, and the thousand naturall shocks
> That flesh is heire to; tis a consumation
> Deuoutly to be wisht to die to sleepe,
> To sleepe, perchance to dreame, I there's the rub,
> For in that sleepe of death what dreames may come
> When we haue shuffled off this mortall coyle
> Must giue vs pause, there's the respect
> That makes calamitie of so long life:
> For who would beare the whips and scornes of time,
> Th'oppressors wrong, the proude mans contumely,
> The pangs of despiz'd loue, the lawes delay,
> The insolence of office, and the spurnes
> That patient merrit of th'vnworthy takes,
> When he himselfe might his quietas make
> With a bare bodkin; who would fardels beare,
> To grunt and sweat vnder a wearie life,
> But that the dread of something after death,
> The vndiscouer'd country, from whose borne
> No trauiler returnes, puzzels the will,
> And makes vs rather beare those ills we haue,
> Then flie to others that we know not of.
> Thus conscience dooes make cowards,
> And thus the natiue hiew of resolution
> Is sickled ore with the pale cast of thought,
> And enterprises of great pitch and moment,
> With this regard theyr currents turne awry,
> And loose the name of action. Soft you now,
> The faire Ophelia, Nimph in thy orizons
> Be all my sinnes remembred. (TLN 1710–1744)

If we were to summarise the differences between the two speeches, we might say that Q1, despite its reputation, offers a fairly logical lesson in Stoicism. It asks whether one should live or pursue actions that may result in death – effectively suicide. If death was simply like untroubled sleep, there would be no problem. But instead, the thought of an afterlife, and an everlasting judge, 'pusles the braine, / and doth confound the sence'. The key point from a Stoic perspective is that these checks on our behaviour are imaginative projections: they describe an 'undiscovered country', 'From whence no passenger euer retur'nd'. Our 'hope' of reward ('the happy smile'), and fear of punishment ('the accursed damn'd') are potentially illusions, and outweighed by the harsh realities of our present existence: its 'hunger', 'sweat' and a 'thousand more calamities be sides'. Compared to the canonical version of the speech, Q1 therefore seems more direct, logical and consistent.[10] Whereas Q2 raises a 'question' that remains perhaps undecided at the end of the speech, Q1 arrives at a clearer 'point': thoughts of the afterlife illogically intrude upon our reasonings and valour.

When we then turn to Q2, this simple Stoic lesson has become complicated. Perhaps the most significant change comes in the second line. No longer is the issue that of living or dying, but of passivity versus activity – 'to suffer the slings and arrowes ... / Or to take up armes'. This lurching gear-change has puzzled actors and readers for centuries: is it the same question as that of the first line, a development of it, or something totally different?

It is therefore interesting that Montaigne's essay 'By diuerse meanes men come vnto a like end' opens with a very similar debate: whether one should conduct oneself passively or actively in the face of a vanquishing force:

> The most vsuall waie to appease those mindes we have offended, when revenge lies in their handes, and that we stand at their mercie, is, by submission to move them to commiseration and pittie: Neverthelesse, courage, constancie, and resolution (meanes altogether opposite) have sometimes wrought the same effect. *Edward* the black Prince of *Wales* (who so long governed our Countrie of *Guienne*, a man whose conditions and fortune were accompanied with many notable parts of worth and magnanimity) ... [11]

Montaigne is clearly influenced by the humanistic tradition of arguing *in utramque partem*, on either side of a question, although in this case about a pressing issue during the violence of the French Civil Wars. But what is interesting from Shakespeare's perspective is how Montaigne moves from the notion of 'revenge', an issue obviously central to *Hamlet*, into a consideration of 'resolution'. This latter word is central to our modern understanding of the canonical 'To be, or not to be' – but it is absent from the Q1 speech. Yet the idea is central to Montaigne's essay, which uses it in a variety of forms: *resolution* (x2), *resolute* (x1), *resolutely* (x1), *resolved* (x2). This is in line with Montaigne's intention in the essay, which rather than the question of living or dying is concerned with questions of conduct, particularly in a military setting, and the effect our behaviour can have on others.

Other words used in these opening two sentences of Montaigne's essay also seem to find echoes in the Q2 additions (Montaigne first):

mindes/minde, opposite/opposing, so long and not least *fortune*. And while Q1's concerns were more squarely philosophical, Q2 seems to have added another question: which is the 'nobler' action? Again, this would seem to be in line with Montaigne's aristocratic register: *courage, conditions, notable, worth, magnamitie* all occurring within his text. The question is no longer what is philosophically valid (Q1), but what form of conduct is most *noble* – a pressing interest for a recently ennobled Gascon gentleman, less so for a prince. And here one also wonders, if Shakespeare was expanding *Hamlet* when he read this passage, might Montaigne's mention of the 'black Prince' have set off a connection in his mind with his own 'solemn black' Prince Hamlet (and 'incky cloake' and 'solembe blacke' are not present in the Q1 text)?[12]

As Montaigne's essay continues, we may see other words and locutions that could be seen to echo the vocabulary and phrasing of the additions to Q2 (bold added):

> ... having bin grievously offended by the *Limosins*, though he by maine force tooke and entred their Cittie, could by no meanes be appeased, nor by the wailefull out-cries of all sorts of people (as of men, women, and children) be moved to any pittie, they prostrating themselves to the common slaughter, crying for mercie, and humbly submitting themselves at his feete, vntill such time as in triumphant manner passing through their Cittie, he perceived three French Gentlemen, who alone, with an incredible and undaunted boldnesse gainestood the enraged violence, and **made head against** the furie of his victorious **army**. The consideration and **respect of so** notable a vertue, did first **abate the dint of his wrath**, and from those three beganne to relent, and shew mercie to all the other inhabitants of the said towne. (1)

Here Shakespeare may have been influenced by 'made head **against** ... army' ('take up armes against') and '**respect of so** notable a vertue' ('**respect**/That makes calamitie **of so** long life'). The idea of a 'dint' – or sword stroke – of wrath being abated might also be seen to look forward to the process by which 'resolution' 'Is sickled ore' or weakened by thought.

Montaigne's essay then takes a more reflective turn, and brings his own self into the frame:

> Either of these wayes might easily perswade me: for I am much inclined to mercie, and affected to mildnesse. So it is, that in mine opinion, I should more naturally stoope vnto compassion, then bend to estimation. Yet is pittie held a vicious passion among the Stoickes.

> They would have vs aide the afflicted, but not to faint, and cosuffer with them. These examples seeme fittest for mee, forsomuch as these **mindes** are seene to be assaulted and environed by these two meanes, in undauntedly **suffering** the one, and stooping under the other. It may peradventure be saide, that to yeeld ones heart unto commiseration, is an effect of facilitie, tendernesse, and meekenesse: whence it proceedeth, that the weakest natures, as of women, children, and the vulgar sort are more subject unto it. (1–2)

Here again, Montaigne's words – *minds, suffering* – seem to reverberate with the revisions to Q2: 'Whether tis nobler in the minde to suffer'.

As we then come to the middle of the essay, Montaigne relates an episode from Diodorus of Sicily's *Bibliotheca Historica*:

> *Dionisius* the elder, after long-lingering and extreame difficulties, having taken the Cittie of *Reggio*, and in it the Captaine *Phyton* (a very honest man), who had so obstinately defended the same, would needes shew a tragicall example of revenge. First, he tolde him, how the day before, he had caused his sonne, and all his kinsfolkes to be **drowned**. To whome *Phyton*, stoutly out-staring him answered nothing, but that they were more happy than himselfe, by the space of one day. Afterward hee caused him to be stripped, and by his executioners to be taken and dragged through the Cittie most ignominiously, and cruelly **whip**ping him, charging him besides with **outragious** and **contumelious** speeches. All which notwithstanding, as one no whit dismaide, he ever shewed a constant and **resolute** heart. And with a cheerefull and bolde countenance went on still, lowdly recounting the honourable and glorious cause of his death, which was, that he would never consent to yeelde his Countrie into the hands of a cruell tyrant, menacing him with an imminent punishment of the Gods. *Dionisius* plainly reading in his Souldiers lookes, that in liew of animating them with braving his conquered enemie, they in contempt of him, and **skorne** of his triumph, seemed by the astonishment of so rare a vertue, to be moved with compassion, and inclined to mutinie, yea, and to free *Phyton* from out the hands of his *Satellites*, caused his torture to cease, and secretly sent him to be drowned in the **sea**. (2)

Here again, words, ideas and scenarios seem to echo the Q2 additions – *drowned* ('sea of troubles'), *whipping* ('whips'), *outragious* ('outragious'), *contumelious* ('contumely') and *sea* ('sea of troubles'). The past tense verb 'scorned' is of course present in Q1, but in Q2 has become the plural nouns 'scornes' – perhaps closer to the singular noun of Montaigne's essay.

The general lexis of Montaigne's 9,496-word essay might also seem to be echoed in the Q2 text – that is, to summarise, with Shakespeare in italics: *mind* (mind/s x4); *suffer* (co-/suffer/ing x3); *armes* (army x2, armes x1); *against* (3); *opposing* (opposite 2); *hart-ake* (heart x3); *thousand* (x2); *naturall* (natural x2, naturally x3); *mortal* (x1); *must* (x1); *respect* (respect/ed x2); *whip* (whipping x1); *time* (x2); *contumely* (contumelious x1); *love* (x1); *beare* (x1); *resolution* (resolution x2, resolved x2, resolutely x1, resolute x1); *great* (x2); *name* (x1). A number of Montaigne's images also resemble certain other of the Q2 revisions. There are two mentions of drowning (the idea of ending life in a 'sea of troubles'). He also tells of how the Emperor Conrad told the besieged people of Guelph that only their women were allowed safe passage out of the city, bringing with them only what they could carry. They responded 'with an vnrelenting courage [and] advised and resolved themselves (neglecting all other riches or jewels) to carry their husbands, their children, and the Duke himselfe, on their backes' (2). The image that could be said to inform Hamlet's sense of strenuous forbearance in the face of life's vicissitudes: 'who would fardels beare'.

A case might therefore be made for the linguistic influence of Montaigne's essay. But what about its intellectual impact? The Stoic lessons of Q1 were commonplaces in Elizabethan England. The grammar school system guaranteed an exposure to the moral temper of Cicero and Seneca, as Verena Lobsien affirms: 'Elizabethan students and grammar school boys ... would have imbibed the kind of everyday Stoicism that provided the mainstay of early modern English *romanitas*'.[13] But Montaigne's essay subjects this Stoic ideology to a sceptical circumspection that looks forward to his later essays. Sometimes Stoic resolution works; sometimes it doesn't. This then leads onto a more general insight that might serve as epigraph for the *Essays* as a whole: 'Surely, man is a wonderfull, vaine, divers, and wavering subject: it is very hard to ground any directly-constant and uniforme judgement vpon him' (2).

It is this questioning of the Stoic model that seems to find its way into Shakespeare's revision. But what is also important – and this is why the textual history is so crucial to our understanding of the speech – is that the process of reflection seems to arise in the context of revision itself. We see words and images being transformed in the transition of Q1 into Q2: the 'euerlasting Iudge' of

Q1 has disappeared, but seems to be revived in 'the lawes delay'. '[B]orne', used as the verb by which we are placed before the judge, has now become a noun, the sceptical boundary from which 'no traveller returns'. And while Shakespeare had started with a speech that seemed assured in its philosophical 'point' – the illogicality of our fear of death – revisiting the speech, and rereading it and revising it in conjunction with Montaigne, seems to alter Shakespeare's outlook. Now the ethical dilemma has also become a cognitive, epistemological dilemma in line with the lexis of 'mind' that pervades Montaigne's essay. It is not only Hamlet, but *Shakespeare*, who is clouding over the over-confident Stoicism of the previous text with editorial reflection, and the uncertainty that follows on from it. Self-consciousness thus arises from self-editing. The 'natiue hiew' of Q1's Stoic certitude is 'sickled ore with the pale cast of' Shakespeare's second thoughts.

Self-editing, textual revision, linguistic reflection is therefore an object lesson in the fact that man is a 'vaine, diverse, and wavering subject', something that Montaigne himself was aware of through the successive revisions of his own *Essays*. Obviously, in terms of *Hamlet* this interpretation rests on the wider argument about the probability of Q2 being a revision of Q1. But one very simple fact makes the likelihood of 'By diuerse meanes' being an influence much more likely. It is the *very first essay* in Montaigne's text. Montaigne placed it there for a good reason. Although not the first essay he composed, it was the one that laid down an important motif: the uncertainty and variability of human nature. But in placing it first, Montaigne also put it in a prime position in terms of its possible influence: Shakespeare was able to find inspiration for his (1603?) revision of *Hamlet* by turning to the first three pages of the translation of Montaigne's *Essays* published in early 1603.

The obvious question that then arises is: can Shakespeare's reading of Montaigne be detected in any of the other differences between Q1 and Q2? Certainly the claim has been made of the canonical play as a whole, and the more philosophical tone of Q2 would seem to be informed by a Montaignean sensibility. The Q2-added speech, 'How all occasions doe informe against me' (5.4), seems a very deliberate (and somehow unsatisfactory) rehash of rather obvious Montaignean themes, with its talk of 'beast', 'large discourse', 'godlike reason', 'thinking' and 'thought' (TLN 2743.26–2743.36). Certain collocations from elsewhere in the play also seem to be inspired by

Shakespeare's reading: Hamlet's words, 'your worme is your onely Emperour for dyet' (TLN 2687), would seem to recall Montaigne's 'The heart and the life of a great and triumphant emperor are the dinner of a little worm' (266).

But one further example might come from an episode that seems to have been almost arbitrarily added to the play: Hamlet's encounter with the pirates, an event described by Alan Sinfield as 'improbable, and ... unnecessary to the plot'.[14] In Q1, Hamlet is set back ashore after his ship is blown in the wrong direction: the 'subtle treason that the king had plotted, / Being crossed by the contention of the windes' (TLN 2985.2–3). But in Q2, he is captured by pirates, who then agree to release him, an episode reported as Horatio reads out Hamlet's letter to him:

> HOR. Horatio, when thou shalt haue ouer-lookt this, giue these fellowes some meanes to the King, they haue Letters for him: Ere wee were two daies old at Sea, a Pyrat of very warlike appointment gaue vs chase, finding our selues too slow of saile, wee put on a compelled valour, and in the grapple I boorded them, on the instant they got cleere of our shyp, so I alone became theyr prisoner, they haue dealt with me like thieues of mercie, but they knew what they did, I am to doe a turne for them, let the King haue the Letters I haue sent, and repayre thou to me with as much speede as thou wouldest flie death, I haue wordes to speake in thine eare will make thee dumbe, yet are they much too light for the bord of the matter, these good fellowes will bring thee where I am, Rosencraus and Guyldensterne hold theyr course for England, of them I haue much to tell thee, farewell. So that thou knowest thine Hamlet. (TLN 2984–3001)

Some have argued that Shakespeare's source was a passage from Alfred North's 1579 translation of Plutarch,[15] who begins his life of Caesar with an account of him being taken hostage at sea:

> When he had been with him a while, he took sea again, and was taken by pirates about the Isle of Pharmacusa: for those pirates kept all upon that sea-coast, with a great fleet of ships and boats. They asking him at the first twenty talents for his ransom, Caesar laughed them to scorn, as though they knew not what a man they had taken, and of himself promised them fifty talents. Then he sent his men up and down to get him this money, so that he was left in manner alone among these thieves of the Cilicians (which are the cruellest butchers in the world), with one of his friends, and two of his slaves only: and yet he made so little reckoning of them, that, when he was desirous to sleep, he sent unto them to command them to make no noise. Thus was he eight-and-thirty days among them, not kept as prisoner,

but rather waited upon by them as a prince. All this time he would boldly exercise himself in any sport or pastime they would go to. And other while also he would write verses, and make orations, and call them together to say them before them: and if any of them seemed as though they had not understood him, or passed not for them, he called them blockheads and brute beasts, and, laughing, threatened them that he would hang them up ... So, when his ransom was come from the city of Miletus, they being paid their money, and he again set at liberty, he then presently armed, and manned out certain ships out of the haven of Miletus, to follow those thieves, whom he found yet riding at anchor in the same island. So he took the most of them, and had the spoil of their goods, but for their bodies, he brought them into the city of Pergamum, and there committed them to prison, whilst he himself went to speak with Junius, who had the government of Asia, as unto whom the execution of these pirates did belong, for that he was Praetor of that country. But this Praetor, having a great fancy to be fingering of the money, because there was good store of it, answered, that he would consider of these prisoners at better leisure. Caesar, leaving Junius there, returned again unto Pergamum, and there hung up all these thieves openly upon a cross, as he had oftentimes promised them in the isle he would do, when they thought he did but jest.[16]

The facts of the incident are the same, certainly. But the tenor of the scene seems very different to Hamlet's encounter. Plutarch uses the episode to illustrate Caesar's ruthless determination. Upon being taken, he openly insults his captors, 'laughed them to scorn', and after turning the tables, and growing impatient with the procrastination of Junius, has them brutally crucified. By contrast, Hamlet attests to a sort of mutual respect between himself and his captors: 'they haue dealt with me like thieues of mercie, but they knew what they did, I am to doe a turne for them' – that is, a favour in return (the Folio reads 'a good turne' as if to make this explicit). Whereas Plutarch stresses resolution and revenge, Hamlet is all for forgiveness and reciprocity.

It is therefore interesting that Montaigne tells the same story in 'Of Crueltie'. Eleanor Prosser convincingly argues that this essay was an important influence on Shakespeare elsewhere, its opening lines influencing *The Tempest*, specifically in Prospero's recognition that, 'The rarer action is / In virtue than in vengeance' (5.127–128).[17] The main thrust of Montaigne's essay is that while virtue is traditionally seen to be achieved with difficulty, there are some (like Socrates) who achieve goodness with ease, and some (like himself) who find that an abhorrence of cruelty occurs naturally within himself: 'I cannot endure to behold the execution with an unrelenting eye'. He goes on to quote from Suetonius's *Life of Caesar*, which presents a more sympathetic portrait than that of Plutarch:

> Some one going about to witnesse the clemencie of *Iulius Cæsar;* 'He was (saith he) tractable and milde in matters of revenge. Having compelled the Pirates to yeeld themselves unto him, who had before taken him prisoner and put him to ranzome, forasmuch as he had threatned to have them all crucified, he condemned them to that kind of death, but it was after he had caused them to be strangled'. *Philemon* his secretarie, who would have poysoned him, had no sharper punishment of him than an ordinarie death. (248)

Although strangling might seem still rather cruel, the tenor of the passage ('tractable and milde') seems much closer to the spirit of Hamlet's encounter than Plutarch. Here, Hamlet, like Prospero, opts for the 'rarer action' of virtue over vengeance. And again, certain words might be seen here to echo the Q2 additions, 'compelled the pirates' perhaps being echoed in Shakespeare's 'compelled valour'.

If Montaigne was an important source for Shakespeare's possible revision of Q1 into Q2, one question remains: what are we finally to make of Shakespeare's 'borrowings'? Are they purloining, graftings, rewritings? Are they plagiarism? Certainly it seemed to be a pressing issue at the time. In his address 'To the Curteous Reader' at the start of his translation, Florio defends translation as being different to 'usurping', but says that it is ultimately ourselves as readers who are to decide:

> What doe the best then, but gleane after others haruest? borrow their colors, inherit their possessions? What doe they but translate? perhaps, vsurpe? at least, collect? if with acknowledgement, it is well; if by stealth, it is too bad: in this, our conscience is our accuser; posteritie our judge: in that our studie is our aduocate, and you Readers our jurie. (A5r–v)

In *Volpone*, Jonson makes a related claim when Lady Politic Would-be identifies Montaigne as a popularly plundered author:

> All our English writers,
> I mean such as are happy in th' Italian,
> Will deign to steal out of this author mainly,
> Almost as much as from Montaignié. (3.6.87–90)

But the key distinction for Florio is whether it is done with 'acknowledgement' or 'stealth'. Might some – Florio possibly – here lay the charge of 'stealth' at Shakespeare's door?

At this moment we might turn to another Q2 addition to *Hamlet*, in Hamlet's lines to his mother in the closet scene. His words are suffused with Montaignean ideas. He speculates that her senses may be 'apoplexed', recalling ideas from 'An Apologie for Raymond Sebond'. He refers to 'That monster custome, who all sence doth eate' (TLN 2544.1) – a key interest for Montaigne's readers at the time, and one recalled in Samuel Daniel's reference to 'Custome, the mightie tyrant of the earth' (¶r) in his dedicatory poem to Florio's volume.[18] But Hamlet also holds up to her two pictures, one showing the graceful brow of her dead husband, the other the lecherous face of Claudius:

> This was your husband, looke you now what followes,
> Heere is your husband like a mildewed eare,
> Blasting his wholsome brother, haue you eyes,
> Could you on this faire mountaine leaue to feede,
> And batten on this Moore ... (TLN 2448–2451)

Most editors modernise the spelling, making the allusion to a physical mountain more explicit. But some comment on the illogicality of the comparison. Surely a moor or level plain would be more lush than a rocky mountain?[19]

One possible explanation is that Hamlet's 'faire mountaine' is not a metaphor, but rather an acknowledgement, a footnote, a reference to the urbane and humane Frenchman celebrated in Matthew Gwinne's ('Il Candido') dedicatory sonnet to Florio and Montaigne at the start of Florio's translation:

> Who never shootes, the marke he never hitt's.
> To take such taske, a pleasure is no paine;
> Vertue and Honor (which immortalize)
> Not stepdame *Iuno* (who would wish thee slaine)
> Calls thee to this thrice-honorable prize;
> *Montaigne*, no cragg'd Mountaine, but faire plaine. (A7r)

If Hamlet's words are an allusion to Gwinne's poem (as may be possible), it also proves that Shakespeare was not working from the manuscript of a translation, as such a poem would only be included at the time of publication. Rather, it shows that as Shakespeare sat down to compose what was to become the canonical form of *Hamlet*, he had two books in front of him: the 1603 first quarto of *Hamlet*, and the 1603 folio of John Florio's translation of Montaigne.

Saul Frampton is Senior Lecturer in English Language and Literature at the University of Westminster in London. He studied English Literature and Philosophy at the University of East Anglia, wrote a thesis on the Renaissance concept of discovery at Oxford, and was a Research Fellow at Cambridge. He has published on Homer, Montaigne, Shakespeare and John Florio. His research interests are in John Florio and Shakespeare, the language of scepticism in the early modern period, and the history of proxemics from the Archaic Greek *agora* up until the present.

Notes

1. Douglas Bruster, *To Be or Not to Be* (London: Bloomsbury, 2007), 5.
2. Ann Thompson and Neil Taylor, eds, *Hamlet* (London: Bloomsbury, 2016), 286n.
3. See Paul Werstine, 'The Textual Mystery of Hamlet', *Shakespeare Quarterly* 39, no. 1 (1988), 1–26; Margrethe Jolly, *The First Two Quartos of 'Hamlet': A New View of the Origins and Relationship of the Texts* (Jefferson, NC: McFarland, 2014); Terri Bourus, *Young Shakespeare's Young Hamlet: Print, Piracy, and Performance* (New York: Palgrave Macmillan, 2014).
4. See Jacob Feis, *Shakespeare and Montaigne* (London: Kegan Paul, 1884); J.M. Robertson, *Montaigne and Shakespeare* (London: A. and C. Black, 1897); Elizabeth Robins Hooker, 'The Relation of Shakespeare to Montaigne', in *Publications of the Modern Language Association of America*, vol. xvii (1902); George Coffin Taylor, *Shakespeare's Debt to Montaigne* (New York: Phaeton Press, 1968); Leo Salingar, *Dramatic Form in Shakespeare and the Jacobeans* (Cambridge, MA: Harvard University Press, 1959), 249–253; Robert Ellrodt, 'Self-Consciousness in Montaigne and Shakespeare', *Shakespeare Studies* 28 (1975), 37–50; Stephen Greenblatt and Peter G. Platt, eds, *Shakespeare's Montaigne: The Florio Translation of the Essays* (New York: New York Review of Books, 2014); William Hamlin, 'Montaigne and Shakespeare', in *The Oxford Handbook of Montaigne*, ed. Philippe Desan (Oxford: Oxford University Press, 2016), 328–346.
5. Harold Jenkins, ed., *Hamlet* (London: Routledge, 1982), 110; Walter N. King, *Hamlet's Search for Meaning* (Athens, GA: University of Georgia Press, 2011), 58.
6. Gary Taylor and Gabriel Egan, eds, *The New Oxford Shakespeare: Authorship Companion* (Oxford: Oxford University Press, 2017), 542.
7. Richard Dutton, '*Hamlet* and Succession', in *Doubtful and Dangerous: The Question of Succession in Late Elizabethan England*, ed. Susan Doran and Paulina Kewes (Manchester: Manchester University Press, 2014), 173–191.
8. Taylor and Egan, *The New Oxford Shakespeare*, 543.
9. Line references to Q1 and Q2 are to the Internet Shakespeare Editions at http://internetshakespeare.uvic.ca/doc/Ham_Q1/complete/#tln-2985.3 and http://internetshakespeare.uvic.ca/doc/Ham_Q2/complete/#tln-2743.25

10. See András Kiséry, *Hamlet's Moment: Drama and Political Knowledge in Early Modern England* (Oxford: Oxford University Press, 2016), 150; Zachary Lesser, *'Hamlet' After Q1: An Uncanny History of the Shakespearean Text* (Philadelphia: University of Pennsylvania Press, 2014), 204–205
11. Michel de Montaigne, *The essayes or morall, politike and millitarie discourses of Lo: Michaell de Montaigne* (London: Edward Blount, 1603), 1. All subsequent references will be placed in the text.
12. A suggestion I owe to Terri Bourus in a personal communication.
13. Verena Lobsien, 'The Household of Heroism: Metaphor, Economy and Coriolanus', *Shakespeare Survey* 69 (2016), 198–227, here 221, doi:10.1017/SSO9781316670408.017.
14. Alan Sinfield, 'Hamlet's Special Providence', *Shakespeare Survey* 33 (1980), 89–98, here 92, doi:10.1017/CCOL052123249X.009.
15. Robert S. Miola, *Shakespeare's Reading* (Oxford: Oxford University Press, 2000), 99; Jenkins, *Hamlet*, 104n.
16. C.F. Tucker Brooke, ed., *Shakespeare's Plutarch* (London: Chatto and Windus, 1909), 2–3.
17. Eleanor Prosser, 'Shakespeare, Montaigne, and the Rarer Action', *Shakespeare Studies* 1 (1965), 261–264.
18. See William M. Hamlin, 'Florio's Montaigne and the Tyranny of "Custome": Appropriation, Ideology, and Early English Readership of the Essayes', *Renaissance Quarterly* 63, no. 2 (2010), 491–544.
19. Thompson and Taylor comment: 'The contrast must be between "high" and "low", since there would not be much in terms of quality of pasture' (370n).

Chapter 8
Shakespeare, Virgil and the First *Hamlet*

John V. Nance

> Thou commest in such questionable shape,
> That I will speake to thee,
> I'll call thee *Hamlet*, King, Father, Royall Dane
> —C3r, STC 22275 (1603)

Hamlet does not recognise this father *as* his father. He acknowledges the figure (the 'it' of 'it comes') by what it lacks in a condition of similitude with what came before.[1] For Hamlet, the spectre – the ghost of his own father and his own becoming – is an occasion for comparison (as rumour has asserted: 'a figure, like your father') and dialogue ('I will speak to thee').[2] It is also an instance where the repetition of Hamlet's origin is framed as disappearance. For many scholars and critics, Hamlet's difficulty in accepting the ghost-as-father could provide an easy analogue to the 'questionable shape' of Q1 *Hamlet* when it is compared to the prevailing authority of Q2 and F. Q1 may resemble '*Hamlet*' enough to warrant contrast and discourse, but 'it' is not quite *Hamlet*.[3] To most, it is merely a

Notes for this section begin on page 159.

ghost: a less substantial and inferior departure from the fuller form of *Hamlet* embodied by the *Hamlets* that were known before. Burnbury's unexpected encounter with Q1 in 1823 marks the ghostly reappearance of *Hamlet*'s absent primogenitor: a sudden body that seemed to declare an unexpected anteriority to Q2 (printed 1604–1605) and F (printed 1623). The return of Q1, the earliest printed version of the play, asked us to accept the spectre as originary. Like the Ghost, the appearance of Q1 instantiated the condition of disappearance *as prior*. We tend to see and experience Q1 in the same way that Hamlet sees and experiences his 'father'. For many, contending with what Zachary Lesser calls the 'uncanny historicity' of Q1 is a paradoxical demand ('What may this mean') that often leads to doubt and, in some cases, outright denial.[4]

Since the nineteenth century, traditional notions of Q1 and its relationship to '*Hamlet*' have often evoked elaborate and sweeping condemnations of its style. The most popular explanations for the presence of Q1 have often involved labelling it as a memorial reconstruction, an analytical procedure that can recall the hermeneutics of spectrality itself.[5] Ghosts are something like memorial constructions in the sense that they are considered derivative and residual constructs. They are becoming-present echoes of prior duration. Ghosts are also spurious figures withdrawn from the centre from which they ultimately derive, identifiable only through a process of recollection that often resists total or absolute identification.[6] 'Is it not like the king?' Is it not like *Hamlet*? The syntax of resemblance does not accommodate equivalence. The idea of Q1 as a spectral text subsequently undermined its claims to antedate Q2 and F: as long as the questionable quarto was seen as a derivative reiteration of a play first performed around 1600–1604 (represented in turn by Q2 or F or both), it could be safely reconciled with the earlier/later bodies of the play. For the long history and tradition surrounding the transmission and reception of Q1, to accept the prior authority of Q1 was to seemingly depend upon the word of a 'spirit' or 'devil' seeking to abuse and damn the integrity of what was both conflictingly before and after the ghost (Hamlet / '*Hamlet*'). We may be compelled, nay bound, to 'remember' the spectre but we must also recall that memory, as both the beneficiary and residue of all spectres, is also the inheritance of departure. To most auditors, the apparitional *Hamlet* of 1603 represents only what is absent or has disappeared from the more familiar *Hamlets* of 1604–1605 and 1623. Spectres may complicate the residual conditions of the play, but too often our scholarship demands that *Hamlet*'s memory constructs recede from view and hie to their confines. *Hamlet* is a haunted play. It is also a play that haunts itself.

Recent developments in the field of textual studies provide new evidence that Q1 *Hamlet* represents Shakespeare's first draft of the play as it was first performed in 1588–1589.[7] This significant development (itself a return to what-has-been in our scholarship) could be seen to mirror that of *Hamlet* himself when he comes to 'take the Ghosts word' as a signifier of its legitimacy (F4v).[8] Bourus's analysis in particular reinstates the authority and priority of the spectre haunting *Hamlet* by rewriting the ghost of Q1 in terms of authentic emergence as opposed to merely difference and departure. This contemporary impression of Q1 challenges the dominant New-Bibliographical paradigm of memorial reconstruction by demonstrating: a) there is no such thing as an *Ur-Hamlet*, and b) Q1 *Hamlet* is most likely *not* a bad, surreptitious text. This perspective also reinstates the theory of revision as a primary analytical paradigm for interpretations of Q1. Methodologically speaking, this means that we should be encouraged to observe the differences between the three texts of *Hamlet* as the product of a developing textual scene as opposed to asserting and reifying claims for a singular, superlative version of the play. We could, on the basis of subjective judgement, still observe the relative merits of one version of the play over another (I did not read Q1 after my mother's suicide), but Bourus's argument convincingly demonstrates that Shakespeare independently authorised *three* singular visions of the play, each responsive in specific ways to evolving theatrical and aesthetic conditions throughout his career. Q1 *Hamlet* may have been 'Shakespeare's first play, or the first play that he wrote without a collaborator; it would seem to have been the earliest surviving play entirely by Shakespeare that reached print'.[9] This claim enables a reading of Q1 that aligns its perceived lack of eloquence more precisely with theatrical trends of the late 1580s as opposed to the late 1590s, a critical development that liberates our ingrained tendency to observe the relative deficiencies of Q1 as an inferior version of the play written in the middle of Shakespeare's career. Bourus's work expertly demonstrates how the text of Q1 (initially performed in 1589) was later revised and expanded by Shakespeare to the shape of the Folio version of the play in 1602, and then revised and expanded again to the canonical shape of Q2 at some point in 1603–1604.¹⁰ This general trajectory signifies Shakespeare's consistent and renewed interest in remaking *Hamlet* from the beginning of his career until the ascension of King James I.

Bourus's significant argument is persuasive but her position is potentially undermined by evidence recently gathered by Martin Wiggins in his catalogue of *British Drama*. Wiggins believes Q1 *Hamlet* is a bad quarto derived from Q2, 'the author's original version', so the analytical affordances gleaned from his entry on the play are grounded firmly in a line of textual succession that begins in 1600 (his 'best guess' for the composition of Q2). This date justifies the inclusion of thirty-three verbal links (i.e. 'sources') in the form of quotations including names, imitations and parodies often 'at the level of short passages' between Q2 *Hamlet* and other early modern texts, ranging from the Bible to the plays of Ben Jonson.¹¹ He indicates that Q1, as a derivative form of Q2, demonstrates a connection to only fifteen external texts ('links'). This version of the play is thus less reliant on the vast textual field encircling the act of composition and this fact demonstrates yet another way in which Q1 and Q2 deviate from one another stylistically. Notable verbal omissions in Q1 but present in Q2 include Horace, Persius, Seneca and Plutarch – authors with a certain intellectual and literary-conceptual cache on the early modern stage. In turn, the second quarto is demonstrably more invested in citations from classical antiquity and this observation could contribute to the apparent deficiencies of expression in Q1 when compared to the supposed idiomatic grandeur of the canonical text. However, if we approach Wiggins's verbal sources for Q1 *Hamlet* with the notion that it is not a bad quarto and instead represents a play that was first written and performed in 1588–1589 (as Bourus suggests), many of the intertextual relationships he establishes in the form of verbal sources could become incongruous and unstable. They also have the potential to disprove Bourus's early date for Q1 *Hamlet*. Of the fifteen verbal links Wiggins associates with Q1, at least three would not have been materially accessible to Shakespeare in the form of a printed book in 1588–1589: Kyd's *The Spanish Tragedy* (first printed in 1592), Marlowe and Nashe's *Dido, Queen of Carthage* (first printed in 1594) and Ben Jonson's *Every Man in His Humor* (first printed in 1601). However, the fourth volume of Wiggins's *British Drama* (1598–1602) – where he discusses *Hamlet* – was published in the same year as Bourus's book, so neither argument could have taken account of the other. Wiggins's brand of scholarship also represents a different approach to the play that uses different types of evidence. In turn, it seems necessary at this point in *Hamlet* studies to observe the relationship between these competing portraits of Shakespeare's play and analyse the source (or 'sources') of their divergence.

The most troublesome source noted by Wiggins for a 1588–1589 Q1 *Hamlet* concerns the play's most famous and recognisable intertextual reference: the entirety of 'Aeneas's tale to Dido' (henceforth referred to as 'the Troy speech').[12] Edward Capell was the first editor to suggest the possible influence of Marlowe and Nashe's *Dido, Queen of Carthage* on Shakespeare's play, although this insinuation was based exclusively on his knowledge of the *title* alone. Writing in 1768, Capell notes that he has 'not seen the play' but understandably so: the earliest observed edition after the 1594 Quarto is Oxberry's in 1818.[13] George Steevens was the first Shakespearean editor to directly consult the text of *Dido* and his examination of Capell's claims admitted potential parallels regarding the death of Priam – specifically Priam's fall and Pyrrhus's hesitation – but concluded that only a slight resemblance between the two passages could be detected.[14] However, Steevens's position was unique and privileged: his copy of the original quarto, now at the Folger, was one of only three surviving copies of the play. The extracts from *Dido* provided in his discussion became the basis for subsequent interpretations through the eighteenth century. Joseph Ritson reached the same conclusion: 'the parallel passage in Marlowe and Nashe's *Dido* will not bear the comparison'.[15] *Dido* was not accessible to a wide academic audience until the nineteenth century, when it benefitted from the renewed Romantic interest in Marlowe. The publication of *The Works of Marlowe* in 1826 provided the first editorial treatment of *Dido* (edited by George Robinson) within the context of an authorial canon.[16] However, this edition does not mention a putative likeness between the plays. At this point in the editorial tradition, the question of influence seemed settled. For the majority of the eighteenth century, most editors and interpreters of the Troy speech in *Hamlet* were more interested in proving or disproving Shakespeare's irony than analysing its debt to *Dido*. The most contentious debates involved conflicting interpretations of Hamlet's laudatory introduction of a play written in a naturalistic style and the contradictory presentation of highly bombastic and artificial lines from that play. This matter was important for these early critics as they attempted to reason through Shakespeare's intentions behind this potentially capricious alteration: was Shakespeare aware of the perceived over-laboured beauty in the Troy speech? If so, was he attempting an ironic aesthetic statement about theatrical taste or is Hamlet's praise actually genuine? Is Shakespeare actually praising himself? Was Shakespeare attempting to imitate an older style of drama from the 1580s?[17] Was he instead attempting to capture the distinguishing character of ancient Greek drama?[18] Did he even write it? These are still attractive interpretive questions – both inside and outside the classroom – as we continue to weigh the intellectual significances of form and dramatic character in *Hamlet*. No one now believes that someone other than Shakespeare wrote these lines. The Troy speech (and Hamlet's prose introduction to it) are now most commonly seen to instigate the play's recurrent and explicit metatheatricality, aspects of Shakespeare's tragedy (and his art more generally) that influence our examination of Shakespeare's attitudes about the theatre and his own artistic practices. Assessments of Shakespeare's stylistic strategies in the Troy speech can thoroughly influence these perceptions, and eighteenth-century critics provided the foundation for some of our more modern insights.

The question of influence between *Dido* and *Hamlet* was revived after the discovery of Q1 *Hamlet* in 1823 and more particularly following the appearance of Alexander Dyce's *Works of Marlowe* in 1850 (revised in 1858).[19] Dyce's editorial judgement transformed interpretations surrounding the relationship between these two texts for subsequent generations of scholarship. The *volta* for this once-dormant problem took the shape of a single emendation. It appears in Marlowe and Nashe's play during Aeneas's speech about the death of Priam, a passage that is topically equivalent to the Troy speech in *Hamlet*. Here are the lines in question from *Dido* as they appear in the 1594 quarto:

> Whereat he lifted up his bedred lims,
> And would have grappeld with Achilles sonne,
> Forgetting both his want of strength and hands,
> Which he disdaining whiskt his sword about,
> And with the wound thereof the King fell downe;
> Then from the navel to the throat at once,
> He ript old Priam: ... (C1v)[20]

Dyce, accepting John Payne Collier's conjectural emendation (which was published separately), substitutes 'wind' for 'wound'. Collier's rationale is curious: he believes 'wind' is 'in conformity, probably, with the author's meaning', and 'with the corresponding lines in *Hamlet*' for which he cites the following:[21]

> Pyrrhus at Priam drives; in a rage strikes wide,
> But with the whiff and wind of his fell sword
> The unnerved father falls. (E4r)

Q1 *Hamlet* has 'whiff' for Dido's 'whiskt', thus linking Pyrrhus's action to air or 'wind' more strongly. Q1 *Hamlet* thus encourages an elemental reading of the connection between the two terms. *Dido* does not. However, this did not seem to matter to earlier commentators. By transforming *Dido*'s text through recourse to the text of *Hamlet*, Dyce unilaterally cements the previously contested relationship between the two plays. The Collier-Dyce emendation singlehandedly *enforces* the impression that this relationship should be observed and accepted. Collier's unusual line of reasoning is further supported by claims related to sense, but such aspects of his argument are contestable. Collier implies that 'the *wound* was given subsequently, as is evident from the lines that succeed' (his italics), but this assumes Priam, or any combatant, can only be wounded once during an armed encounter. Yet the preceding lines in this sequence from *Dido* indicate that Pyrrhus has already cut off Priam's hands.[22] Collier's logic is inconsistent: his emendation implies Priam can only suffer a single injury, namely being ripped 'from the navel to the throat' (describing that as a 'wound' seems a bit of an understatement), yet Priam is already wounded (i.e. hands) when the killing stroke occurs. It is possible that Priam could indeed be 'wounded' again by Pyrrhus's 'whisking' sword and then killed. On the basis of narrative sense alone, 'wound' is not an inconceivable reading. Where does that leave the validity of Collier's emendation?[23]

In the course of defending his suggested emendation to *Dido*, Collier specifically cites the lines from *Hamlet* as they appear in Q2 and this is because he believed the text of Q1 to be a surreptitious amalgam of 'short-hand' and memorial reconstruction and/or the work of an inferior play-patcher.[24] In fact, we owe the first articulation of Q1's dubious provenance to Collier himself on the basis of these suppositions. Bourus has recently demonstrated that there is 'no proof' for this 'story' and she indicates the degree to which Collier, like many Q1 commentators, 'treats his conclusions as self-evidently true'.[25] Collier believed that Q1 was pirated and he suggested an emendation to the text of *Dido* by assuming it influenced the Troy speech in Q2 *Hamlet*. These notions are not unrelated. In 1843, Collier's impression of Q1 as a pirated text challenged the theory that the first quarto may have represented Shakespeare's first draft of the play or his revision of the imaginary *Ur-Hamlet*. Charles Knight, Collier's intellectual rival, believed that Q1 was an original sketch of the canonical *Hamlet*, initially composed by Shakespeare in the late 1580s and alluded to by Lodge and Nashe. For Collier, disproving Knight's thesis also meant disproving an early date for Q1.[26] By dismissing Q1 on account of bad provenance, Collier was able to expedite an uncomplicated linearity that clearly made *Hamlet* (1604) the borrower of *Dido* (1594). Indeed, this impression is *dependent* on the bad quarto thesis. However, all three texts of *Hamlet* agree on the specific nature of Priam's fall. Here are the equivalent lines in Q1:

> *Pyrrhus* at *Priam* drives, but all in rage
> Strikes wide, but with the whiffe and winde
> Of his fell sword, th'unnerved father falles. (E4r)

The lineation is slightly different here than in Q2 (wide / sword / Illium) and Q2 has removed the conjunction 'but' and adjective 'all' from the first line (Q2's reading thus becomes more assonant and aggressive), but Priam's descent is still caused by 'the whiff and wind' of Pyrrhus's sword. The causal quadgram used as Collier's basis for the emendation in *Dido* is identical. In turn, the *text* of Q2 is not required to justify Collier's perceived refinement of Marlowe and Nashe's play. Collier would have had recourse to the same language and thought in Q1 that he observed in Q2. This important textual agreement implies that Collier's unsubstantiated suppositions regarding the inferiority of Q1 authorised this emendation of *Dido*. Labelling Q1 as 'surreptitious' enables an uncontested negotiation of *Hamlet*'s position in Shakespeare's chronology to accommodate notions of appropriation. Shakespeare could not have used *Dido* as a printed source if *Hamlet* was originally written in the late 1580s and scholars still debate if *Dido* was ever performed.[27] Collier's entire thesis of resemblance is therefore conditional on the validity of this thesis regarding piracy. However, these interrelated postulates are consequential only if we believe *Dido* and *Hamlet* share a resemblance in the first place. Are these speeches (as they originally appear) really so similar?

Let's begin with the emergence of Pyrrhus in each text's narration of the equivalent events, as this is the description that commences the Troy speech in *Hamlet*. Here are the relevant lines as they appear in the first quarto of Shakespeare's play:

> The rugged *Pirrus*, he whose sable armes,
> Blacke as his purpose did the night resemble,
> When he lay couched in the ominous horse,
> Hath now his blacke and grimme complexion smeered
> With Heraldry more dismall, head to foote,
> Now is he totall guise, horridely tricked
> With blood of fathers, mothers, daughters, sonnes,
> Back't and imparched in calagulate gore,
> Rifted in earth and fire, olde grandsire *Pryam* seekes. (E4r)

And the equivalent passage in *Dido*:

> At last came *Pirrhus* fell and full of ire,
> His harnesse dropping bloud, and on his speare
> The mangled head of *Priams* yongest sonne,
> And after him his band of Mirmidons,
> With balles of wilde fire in their murdering pawes,
> Which made the funerall flame that burnt faire *Troy:*
> All which hemd me about, crying, this is he. (C1v)

These speeches visualise the son of Achilles in different tones: the Troy speech in *Hamlet* initially associates Pyrrhus with 'blacke' resolution and dark night, a strong visual impression that also recalls the cavernous gloom of the Trojan 'horse'. Shakespeare's description is then further embellished, in the style of a determined elaboration, by the emulsive hues of calamitous gore. Dreadfully dark Pyrrhus is also coated in the heraldry of slaughter and death. This visual intensification of Pyrrhus also reflects an affective movement from Stygian melancholy to calamitous sanguinity, a progression that could also recall the humoral undertones important to Hamlet's character more generally. Pyrrhus is initially signified with the colour black, a hue commonly associated with melancholy (i.e. black bile) in early modern discourses about the human body. In contrast, red (i.e. blood) carries denotations of a choleric (or angry) disposition, as does 'fire' and the other allusions to heat ('baked', 'imparched') throughout these lines. Thus, the descriptive transition from black to red indicates a movement of Pyrrhus's melancholic temperament towards the choleric through bloodletting. This movement is seemingly meant to reflect Pyrrhus's progress through mourning the death of his father to the revenge of his father's death. This is the same type of trajectory that Hamlet, a fellow melancholic and son of a murdered father, wishes for himself.[28]

The corresponding lines in *Dido* seem monochromatic by comparison. In Marlowe and Nashe's play, blood red is Pyrrhus's exclusive hue. Pyrrhus is angry, but he is not black or potentially melancholic. Notably, *Hamlet* and *Dido* seem to play on a description of Pyrrhus found only in Stanyhurst's translation: 'There I saw in bouchererye bathed / *Fyrye* Neoptolemus' (F4v).[29] The account in *Dido* also includes a detail not present in *Hamlet* but unique to Phaer's translation: 'Duke Pyrrhus in brazen harneis bright with burnisht brand' (C2r).[30] There is no 'harness' in translations of this episode by Caxton, Lydgate or Stanyhurst, nor is there a mention of a 'harness' in any of the three versions of this speech in *Hamlet*. Marlowe or Nashe describes Pyrrhus's 'harnesse dropping bloud' and this suggests *Dido* shares a descriptive link with a material object unique to the Phaer translation of 1573. Further, the speech from *Dido* includes an additional image of carnage that has no equivalent in *Hamlet*, Virgil or any early modern or medieval rendition of *The Aeneid*. The death of Polites (i.e. 'Priam's youngest son') figures prominently in all extant versions of *The Aeneid* – it is an essential element of the Troy mythos that highlights the savage *furor* of Pyrrhus that ultimately foreshadows Aeneas's own. The author of this speech in *Dido* rewrites the death of Polites as an exercise in the grotesque: no extant remediation of the fall of Troy includes a description of Polites' 'head' on a 'spear'. The author of Aeneas's speech in *Dido* uses the death of a son to explore the intensification of narrative and character. Where is Polites in *Hamlet*? This omission is a significant deviation from both *Dido* and the literary and narrative tradition evolving out of the fall of Troy. Further differences in these passages from *Hamlet* and *Dido* are abundant. In fact, the only shared lexical features (references to anger, fire and blood) are probably the result of consulting the same general source (Virgil) and the same translation (Stanyhurst). The key differences are likely the result of *Dido*'s additional consultation of Phaer as well as the implementation of different stylistic and artistic strategies with the description and character of Pyrrhus. The portrait stillness of *Hamlet*'s vision of the fall of Troy contrasts heavily with the kinaesthetic carnage of *Dido*.

The following lines in *Dido* have no parallel to the Troy speech in *Hamlet*:

> My mother *Venus* iealous of my health,
> Conuaid me from their crooked nets and bands:
> So I escapt the furious *Pirrhus* wrath:
> Who then ran to the pallace of the King,
> And at *Ioues* Altar finding *Priamus*,
> About whose withered necke hung *Hecuba*,
> Foulding his hand in hers, and ioyntly both
> Beating their breasts and falling on the ground,
> He with his faulchions poynt raisde vp at once,
> And with *Megeras* eyes stared in their face,
> Threatning a thousand deaths at euery glaunce.
> To whom the aged King thus trembling spoke:
> *Achilles* sonne, remember what I was,
> Father of fiftie sonnes, but they are slaine,
> Lord of my fortune, but my fortunes turnd,
> King of this Citie, but my *Troy* is fired,
> And now am neither father, Lord, nor King:
> Yet who so wretched but desires to liue?
> O let me liue, great *Neoptolemus*,
> Not mou'd at all, but smiling at his teares,
> This butcher whil'st his hands were yet held vp,
> Treading vpon his breast, strooke off his hands.
> At which the franticke Queene leapt on his face,
> And in his eyelids hanging by the nayles,
> A little while prolong'd her husbands life:
> At last the souldiers puld her by the heeles,
> And swong her howling in the emptie ayre,
> Which sent an eccho to the wounded King: (C1r–v)

This conflict is similarly protracted by Priam's outburst to Pyrrhus regarding his rank, suffering and renown in Virgil, Phaer and Stanyhurst, but there is no equivalent to this aspect of the tale in *Hamlet*, Caxton or Lydgate. In this way, *Hamlet*'s compressed version of the Troy speech has more in common with Caxton and Lydgate than the other authorities. It is interesting to note that *Dido* again adds elements to this episode in the Troy legend: the detail of Pyrrhus cutting off Priam's hands is not present in any extant version of Priam's death. Like Polites' head on Pyrrhus's spear, these are supplements to traditional accounts of the story that heighten *Dido*'s focus on the gruesome and macabre topographies of a Trojan necropolis.

Further, the details surrounding Hecuba in *Dido* are not comparable to Hecuba in *The Aeneid*. Here, Hecuba simply chastises Priam for attempting to fight the wrathful son of Achilles. However, the details involving Hecuba 'leaping' on an attacker and scraping his 'eyes' are important features of Hecuba's response to the death of Polydorus. In depictions of this event in both Ovid and Euripides, Hecuba retaliates against Polymnestor by doing violence to his 'hapless eyes'. In Euripides' *Hecuba*, this is done with a hairpin and the help of other Trojan women.[31] In *Ovid's Metamorphosis*, Hecuba, in response to her son's death, 'Did in the traitor's face bestowe her nayles and scratched out / His eyes' (P4r).[32] The author of this speech in *Dido* seems to have conflated classical accounts of the death of Priam with the death of Polydorus. Further parallels to Ovid may include Hecuba's 'howling'. *The Metamorphoses* includes details extant in the mythological tradition indicating Hecuba's transformation into a dog: 'And as she opte her chappe / To speake, in stead of speeche shee barkt' (P4r).[33] As a result of these allusions, *Dido*'s speech seems more Ovidian than *Hamlet*'s.

The next segment of the Troy speech in Q1 *Hamlet* includes a version of the lines cited above that Collier referenced to emend the text of *Dido*:

> Anone he finds him striking too short at Greeks,
> His hand rebellious to his Arme,
> Lies where it falles, vnable to resist.
> *Pyrrus* at *Pryam* driues, but all in rage,
> Strikes wide, but with the whiffe and winde
> Of his fell sword, th'unnerued father falles. (E4r)[34]

Compare to the equivalent lines in *Dido*:

> Whereat he lifted vp his bedred lims,
> And would haue grappeld with *Achilles* sonne,
> Forgetting both his want of strength and hands,
> Which he disdaining whiskt his sword about,
> And with the wound thereof the King fell downe:
> Then from the nauell to the throat at once,
> He ript old *Priam:* at whose latter gaspe
> *Ioues* marble statue gan to bend the brow,
> As lothing *Pirrhus* for this wicked act:
> Yet he vndaunted tooke his fathers flagge,
> And dipt it in the old Kings chill cold bloud,
> And then in triumph ran into the streetes,
> Through which he could not passe for slaughtred men:
> So leaning on his sword he stood stone still,
> Viewing the fire wherewith rich *Ilion* burnt. (C1v)[35]

Here, in agreement with all versions of *The Aeneid*, ineffectual Priam and furious Pyrrhus face one another in armed combat. In *Hamlet*, Priam is driven to the ground by a wide stroke of Pyrrhus's sword: the very wind of the blow is powerful enough to send the frail king plummeting. This version of the attack emphasises the futility of Priam's enfeebled resistance. He is battling time as much as he is battling Pyrrhus. In the 1594 text of *Dido*, Pyrrhus attacks a handless Priam, and with a 'wisk' or sweep of his sword wounds him again and disables him. *Dido*'s narrative thus emphasises the cruelty of Pyrrhus and his untamed, savage propensity for violence and 'wicked acts'. After the murder of Priam, the author of the *Dido* speech uses images associated with the death of Polites in Virgil (triumphantly dipping regal cloth into blood) to attach further dramatic weight to the death of Priam. This follows the general outline of *The Aeneid* by underscoring Pyrrhus's cruelty and his arrogant dismissal of devotional *pietas*. Cosmic concerns about propriety are not present in *Hamlet*'s Troy speech. Many scholars have noted the similar rendering of Pyrrhus's pause in both *Hamlet* and *Dido* – an image not found in Virgil, Caxton, Lydgate, Phaer or Stanyhurst – as evidence that the two plays are in some way related to one another. However, there is no parallel for Pyrrhus's 'stone still' pose in Q1 *Hamlet*; it is first included in an extended version of this speech first published in the second quarto (1604–1605).[36] Thus, the only shared feature of these speeches not found elsewhere in other representations of Priam's death is from Q2, a text that all editors agree postdates the publication of *Dido*.

In *Dido*, Aeneas's tale about the death of Priam ends with Pyrrhus watching Troy burn, but the speech continues in Q1 *Hamlet* to consider Hecuba:

> PLAY. But who O who had seene the mobled Queene?
> COR. Mobled Queene is good, faith very good.
> PLAY. All in the alarum and feare of death rose vp,
> And o're her weake and all ore-teeming loynes, a blancket
> And a kercher on that head, where late the diademe stoode,
> Who this had seene with tongue inuenom'd speech,
> Would treason haue pronounced,
> For if the gods themselues had seene her then,
> When she saw *Pirrus* with malitious strokes,
> Mincing her husbandes limbs,
> It would haue made milch the burning eyes of heauen,
> And passion in the gods. (E4r–v)[37]

Hamlet's Hecuba does not reach for Pyrrhus with vicious nails. Instead, this Troy speech emphasises her status as a figure of dramatic suffering. Exchanging her 'diademe' for a 'blanket' and 'kercher', she is transformed from a queen to a beggar, not (as in *Dido* and Ovid) from a woman into a dog. Divine justice is determinedly absent from this scene of cruelty and we are left with a barbarically indefinite image of grief. Thus, the author of this speech represents Hecuba as a silent model for misery and distress, rather than an archetype of maternal rage. What the gods would have seen in Hecuba (if they had seen) potentially finds its articulation in the strained agonies of Hamlet himself.

These passages from *Hamlet* and *Dido* are similar in that they dramatise events from Virgil's *Aeneid*. Beyond this shared source, however, there is very little that could link them together in terms of how they choose to interpret, narrate and relate the death of Priam in their theatrical compositions. They clearly represent two entirely different renderings of the same popular story. The function of these observed discrepancies can influence arguments about the early date of Q1 *Hamlet*: the lack of a demonstrable connection between these plays supports the emergent consensus that Q1 is not a bad quarto and it also negates traditional narratives of borrowing that would seem to invalidate Bourus's 1588–1589 date for Q1 *Hamlet*. Despite these obvious differences, Collier manufactured an impression of similitude between *Dido* and *Hamlet* with his substitution of *Dido*'s 'wound' for *Hamlet*'s 'wind', and this reading has been unanimously accepted in the editorial community since 1850. Editions of Marlowe's collected works by Francis Cunningham (1870),[38] A.H. Bullen (1884–1885),[39] C.F. Tucker Brooke (1910),[40] Roma Gill (1986)[41] and Fredson Bowers (1973) include this 'sophistication'. It is also echoed in single-play editions of *Dido* by Tucker Brooke (for Methuen, 1930)[42] and H.J. Oliver (Revels, 1968)[43] as well as editions of the complete works of Nashe by Alexander Grossart (1885) and R.B. McKerrow (1904).[44] This micro-history of an emendation demonstrates that all editions of Marlowe's complete works since Dyce (and every single edition of Nashe's complete works) accept 'wind' in place of 'wound' in their texts of *Dido*. This widespread acceptance of the Collier-Dyce emendation also signals the widespread and unequivocal acceptance of *Dido*'s influence on the Troy speech in *Hamlet*. In turn, *Dido* has been subsequently embroiled in larger critical narratives concerning Marlowe's influence on Shakespeare.[45]

Such investigations have been at times useful from the perspective of literary and stylistic histories, but they have also occasionally occluded more innovative assessments of their professional and canonical relationships. For example, imitation or influence has been cited as a primary rebuttal to claims that Shakespeare and Marlowe collaborated with one another on the *Henry VI* plays – a theory prevalent since the eighteenth century, and now strongly supported by a series of recent attribution studies.[46] Despite the observable and quantifiable difference between imitation and identity, some scholars have asserted and others still contend that Marlowe can be detected in these plays because Shakespeare is simply mimicking Marlowe's style.[47] Others have indicated that the Marlovian influence in Shakespeare's plays is the result of professional rivalry – a more influential concept in both theory and popular culture. Yet these mainstream beliefs present simple and contestable reifications of old ideas that are not compatible with modern scholarship. Emulation or anxieties related to influence have become so engrained in our readings of these playwrights that we have come to accept them as incontrovertible characteristics of Shakespeare's artistry. However, Marlowe is now credited on the title page of all three *Henry VI* plays as a collaborator (not influencer) in the *New Oxford Shakespeare*. Collaboration is a different form of influence defined primarily by the interaction of individual minds and hands engaged with the material and institutional conditions of literary production for the early modern stage. Collaboration requires elements of discursive concurrence – both temporal and spatial – that mere emulation could never duplicate. As collaborators, Shakespeare and Marlowe (and others) would have individually impacted the plays with their respective, individual contributions. All of this suggests that we may have overestimated the degree to which Marlowe has strictly *influenced* Shakespeare's works. This is not to say that Shakespeare was indifferent to Marlowe's abilities as a writer, nor is it to suggest that Shakespeare never imitated Marlowe. Instead, I wish to stress that 'Marlovian Emulation' has become a brand of scholarship on which we have become at times over-reliant. From the perspective of literary inheritance, this dependency has fashioned potentially misleading assumptions about Shakespeare's relationship to Marlowe. Such a view brings the text of *Dido* back into focus.

If (as it seems) the Troy speech in *Hamlet* does not derive from Marlowe and Nashe's play, then it almost certainly derives from

Book II of Virgil's *Aeneid*, a view suggested by Robert Miola in 1983 and most recently supported by Colin Burrow (2013).[48] However, Virgil is not included in Wiggins's list of sources for *any* version of *Hamlet* because the Troy speech, the longest, most sustained and most recognisable Virgilian allusion in the Shakespearean canon, is most often interpreted by editors as a creative adaptation or competitive response to Aeneas's speech as it is dramatised in *Dido, Queen of Carthage*.[49] As is well documented, Virgil's epic was one of the most respected, influential and most widely read texts in early modern England. While in grammar school, Shakespeare would have read, translated and imitated *The Aeneid* in Latin, and throughout his professional life he would have recourse to English translations by Phaer, Twyne and Stanyhurst. It is commonly suggested that Shakespeare used one or more of these editions as verbal sources in *Titus, Venus and Adonis, Troilus and Cressida, Antony and Cleopatra* and *The Tempest*. Other critics have noted potential borrowings in *Henry V, Cymbeline* and *Macbeth*. Ovid may have been Shakespeare's favourite and most commonly emulated classical author, but Virgil's epic was still a prominent fixture of his literary imagination throughout his professional career. It is a notable omission from Wiggins's sources for *Hamlet* and other mainstream memory institutions that have decided the play's debt to *Dido*.

All principal interpretations of classical antiquity in *Hamlet* depend upon Q2, a text that has been widely considered the primary and canonical text of the play since the nineteenth century. However, the widespread analytical rootedness in Q2 has concealed a consideration of *Hamlet*'s classicism as it relates to the play's complex transmission history. In particular, we do not have a concrete understanding of how the three texts of *Hamlet* may articulate their classicism in different ways. More specifically, we currently lack an investigation that delineates Q1's independent relationship to classical sources, especially *The Aeneid*. This aspect of Q1 could influence arguments related to Shakespeare's canon and chronology and it could provide a more nuanced view of Shakespeare's handling of classical contexts and intertexts as he revised *Hamlet* throughout his career. A comprehensive investigation of this type is beyond the scope of the current article, but there is one particular aspect of the Troy speech in Q2 that bears some discussion.

In addition to slight alterations of the lineation and word choice to the Troy speech as it appears in Q1, the 1604 text of *Hamlet* also adds twenty-three lines. This addition includes Pyrrhus's 'pause' as well as an allusion to 'And never did the Cyclops' hammers fall / On Mars's armor, forged for proof eterne'. Following Robert Root, Miola notes that these lines directly refer to *The Aeneid*:

> Cyclops under Aetna,
> Drop the work begun. Here is our task:
> Armour is to be forged for a brave soldier.
> Now we can use your brawn, and your deft hands,
> Your craft, your mastery.
> ... and the cavern
> Groaned under the anvils they set down.
> Now this, now that one, for a mighty stroke
> Brought up his arms in rhythm, as they hammered[50]

If we accept Miola's suggestion, the addition of this image suggests Q2 is more demonstrably aligned with *The Aeneid* than Q1. This line of reasoning coincides with notions that Shakespeare was reading *The Aeneid* in 1600–1602, around the assumed date of *Hamlet*'s first performance, as a source for *Troilus and Cressida*. This period also marks a specific type of return to Virgil for Shakespeare, perhaps in response to Jonson's treatment of *The Aeneid* during the War of the Theatres. It has been suggested that the presence of Virgilian elements in *Hamlet* (beyond the Troy speech) was the result of Shakespeare's consultation of *The Aeneid* in the seventeenth century. But Shakespeare did not read *The Aeneid* once, nor did he include references to Virgil's epic in only one play. The newly added and specifically Virgilian image of the Cyclops forging Aeneas's armour in Q2 could indicate Shakespeare was *revising* the Troy speech and incorporating additional elements of *The Aeneid* in the second quarto as a result of interacting with one of *Troilus*'s primary sources at a time when returning to Virgil was of professional and interpersonal interest for Shakespeare. The additions to the Troy speech in Q2 seem to align with the revision hypothesis and they also demonstrate *Hamlet*'s evolving relationship to Virgil's epic.

The long history and tradition of Shakespearean textual scholarship has viewed the first quarto as something like *Hamlet*'s ghost. Similar to Hamlet's father, the unexpected recurrence of Q1 occasioned a return of the no-thing that has been again. This double movement of return both in *Hamlet* (narratological) and among *Hamlets* (bibliographical) is that of a revived originator, or the original cause that signals the past non-being of the no-thing that came before. Hamlet's encounter with the Ghost (an inciting event central to all versions of the play) stages the concept of origin as a haunting in the form of a spectral repetition of his absent father. The *fons et origio* of being, the 'that which came before' of Hamlet himself, is thus a ghostly matter. As a consequence of their shared paradoxical temporality embodied by the return of the no-thing, the phantasmagoric origins of Hamlet and *Hamlet* are also correspondingly troubled by illegibility. Hamlet may indeed *see* the Ghost (but also the no-thing, the 'it' of 'it comes!') and recognise its embodied claims to priority (i.e. the return of that which came before), but it is only the ontological condition of the spectre as difference that remains legible to him. The spectral nature of the text Q1 *Hamlet* may have perpetuated narratives of disavowal, but Terri Bourus believes the ghost. She demonstrates, Hamletlike, the authority of the spectre by taking us into the theatre. In an attempt to provide 'sounder proof' for her claims of a 1588–1589 *Hamlet*, I have listened to one particular ghost that Wiggins sees in the text: *Dido, Queen of Carthage* – arguably the most important source that troubles claims for this early date. This analysis has also provided evidence that suggests Wiggins (and many other scholars) did not properly recognise Q1's most important spectre: Virgil's *Aeneid* – long accepted as a potential source of Q2 and F but not Q1. The first quarto's relationship to Virgil can encourage new lines of analysis that consider early Shakespeare experimenting with a specifically Virgilian brand of tragedy. His subsequent revisions to *Hamlet* through Virgil indicate the play's importance for returning to and articulating Virgilian themes throughout his career. Like Hamlet, Aeneas is haunted by the death of his king, the 'father' of Troy. As Hamlet sees the ghost on the battlements of Elsinore, Aeneas, when he arrives in Carthage, sees the statue of Priam. Hamlet is haunted by his memory of the *Aeneid*, by Aeneas himself as the exemplary son (who saves his father), and in particular haunted by the emblematic, violent revenge of a son (Pyrrhus), whose father has been killed. Aeneas's mother is Venus, the goddess of sex. Hamlet is haunted by his mother's sexuality, which he rejects, just as Aeneas proves his epic destiny and manhood by rejecting his lover Dido.

John V. Nance, an independent scholar and freelance writer, is an Associate Editor of *The New Oxford Shakespeare: Complete Alternative Versions* (forthcoming). He has published essays on attribution issues in *Edward III*, *1 Henry VI*, *2 Henry VI*, *Double Falsehood*, *All's Well that Ends Well*, and the manuscript verses 'To the Queen' ('As the dial hand . . .').

Notes

'Q1' refers to the 'first quarto' or 'first edition' of *Hamlet*, printed in 1603.
1. C3r, STC 22275 (1603). Here and elsewhere, all quotes from the first quarto of *Hamlet* and *Dido* are taken from original text facsimiles available on *Early English Books Online*. All references cite the signature and the accompanying Short Title Catalogue identifier.
2. B4v, C3r, STC 22275 (1603).
3. For more on the problem of returning for the first time in the context of *Hamlet*, see Jacques Derrida, *Specters of Marx* (London: Routledge, 2006), 1–21.
4. See Zachary Lesser, *Hamlet After Q1: An Uncanny History of the Shakespearean Text* (Philadelphia: University of Pennsylvania Press, 2015), 1–37. Lesser's approach to the troubling temporality of Q1 *Hamlet* dresses in Freudian terminology but it does not draw heavily from theoretical discourse, psychoanalytic or otherwise. Most importantly, Lesser does not consult Derrida's influential Marxist interpretation of the Ghost in *Hamlet* or consider how this reading could be adapted into his theoretical apparatus.
5. For a summary of the intellectual context of bad quarto theory, see Laurie McGuire, *Shakespearean Suspect Texts* (Cambridge: Cambridge University Press, 1996), 21–91.
6. For more on the theoretical paradigm of spectrality, see the collected essays in Maria Del Pilar Blanco and Esther Peeren, eds, *The Spectralities Reader: Ghosts and Haunting in Contemporary Cultural Theory* (London: Bloomsbury, 2013).
7. The current basis for this claim is provided by Terri Bourus, *Young Shakespeare's Young Hamlet: Print, Piracy, Performance* (New York: Palgrave Macmillan, 2014). For a useful précis of this evidence, see Gary Taylor and Rory Loughnane, 'The Canon and Chronology of Shakespeare's Works', in *The New Oxford Shakespeare: Authorship Companion*, ed. Gary Taylor and Gabriel Egan (Oxford: Oxford University Press, 2017), 542–548.
8. STC 22275 (1603).
9. Bourus, *Young Shakespeare's Young Hamlet*, 181.
10. Ibid., 181–207.
11. See Martin Wiggins, #1259, in *British Drama 1533–1642: A Catalogue, Volume IV: 1598–1602* (Oxford: Oxford University Press, 2014), 246 (summarising narrative and verbal sources for all three texts, and labelling the first printed edition, Q1, as the last in chronological order, 'C').

12. The allusions to Kyd and Jonson can be explained without recourse to printed texts of either play or to the text of Q1 *Hamlet*, specifically. Due to spatial constraints, I am unable to discuss these examples at length. Forthcoming work will provide an extended argument on why these sources are not problematic for a 1588–1589 *Hamlet*.
13. Edward Capell, *Notes and Various Readings to Shakespeare* (London: Henry Hughes, 1774), 1.134.
14. See Ben Jonson and George Steevens, eds, *The Plays of William Shakespeare* (London: T. Longman etc, 1793), 15.368–369.
15. Ibid., 15.369.
16. George Robinson, ed., *The Works of Christopher Marlowe*, 2 vols (London: William Pickering, 1826).
17. Jonson and Steevens, *Plays*, 15.368.
18. William Warburton, ed., *Works of Shakespeare*, 8 vols (Dublin, 1748), 8.240.
19. Alexander Dyce, ed., *The Works of Christopher Marlowe* (London: Routledge and Sons, 1850).
20. STC 17441 (1594); see also 2.1.250–256 in Bowers' edition of *Dido*, in Fredson Bowers, ed., *The Complete Works of Christopher Marlowe*, 2 vols (Cambridge: Cambridge University Press, 1973).
21. J. Payne Collier, *The History of Dramatic Poetry* (London: John Murray, 1831), 1.226.
22. 'Not mov'd at all, but smiling at his teares, / This butcher whil'st his hands were held up, / Treading upon his breast, stroke off his hands' (C1v). See also Bowers, *Complete Works*, 2.1.240–242.
23. Due to spatial constraints, I am unable to accommodate a complementary empirical approach that inflects extant work surrounding the authorship of *Dido*. Future work will approach the uncertainty of Collier's emendation with the assistance of modern digital databases.
24. Collier, *History of Dramatic Poetry*, 1.281.
25. Bourus, *Young Shakespeare's Young Hamlet*, 72.
26. For further accounts of their disagreements, see Lesser, *Hamlet After Q1*, 42–58.
27. This debated aspect of *Dido*'s history has been thought to parallel the remembered circumstances of the unknown play that Hamlet recalls at court: 'it was never acted – or, if it were, never above twice' (Q1 7.238–239). Q2 and F both read 'never above once'. This variant – and the paradoxical assertion that Hamlet has heard a speech by the Player from a play that was never acted – is possibly more reflective of the misleading and deceptive characteristics of Hamlet's own role at this point in the play. It is possible that Shakespeare knew of a play by Marlowe and Nashe called *Dido* prior to its publication in 1594, but if Hamlet is indeed alluding to this play here and in the speech that follows, it is more likely to be a conjectural recreation than a direct reference. There is no evidence that *Dido* circulated independently in manuscript form and the extreme differences between the Troy speeches in both texts (see below) betray the notion that the speech in *Hamlet* is based on it or any prior play.
28. For more on the humoral aspects of the Troy speech and *Hamlet* more generally, see Gail Kern Paster, *Humoring the Body: Emotions and the Renaissance Stage* (Chicago: University of Chicago Press, 2004), 45–46.
29. STC 24806 (1572).

30. STC 24801 (1573).
31. For a modern rendering of this episode, see David Grene and Richmond Lattimore, eds, *Euripides*, 5 vols (Chicago: University of Chicago Press, 2013), 2.1133–1177.
32. STC 18956 (1567).
33. STC 18956 (1567).
34. STC 22275 (1603).
35. STC 17441 (1594).
36. See also James Black, 'Hamlet Hears Marlowe; Shakespeare Reads Virgil', *Renaissance and Reformation* 18, no. 4 (Fall 1994), 19.
37. STC 22275.
38. Cunningham, ed., *The Works of Christopher Marlowe* (London: Albert J. Croker Brothers, 1870), 339. The revised edition of 1902 replicates this emendation.
39. Alexander Bullen, ed., *The Works of Christopher Marlowe*, 3 vols (London: John C. Nimmo, 1885), 2: 326.
40. C.F. Tucker Brooke, ed., *The Works of Marlowe* (Oxford: Clarendon Press, 1910), 407.
41. Roma Gill, ed., *The Complete Works of Christopher Marlowe*, 5 vols (Oxford: Oxford University Press, 1986), 1: 140.
42. C.F. Tucker Brooke, ed., *The Tragedy of Dido, Queen of Carthage* (London: Methuen, 1930), 160. This edition was reprinted in 1960 by Gordian Press.
43. H.J. Oliver, ed., *Dido, Queen of Carthage and The Massacre at Paris* (Boston, MA: Harvard University Press, 1968).
44. Alexander Grossart, ed., *The Complete Works of Thomas Nashe*, 6 vols (London: Huth Library, 1885), 6: 29; R.B. McKerrow, ed., *The Works of Thomas Nashe*, 5 vols (London: Blackwell, 1904), 2: 358.
45. For a thorough treatment of this brand of scholarship, see Robert A. Logan, *Shakespeare's Marlowe: The Influence of Christopher Marlowe on Shakespeare's Artistry* (New York: Routledge, 2007).
46. For a useful summary of these claims and their sources, see Taylor and Egan, *Authorship Companion*, 493–499, 513–517.
47. For more on the difference between imitation and identity, see Gary Taylor and John V. Nance, 'Imitation or Collaboration? Marlowe and the Early Shakespeare Canon', *Shakespeare Survey* 68 (2015), 32–47.
48. Robert S. Miola, 'Aeneas and *Hamlet*', *Classical and Modern Literature* 8 (1988), 281–286; Colin Burrow, *Shakespeare and Classical Antiquity* (Oxford: Oxford University Press, 2013), 67–71.
49. Virgil is listed as a 'source' for Marlowe and Nashe's *Dido, Queen of Carthage* in Wiggins, *Catalogue*, #820.
50. Miola, 'Aeneas and *Hamlet*', 283.

Chapter 9
Unique Lines and the Ambient Heart of Q1 *Hamlet*

Laurie Johnson

In the maelstrom of debates about the provenance of *Hamlet* and the relationship between the three early versions of the play, scholars inevitably feel called upon to declare their position on questions of transmission and chronology. The pressure to do this might explain why the study of the first quarto (Q1, 1603) has for the most part been characterised by analysis of its degree of similarity, however small this is usually made out to be, to the second quarto (Q2) and Folio (F) versions. What gets lost, as a result, is any detailed consideration of the unique lines in Q1 – that is, lines for which there is no obvious analogue in either Q2 or F. There are many scholarly analyses of the unique lines in Q2 or F – those lines in one of these versions that are not in the other – with discussion of Q1 focusing instead on whether it 'cuts' or 'remembers' any of these lines.[1] By contrast, my focus here will be on Q1 lines that are without analogues in Q2 or F – which I have undertaken with no desire in the

Notes for this section begin on page 177.

first instance to adopt or defend any specific position on transmission or chronology. Even the 'solution' I proposed in *The Tain of Hamlet* took no account of these unique lines in any systematic way.[2] While not defending any single position, I will however contend that the unique lines in Q1 present a significant problem for the 'note-taker' explanation proposed by Ambrose Gunthio (possibly a pseudonym of John Payne Collier) in 1825 and repackaged for a new readership by Tiffany Stern in 2013.[3] My principal objective here is to demonstrate the consistent presence of a key image – *the heart* – and its association with the character of Corambis (Polonius in Q2 and F) in lines that are unique to Q1. This consistency means that whichever model of transmission or provenance one may accept, some account is needed of the prospect that these unique lines were either cut or added systematically in conjunction with the change of the name of the King's counsellor.

In *Tain*, I proposed that the three abiding positions on *Hamlet* transmission – the first draft, memorial reconstruction, and abridged performance text theories – could all be correct in some degree so long as the proponents of each could abandon their adherence to a singular text. Each of the three versions could, in its own way, be a product of multiple theatrical and textual processes, and for the Q1 *Hamlet* my solution involved the proposition that the actor central to the memorial reconstruction explanation need not have been remembering a single performance of the text. Instead, over many years, he could have performed in various roles during earlier performances, so his memory was not a flawed recollection of a performance based on Q2, F or some other version; rather, Q1 could record his memory of much earlier performances, while his cue script from the later performance provided the more solid core of several scenes in the first half of the play. Topical material was used to construct a possible timeline of revision to the lost earliest version. Since *Tain* was published, Terri Bourus's *Young Shakespeare's Young Hamlet* has sparked renewed interest in the idea that Q1 is the first version of the play, which remained relatively intact between 1589 and 1603,[4] and Zachary Lesser's *'Hamlet' After Q1: An Uncanny History of the Shakespearean Text* offered a more chronological and broadly cultural account of the various approaches to Q1 and how they reflected the views of the Romantics, the Bard worshippers, the antiquarians, the New Bibliographers, and others who developed them.[5] Lesser does not align himself with any single position, but his analysis of the specific historical situatedness of each approach explains why their proponents might never be so willing or able to accept a compromise solution of the kind that I have proposed. Most recently, the *New Oxford Shakespeare* and, in particular, Gary Taylor and Rory Loughnane's chapter on the chronology of the plays, establishes further grounds for thinking that Q1 does at least retain a significant residue of the earliest version of the play *circa* 1589, while also providing a range of different types of evidence for dating Q2 to 1602 or 1603.[6] As the perceived gap between the earliest version of the play and its more familiar iterations widens, the study of the unique lines of Q1 becomes more urgent, providing a potential new window into the early dramatic vision to which the text of Q1 gives expression.

Let me begin by clarifying what constitutes a 'unique' line. It is of course a staple of the memorial reconstruction theory and related 'bad quarto' investigations that there are eighty-seven lines – those of the parts of Marcellus, Lucianus (player) and Voltemar – that are repeated verbatim in Q1, Q2 and F. The fact that two of these lines are not lexically verbatim, or that some also differ from Q2 and F in punctuation, is often cited as an objection to the memorial theory, since the idea is that the so-called 'pirate' had these lines in hand and so they should not differ in any way from the other versions. The prospect of a memorial reconstruction also containing revisions is not normally entertained, but it would explain such minor discrepancies. To my purpose here, the suggestion that eighty-seven lines are identical might be taken to mean that of Q1's 2,221 lines there must be 2,134 lines that are not identical.[7] This is one of the faults with the standard memorial reconstruction argument, as Paul Werstine deftly demonstrated when analysing the lack of 'decline' in many sections of Q2 where the actor-reporter was not on stage[8] – in other words, there are many other lines in Q1 that are near enough to identical to Q2 or F as to suggest that the memory of a single 'pirate' cannot explain such variations in degree of similarity through the whole of the play. At what degree of difference, then, does a line cease to be similar and can be classified as unique to Q1? I take my cue here from Paul Bertram and Bernice Kliman, whose *Three-Text Hamlet* identifies analogous lines across the three versions, with Q1 lines being assessed for correspondence 'sometimes where only a faint trace of resemblance can be found'.[9] Following this reasoning, it might be determined that a line can be considered unique if it fails even the generous test of resemblance applied by Bertram and Kliman.

For an example of their generous spirit, consider the King's initial question to Hamlet, rendered in Q2 as 'How is it that the clowdes still hang on you' (TLN 246)[10] and F as 'How is it that the Clouds still hang on you?' (substantially identical, but differing in punctuation and capitalisation). By contrast, Q1 reads: 'What meanes these sad and melancholy moodes?' (Q1 TLN 173). The Q1 version does not contain a single word present in the Q2/F version. It is clear in both that the King inquires after Hamlet's state of mind, yet the language is markedly different: 'how is it' is a question of cause with a metaphor leaving Hamlet without agency (the clouds simply 'hang' on him), whereas 'what means' asks after the intention behind the moods. Yet in a manner that could potentially be explained by the 'note-taker' theory, 'how is it' might be a failed attempt to translate from the equivalent form 'by what means' or *vice versa*, since Q1 merely lacks the preposition.[11] In any case, whether it could be explained as a misinterpreted note, a misremembered line or a deliberate revision, the Q1 text here clearly differs significantly in wording from Q2 and F, but it has been counted as possessing enough resemblance to count as an analogous line: it is a single iambic pentameter line asking a question. Considering how broadly 'resemblance' is defined in a case like this, it would be fair to say that any line Bertram and Kliman do *not* consider analogous is lacking any conceivable similarity and must surely therefore count as unique to Q1. The total number of lines that fit into this category – no analogue identified in Q2 or F – is 272 (including five stage directions), which constitutes 12.25% or just a shade under one in every eight lines. This is a significant percentage of lines to be demonstrably unique to this version of the play, especially when almost every study of the relationship of Q1 to Q2 and F focuses only on what it cuts, remembers or misremembers.

This percentage may be particularly damning for the 'note-taker' theory. Stern offers a great deal of evidence that note-taking was prevalent and indeed expected at churches in the early modern period to aid parishioners in remembering the preacher's lessons, and outlines a number of methods that note-takers were instructed to use to facilitate accuracy.[12] She further argues that evidence exists for the prevalence of note-taking at playhouses, offering examples of plays that parody note-taking as well as some that decry the presence of note-takers in the audience, and Thomas Heywood's lament in *If You Know Not Me, You Know Nobody* is, for me, compelling: he reminds the audience in a new prologue that the printed version of 1605 came about 'by Stenography ... scarce one word trew'.[13] Earlier, in 1608, Heywood had also complained that some of his plays were 'accidentally' passed onto printers, 'coppied onely by the eare'.[14] As Bourus has shown in her detailed critique of Stern's argument, parodies of note-taking and Heywood's belief that his plays had been stolen by stenographers do not in fact constitute evidence of the widespread nature of the practice as early as 1603.[15] Bourus is right, although I am inclined to think that note-taking *was* prevalent as a cultural practice for the individual to remember commonplaces, memorable turns of phrase and such like for transferring into their journals during evening stints at the writing desk – and Bourus would agree.[16] This is of course different from what Stern proposes, whereupon note-taking is used to generate copies of whole plays for printing. Given the evidence for sermons having been printed from notes, it is likely that somebody at some point would have struck on the idea of transferring the practice to the playhouse, so my inclination is to accept that note-takers might have generated copies of some plays, but I am equally inclined to agree with Bourus that there is insufficient evidence to assume that it was a widespread practice. More to the point, when discussing Q1 *Hamlet*, even if the reader was persuaded by Stern that the practice was widespread, her explanation of how this text carries the tell-tale traces of having been produced from notes is uncharacteristically inconsistent and unconvincing.

I need not replicate here the detailed critique that Bourus provides – the reader is well advised to read her chapter on the 'piratical reporter' in *Young Shakespeare's Young Hamlet* to get its full gist.[17] Yet, pursuant to my observations about unique lines in Q1, a number of additional points of critique are worth providing. In an ill-conceived afterthought, offered in the conclusion to her article, Stern proposes that the changes to the names of Polonius and Reynaldo (to Corambis and Montano) might be a record of 'specific performance variants' from a performance of *Hamlet* in Oxford, as a result of the note-taker mishearing the use of the names Pullen (Oxford University's founder, and 'Polenius' in Latin) and Reynolds (then President of Corpus Christi College): '*Hamlet* Q1', Stern adds, 'the only professional play to boast Oxford performance on its title-page, may record the play, or aspects of the play, in a localised version'.[18] The obvious problem here is that Polonius and Reynaldo are the names in Q2 and F, not those used in Q1. Whence Corambis and Montano for an Oxford variant?

Stern is on surer footing when handling minor alterations to names, as in the case of Cornelius being Cornelia, Voltemand being Voltemar, and so on, which can result from the advice of Peter Bales to only 'take the two first letters of everie name, and so commit the rest to memorie'.[19] Yet if Q1 is a result of note-taking, based on this advice, the names Corambis and Montano are not so easily resolved, nor for that matter is the rendering of Laertes in Q1 as Leartes, since the first two letters are not retained. To this we can add the concerns raised by the frequency of unique lines in Q1: is there any evidence to suggest that one in eight is an acceptable proportion of unique material in a noted text? I will argue in what follows that the most significant change in name (Corambis/Polonius) can be explained with reference to the frequency of unique lines, once these lines are understood systematically and not simply as products of corruption to Q2 or F. For Stern, though, unique lines represent evidence of the 'patchwork' nature of Q1, just as some sermons were known to have been printed from notes and 'patched ... out of some borrowed notes', and in the case of the play this includes occasional use of lines from other sources.[20] Yet Stern also observes that Q1 is 'filled with gaps' that resemble sermons printed 'with whole lims cut off at once, and cleane left out'.[21] The latter result from noted sermons being sent prematurely to the printer, but the explanation for the patchwork nature of Q1 hinges on examples where at least one additional party was involved in amending the noted text prior to printing: the patchwork Q1 and the Q1 filled with gaps are thus explained by competing models of production.

Something like a patchwork process of amendment could potentially explain the high percentage of unique lines if it were the case, as Stern proposes, that additions were made to *Hamlet* 'to solder its gaps'.[22] This demands closer inspection of more than just the three lines used to demonstrate the point in Stern's article. Is it fair to claim, for example, that the lines in question are covering obvious gaps? Stern's first example is from Leartes, although his Q2/F name of Laertes is used in introducing the example, overlooking her own point about names. When told of his sister's death, Leartes says:

> Too much of water has thou *Ofelia*,
> Therefore I will not drowne thee in my teares,
> Reuenge it is must yield this heart releefe,[23]
> For woe begets woe, and griefe hangs on griefe. *Exeunt.*
>   (Q1 TLN 1897–1900)

The first two lines are recognised by Bertram and Kliman as being analogous with the Q2/F lines, 'Too much of water hast thou poore *Ophelia*, / And therefore I forbid my tears' (TLN 3179), but the couplet is designated as unique. Stern cites only the first line of the couplet as having been patched in by borrowing Hieronimo's 'in revenge my hart would finde releefe' from *The Spanish Tragedy*. Shakespeare in 1589 could, of course, have been influenced by Kyd's then-recent play, and elsewhere scholars do not take evidence of Kyd's influence as proof of memorial reconstruction. We have no way of arbitrating between these two explanations of the echo of Kyd: 'nothing neither way'. But if we accept Stern's theory that the couplet fills a gap, it has been introduced by an amender to complete the scene with lines that the note-taker failed to record: in Q2, the relevant section contains additional lines about the 'speech of fire' that Laertes would have blaze but 'that this folly drownes it' (TLN 3184), his exit, and the King's clumsy lines:

> KING   Let's follow *Gertrard*,
>   How much I had to doe to calme his rage,
>   Now feare I this will giue it start againe,
>   Therefore lets follow.   *Exeunt.*
>   (TLN 3185–3188)

In the Folio, Gertrard is of course Gertrude – is this a note-taker intervening in these texts by retaining only the first two letters of her name? Of course not; there would never be traction for a theory that either Q2 or F was a noted text. More importantly, the King's lines make the fundamental error of beginning with the same words as the final cue, a sin that Stern identifies in the Marcellus part in the opening scene of Q1, enabling her to dismiss the actor-pirate theory because 'it does not take acting into account'.[24] But Q2 fails this same test in this instance. It also gives to Laertes an insensitive turn of phrase ('folly drowns it') moments after he has heard that his sister has drowned – the Folio changes the offending line to 'folly doubts it'.

Moreover, by looking at the unique lines in Q1 in greater detail, it becomes apparent very quickly that this 'added' line is no orphan hived off from *The Spanish Tragedy* to solder a gap in the noted text. According to Bertram and Kliman's standard of resemblance, every line in the first scene has an analogous counterpart in Q2/F, with the first unique line being delivered by Leartes early in Scene 2:

> Now that the funerall rites are all performed,
> I may haue leaue to go againe to *France*,
> For though the fauour of your grace may stay mee,
> Yet something is there whispers in my hart,
> Which makes my minde and spirits bend all for *France*.
>   (Q1 TLN 162–166)

In these lines, the first, third and fourth are designated as unique, whereas the two lines that end in 'France' correspond to TLN 232 and TLN 236 in Q2/F. The sense of the Q1 passage is thus consonant with the corresponding Q2 and F passages, but the content of these three lines within it are so lacking in resemblance as to warrant the designation. The unique Q1 lines do not present as mere gap fillers to suture over forgotten lines, however, if we compare them to the line that Stern would have the amender or noter take from Kyd: revenge is what will yield 'this heart releefe' and it is this 'heart' that Leartes says in his first speech is set for France. Crucially, in all three versions, the King responds to the request by asking if Laertes/Leartes has his father's leave, but in Q2/F this question is posed in response to talk of duty; only in Q1 is the question of the heart of Leartes brought to bear on his request. Thus, in Q1, the leave granted is in accordance with the heart rather than with duty, and this is further reinforced when the King agrees in a line also unique to Q1: 'With all our heart, Leartes fare thee well' (Q1 TLN 170). Thus, the first speech spoken by 'Corambis' in Q1 is surrounded, in Q1, by two speeches that both contain the word 'heart'.

The line 'whispers in my hart' has no analogue in *The Spanish Tragedy* or, for that matter, in any extant text save for one very noticeable exception. Until the publication of Q1 in 1603, the verb 'to whisper *in*' had no other complement than the ear in any text identifiable through *Early English Books Online* except William Basse's *Three Pastoral Elegies* (1602), which uses 'And whisper to himselfe within his hart', followed in the next line of Elegy II with 'How base and euer lasting slaue am I'.[25] Stern cites Basse's *Helpe to Discourse* (1623) as a text that quotes *Hamlet* but with sufficient variation to suggest it was reproduced from notes, and I would now add the earlier *Pastoral Elegies* to the list of Basse texts that borrow from

Shakespeare. While Stern was unable with the later text to determine which version of *Hamlet* was used in the performances from which Basse drew his notes, here I can be very specific: the 'base and euer lasting slaue' could possibly be transposed from any of the three texts – Q2/F has the more famous 'what a rogue and peasant slaue am I?' (TLN 1590) and Q1 has 'what a dunghill idiote slaue am I?' (Q1 TLN 1133) – but only Q1 has 'whispers in my hart'. Basse's earlier text was also published before either of the quartos of *Hamlet*, so it must be that he heard the lines in performance before 1602. Lending support to Stern's claims that Basse drew on notes taken from *Hamlet* in performance does not mean Q1 is a noted text; quite the opposite, it suggests that Basse is far too piecemeal a note-taker to be proof of any systematic recording of whole plays by noters. Yet it does position Q1 in performance as a potential source for a note-taker, rather than in text as the product of this activity.

One might be tempted to dismiss the presence of 'heart' in this first block of unique lines and in the later line about revenge as simply coincidental. But further analysis of the unique Q1 lines shows this specific word to be far more prevalent. Soon after the King grants Leartes his leave and turns his attention to Hamlet's 'sad and melancholy moodes', the King delivers a unique line by describing Hamlet as 'the Ioy and halfe heart of your mother' (Q1 TLN 176) and Hamlet himself then adds to the 'haviour of visage' speech the claim that nothing is 'equall to the sorrow of my heart, Him haue I lost I must of force forgoe' (Q1 TLN 183–184) – the last line here begins the couplet that ends with the more famous 'sutes of woe' line. Of the first seven unique lines in Q1 *Hamlet*, then, four contain 'heart', reinforcing a chain of meaning that is therefore missing from Q2/F – the first two connect Leartes to his father Corambis while speaking to the son's desire to be elsewhere; the next two connect Hamlet to his father and mother, each in their own way distanced from him. Completing the connection is the final unique line in this scene, when the King tells Hamlet to think on all the fathers who have died (which has analogues in Q2 and F), potentially providing the cue to an attentive audience that another father – the most prominent other father in the play being the King's counsellor – is soon to die.[26]

The 'heart' motif continues to dominate the unique lines well beyond the cluster in Scene 2 and its connection to one later line about revenge by Leartes. In Scene 3, Ofelia has her argument with Leartes about Hamlet's vows, and while the sense of their speeches here echoes that of Q2/F in the corresponding exchange, there are unique lines for both characters. Leartes in fact delivers a relevant line that Bertram and Kliman recognise as analogous but which should have been designated unique, when he observes that Hamlet 'Speakes from his heart, but yet take heed sister' (Q1 TLN 343). Bertram and Kliman align this line with TLN 496 ('Feare it *Ophelia*, feare it my dear sister'), but then they also designate Q1 TLN 347 as analogous with the same line – 'Belieu't Ofelia, therefore keep aloofe'. The latter clearly has more in common, but what the first line has in common with the Q2/F lines is simply that it is positioned to introduce the words of wisdom Leartes offers in a mirror of the wise precepts Corambis/Polonius delivers soon afterwards. If we acknowledge that only the second Q1 line constitutes a properly analogous line here, then Leartes earns himself yet another unique heart line in the first. Certainly, the first half of the first line in Q1 is unique; neither of the later texts has any reference to 'heart' here. And Ofelia shortly thereafter delivers another heart line that Bertram and Kliman do designate as unique, when she berates Leartes for 'forgetting what is said to me' (Q1 TLN 354) when he, like a libertine (the word used in Q2/F on TLN 512 and here provided on the analogous Q1 TLN 355), 'Doth giue his heart, his appetite at ful' when his honour dies (Q1 TLN 356). This unique line occupies the same place as Q2/F's libertine who 'Himself the primrose path of dalience treads' but changes the language significantly to accommodate another heart line, which in this instance immediately precedes the entry of Corambis (at Q1 TLN 360).

As Leartes leaves, following Corambis's advice to him, he asks Ofelia to remember his words to her, to which she responds, 'It is already lock't within my hart' (Q1 TLN 383), which is analogous to 'Tis in my memory lockt' (TLN 551), suggesting that it is not only in the unique lines that the 'heart' motif is prevalent – yet many of the uses of 'heart' in Q1's analogous lines are also matched to lines that lack 'heart' in Q2/F. Thus, when Corambis advises Ofelia 'How prodigall the tongue lends the heart vowes' (Q1 TLN 399), the Q2/F analogue renders it as 'how prodigall the soule / Lends the tongue vowes' (TLN 582–583). Similarly, in the later scene where Corambis and the King hatch their plan to spy on Hamlet during the 'To be or not to be' speech – which of course is located earlier in Q1, in a space that matches the sequencing in the Amleth tale[27] – Corambis asks the Queen to leave them, to which she responds 'With all my hart' (Q1 TLN 1687). The analogous line in Q2/F, in the much later Act 3, Scene 1, has the King asking Gertrude to leave, to which she responds 'I shall obey you' (TLN 1687). In Q1, the Queen will later have occasion to use the same 'all my heart' when Corambis and the King plot again to spy on Hamlet (this time fatally, as it happens, for Corambis). The King asks the Queen for her thoughts on the plan, to which she responds with the unique line 'With all my heart, soone I will send for him' (Q1 TLN 1202), and Corambis offers two unique lines of his own: 'My selfe will be that happy messenger, / Who hopes his griefe will be reueal'd to her' (Q1 TLN 1203–1204). More bewildering than perhaps any of these other allegedly analogous lines lacking heart references is the Queen's lament in Q1 that Corambis's death 'Hath piersed so the yong *Ofeliaes* heart' (Q1 TLN 1683), which Bertram and Kliman identify with TLN 2821, in which the Queen recognises that after the death of Polonius they acted over-hastily, 'In hugger mugger to inter him: poore *Ophelia*'. The only correspondence between the two lines is the name (which is not even grammatically or rhythmically correspondent). Finally, when Leartes is advised of his father's death, he declares that to his father's friends, he will 'locke them in my heart' (Q1 TLN 1742), and for the analogue to this line Bertram and Kliman reach all the way back to TLN 551, the same line with which Ofelia's 'lock't within my hart' was identified.

In their quest for analogous resemblances, Bertram and Kliman thus over-hastily paper over several examples of unique lines with the heart motif (or lines that, at the very least, uniquely add a reference to the heart). In all these cases, the motif applies to Corambis or his offspring, especially in the sense that he is fated to die behind that arras, leaving his children insane and vengeful. The 'heart lines' building on this chain of associations continue to pepper the play. Among the string of precepts Corambis offers to Ofelia, there is the unique 'louers lines are snares to intrap the heart' (Q1 TLN 404), and just prior to asking the Queen to leave in the first spying scene, he explains to the King that by listening to Hamlet speak to Ofelia, 'There shall you heare the effect of all his hart' (Q1 TLN 826). Even in the bedchamber scene, soon after Corambis has been slain, his lifeless form on stage apparently compels Hamlet and his mother to adopt the heart motif in their discourse. Hamlet says he will make her 'eyes looke downe into your heart' (Q1 TLN 1514), for which there is the analogous 'let me wring your heart' (TLN 2417), and describes the dead King 'Whose heart went hand in hand euen with that vow' (Q1 TLN 1523), which is identified with the much earlier Ghost's line, 'hand in hand, euen with the vowe' (TLN 736), from Act 1, Scene 4, albeit without the 'heart'. Then, Hamlet asks who would chide the 'hote blood within a Virgins heart' (Q1 TLN 1546), which is identified with the 'flaming youth' of TLN 2459, and the Queen responds 'Hamlet, thou cleaues my heart in twaine' (Q1 TLN 1548), the very line that Gertrude does deliver in Q2/F, but later, after the Ghost has left the chamber. Finally, as unique lines take over the end of the bedchamber scene, the Queen offers two more heart references in lines that are unquestionably unique to Q1: she says it is the 'weakness of thy braine, / Which makes thy tongue to blazon thy hearts griefe' (Q1 TLN 1580–1581), and then agrees 'by that maiesty, / That knows our thoughts, and looks into our hearts' (Q1 TLN 1594–1595) that she will support 'What stratagem soe're thou shalt deuise' (Q1 TLN 1597).

These two heart lines are particularly noteworthy because they accompany the two key sections of dialogue differentiating the Q1 version of this scene from the Q2/F version. Whereas the Queen in Q2/F says barely anything in the scene after the Ghost exits except for the repositioned 'heart in twain' line and a nonplussed agreement not to breathe a word of what Hamlet has said to her, she delivers almost half of the lines (ten lines out of twenty-one) in Q1 in the remainder of the same scene, nearly all of which are unique, in which she denies being in any way complicit in the murder and agrees to do whatsoever Hamlet requires of her to bring about revenge. Margrethe Jolly has observed that the Q1 Queen's comments grammatically and semantically echo those of Geruthe in François de Belleforest's version of the same scene in the Amleth story, making it likely that this Q1 scene is prior to the Q2/F version.[28] Yet it is also worth noting that in transforming the Amleth tale for the stage, Shakespeare constructs a family relationship where none exists in the original: the bedchamber spy becomes Corambis and the temptress becomes Ofelia, who is refigured as the spy's daughter, and the figure of Leartes is added to give the spy a son who will pursue revenge for the spy's death, in a mirror revenge plot that will lead Hamlet to his own demise.[29] I suggest that the proliferating heart lines in Q1 appear remarkably well placed to reinforce this introduced familial structure and its presentation as a mirror of the royal familial crisis. Even when no heart line appears in an exchange between Corambis and Ofelia – as is the case in the scene in which Ofelia describes how she had rejected Hamlet's letters – one appears at the start of the next scene to cement a link: Corambis ends the exchange with Ofelia by insisting that the news of Hamlet's state is to be conveyed immediately to the King, who in the first line of the next scene inquires after Hamlet's state of mind from Rossencraft and Gilderstone: 'our deere cosin Hamlet / Hath lost the very heart of all his sence' (Q1 TLN 717–718). This unique line speaks to Hamlet's sense but in context it also folds back onto the discovery by Corambis that the heart of his sense is Ofelia's love.

The death of Corambis slows down the rate of this proliferation, but the examples that follow the bedchamber scene ensure the connection is not lost in the remainder of the play: in their discussion about the implications of Hamlet killing Corambis, after the Queen observes the effect on 'yong *Ofeliaes* heart' (as I noted above), the King comments on news of Leartes returning from France with the unique line that 'he hath halfe the heart of all our Land' (Q1 TLN 1687); there is of course the statement on revenge by Leartes, which we considered at the outset; and, at the last, the penultimate scene ends with the Queen defending Hamlet's behaviour in the graveyard by protesting that it his madness that is the cause, 'And not his heart, *Leartes*' (Q1 TLN 2073), reinforcing in this unique line the connection between the heart motif, Leartes, and the parallel revenge plots that will come to a fatal head in the final scene to follow.

Why this connection and, more to the point, why not this connection in the Q2/F but only in Q1? The answer may be hiding in plain sight, given that Corambis is at the heart of these heart line connections. The absence of his name from both the Q2/F versions, where the same character bears the name of Polonius, suggests that the absence of the heart lines in these versions and the absence of the name Corambis may be no coincidence. To the reader familiar with what scholars have in the past written about the names in *Hamlet*, this answer is perhaps already abundantly obvious: the name 'Corambis' has long been held to mean 'two-hearted' (from Latin *cor-* for 'heart' and *ambi-* for 'both', although *ambi* can also suggest 'around' as in 'ambient'). The Q1 name is seen by some to represent a deliberate play on the motto of Lord Burghley, William Cecil ('*cor unum via una*' or 'one heart, one way').[30]

The heart of Corambis does indeed seem divided and duplicitous, but through the use of the heart motif in so many unique lines it also very much seems to become a core element in the interweaving of plots from more episodic, disparate elements in the Amleth source tale. This, to be sure, is true of Q1; the lack of these lines in Q2/F and the use of a different name for the King's counsellor and spy means the absence of this core element. This does not mean that Polonius and his family lack the centrality to the parallel revenge plot in Q2 or F; rather, it means that the core nature of the parallel plot is rendered more immediate and visible in Q1 via the presence of the heart lines throughout. The potential to be read topically is also more apparent in Q1, which might even explain the change of name and the absence from Q2/F of the numerous heart lines pointing to the pun that cues the topical reference. In this scenario, I refer to the prospect that the powerful Cecil family took exception to the play and demanded a change of name, just as William Brooke (Tenth Baron Cobham and, from late 1596 to early 1597, Lord Chamberlain) is believed to have prompted the change of the name of Sir John Oldcastle to Sir John Falstaff in *1 Henry IV*.[31] If such a scenario followed the Oldcastle saga, both playwright and company might be expected to exercise more caution and would hardly be likely to sprinkle a new play with so many dangerous puns. Yet if the play Thomas Lodge saw at the Theatre in 1596, with its oyster-wife-sounding Ghost, bore any resemblance to the text of Q1 *Hamlet*, then it becomes altogether reasonable to suspect that the Oldcastle change was ordered at around the same time that the Corambis material was brought to the attention of the Cecils.[32] It is even possible that *Hamlet* was removed from circulation for several years and that the name of Polonius was introduced along with other substantive changes, resulting in the Q2/F variants, after 1599, which fits well with the scenario I am describing here.

No evidence exists for any such censorship or suppression, so it cannot be offered as a firm conclusion. While it certainly suits the topical argument that I offered in *Tain* to have the name Corambis swapped out by 1599 due to censorship, nothing I have offered here clinches the deal. The Corambis-heart lines connection could also feasibly be present in Q1 *circa* 1589 as in the hypothesis by Bourus and others that this version faithfully records Shakespeare's earliest version of the play, revised in 1602 or 1603 with Polonius swapped in and the heart lines removed. Even those who subscribe to the proposition that Q1 comes after Q2 or F (or both) in the chain of transmission need not fear the discovery of a systematic approach to the addition, in this case, of unique lines, so long as they are prepared to accept that the new Q1 material is no mere product of happenstance. That wraps it up for the standard memorial reconstruction argument, I suggest. As I have also sought to demonstrate here, the Corambis-heart lines connection does not support the 'note-taker' theory, as there is nothing in the relevant sections of Q2 or F to indicate that a note-taker or an amender would fill gaps so consistently with heart lines in a way that structurally enhances the parallel revenge plot.

Perhaps there is one heart line in the play that does at least weigh the argument towards those who place Q1 first in the chronology, and I am pleased to say that even my complicated memorial revision argument fits this bill along with the early version arguments. The line has escaped mention to this point because it is not in Q1; rather, it is to be found in Q2 and F, as Hamlet advises Horatio to watch the King closely during the performance of *The Murder of Gonzago*. This play is being used by Hamlet because of its suggestive topicality, which is of course what should trigger the King's guilt reaction. Q1 replicates the same scene, but lacks the section of Hamlet's advice from 'Since my deare soule was mistris of her choice' (TLN 1914) until the statement that 'There is a play to night before the King' (TLN 1926). In these missing lines, Hamlet declares that if he could find a man who is not passion's slave, then he will wear that man in 'my harts core, I in my hart of hart, / As I doe thee' (TLN 1924–1925). The text of F goes further, inserting capital letters for 'Core' and 'Heart'. I am intrigued by the presence of this line, which seems explicitly to cue the audience to recognise the pun that is rife in Q1, even though the name of Corambis and all of the Q1 unique heart lines are not in Q2 or F, in the midst of a speech about the utility of a topical play to trigger the guilt of the powerful.

To my reckoning, it makes no sense for the Q1 author to have added the name of Corambis and numerous heart lines to reinforce the same pun, only to then remove this line, if Q1 comes after Q2 or F in the chain of transmission. More likely, the name of Corambis and the heart lines come first, and are swapped out for the Q2 or F revisions, but the author inserted additional reinforcement about topicality by including an explicit reference to the material that was by necessity removed. It is perhaps also worth noting here that the extra number of lines added to the Q1 speech is one block of twelve lines (TLN 1914–1925) and a second block of five lines (TLN 1934–

1938) of which one line is repeated ('For I mine eies will riuet to his face' – Q1 TLN 1266; TLN 1936). This is to say that the revision of Q1 has in this speech about the uses of topical plays the insertion of 'Some dozen or sixteene lines' (Q1 TLN 1124; TLN 1581). The playwright's own self-referential joke, perchance? Even if we put such speculation to one side, it should be patently clear that the ambient heart motif in Q1 *Hamlet* cannot be the product of coincidence or faulty memory. Instead, it bears witness to the systematic deployment of a pun on the name given in this play to the counsellor-spy character inherited from the Amleth tale, with the effect of enriching the parallel revenge plot by giving this character a name, a family and many hearts.

Laurie Johnson is Professor of English and Cultural Studies at the University of Southern Queensland. He is author of *Shakespeare's Lost Playhouse: Eleven Days at Newington Butts* (2018), *The Tain of Hamlet* (2013) and *The Wolf Man's Burden* (2001), and editor of *Embodied Cognition and Shakespeare's Theatre: The Early Modern Body-Mind* (with John Sutton and Evelyn Tribble, 2014) and *Rapt in Secret Studies: Emerging Shakespeares* (with Darryl Chalk, 2010). He is President of the Australian and New Zealand Shakespeare Association and a member of the editorial board of *Shakespeare* journal (Taylor & Francis).

Notes

1. See, for example, the introduction by Philip Edwards to the New Cambridge edition of *Hamlet* (Cambridge: Cambridge University Press, 1985), 22–32; Kathleen O. Irace's introduction to the New Cambridge edition of *The First Quarto of Hamlet* (Cambridge: Cambridge University Press, 1998), 1–5, 11–13; and Paul Menzer, *The Hamlets: Cues, Qs, and Remembered Texts* (Newark: University of Delaware Press, 2008), 53–63, 80–83.
2. Laurie Johnson, *The Tain of Hamlet* (Newcastle upon Tyne: Cambridge Scholars Publishing, 2013).
3. Tiffany Stern, 'Sermons, Plays and Note-Takers: Hamlet Q1 as a "Noted" Text', *Shakespeare Survey* 66 (2013), 1–23, https://doi.org/10.1017/SSO9781107300699.001.
4. Terri Bourus, *Young Shakespeare's Young Hamlet: Print, Piracy, and Performance* (New York: Palgrave Macmillan, 2014).
5. Zachary Lesser, *'Hamlet' After Q1: An Uncanny History of the Shakespearean Text* (Philadelphia: University of Pennsylvania Press, 2015).

6. Gary Taylor and Rory Loughnane, 'The Canon and Chronology of Shakespeare's Works', in *The New Oxford Shakespeare: Authorship Companion*, ed. Gary Taylor and Gabriel Egan (Oxford: Oxford University Press, 2017), 417–602, here 542–548.
7. The line count is taken from Paul Bertram and Bernice W. Kliman, eds, *The Three-Text Hamlet: Parallel Texts of the First and Second Quartos and First Folio* (New York: AMS Press, 1991).
8. Paul Werstine, 'A Century of "Bad" Shakespeare Quartos', *Shakespeare Quarterly* 50, no. 3 (Autumn 1999), 310–333, here 319, https://doi.org/10.2307/290236110 .2307/2902361.
9. Bertram and Kliman, *Three-Text Hamlet*, 8.
10. Line numbers provided follow the Through Line Number (TLN) system established in 1968 by Charlton Hinman for *The Norton Facsimile* of the First Folio, in which every typographical line in the Folio text is numbered consecutively. TLN counts used here are taken from Bertram and Kliman, *Three-Text Hamlet*, with those marked Q1 following the consecutive line numbers they provide separately for the Q1 text.
11. See *Oxford English Dictionary*, 'how, *adv.* and *n.3* 1.a.' which includes the phrase 'how is it' among examples of the form defined as 'Qualifying a verb: In what way or manner? By what means?' OED Online, Oxford University Press, http://www.oed.com.ezproxy.usq.edu.au/view/Entry/89004 (accessed 26 March 2019).
12. Stern, 'Sermons', 4–8.
13. Ibid., 9–10.
14. Ibid., 10.
15. Bourus, *Young Shakespeare's Young Hamlet*, 88–92.
16. On the use of notes, tables and writing in early modern England, see Peter Stallybrass, Roger Chartier, J. Franklin Mowery and Heather Wolfe, 'Hamlet's Tables and the Technologies of Writing in Renaissance England', *Shakespeare Quarterly* 55 (2004), 379–419. Both Bourus and Stern also refer to this important work, each of course leading to different conclusions.
17. Bourus, *Young Shakespeare's Young Hamlet*, 69–100.
18. Stern, 'Sermons', 22.
19. Ibid., 12.
20. Ibid., 15–16.
21. Ibid., 16.
22. Ibid., 16.
23. Bertram and Kliman's transcription incorrectly gives 'releese' at the end of this line, but it is clearly an 'f' in the quarto and the couplet relies on 'releefe' rhyming with 'griefe'.
24. Stern, 'Sermons', 3.
25. William Basse, *Three pastoral elegies of Anander, Anetor, and Muridella* (London: Valentine Simmes for John Barnes, 1602), D1^v.
26. Q1 also adds at this point the unique lines, 'vntill the / Generall ending. Therefore cease laments' (Q1 TLN 188–189). This 'general ending' goes beyond Q2 and F by pointing not just to past deaths of fathers, since it insinuates that all fathers die, hinting more strongly than Q2/F at the likelihood that at least one other father will meet the general ending before the play is done. Those familiar with the Amleth tale will already know that the King's counsellor is marked for death,

but even those unfamiliar with the source tale may at this point in Q1 be cued to expect the fate awaiting Corambis, which initially motivates Leartes to pursue the revenge that would give his heart relief.

27. See Johnson, *Tain of Hamlet*, 184–185.
28. Margrethe Jolly, '*Hamlet* and the French Connection: The Relationship of Q1 and Q2 *Hamlet* and the Evidence of Belleforest's *Histoires Tragiques*', *Parergon* 29, no. 1 (2012), 83–105, here 98–99, https://doi.org/10.1353/pgn.2012.0016.
29. See, for example, Johnson, *Tain of Hamlet*, 187–188; Anthony Miller, '*Hamlet*, II.ii–III.iv: Mirrors of Revenge', *Sydney Studies in English* 11 (1985–1986), 3–22; Hidematsu Nojima, 'The Mirror of Hamlet', in *Hamlet and Japan*, ed. Yoshiko Uéno (New York: AMS Press, 1995), 21–35; David Scott Kastan, '"His semblable is his *mirror*": *Hamlet* and the Imitation of Revenge', *Shakespeare Studies* 19 (1987), 111–124.
30. Sadly, since J. Thomas Looney pointed to this likely association in 1920, it has become a favourite argument among authorship doubters, despite the publication only a year later of Lilian Winstanley's thorough analysis of topical associations in the play, which was offered without any question of authorship. For a summary of these approaches and further discussion of the potential associations of the name 'Corambis', see Johnson, *Tain of Hamlet*, 203–207.
31. See, for example, Gary Taylor, 'The Fortunes of Oldcastle', *Shakespeare Survey* 38 (1985), 85–100, https://doi.org/10.1017/CCOL0521320267.008.
32. On the broader implications of Lodge's account, see Bourus, *Young Shakespeare's Young Hamlet*, 144–152; Johnson, *Tain of Hamlet*, 50–53.

Chapter 10
'Brief Let Me Be'
Telescoped Action and Characters in Q1 and Q2 *Hamlet*

Tommaso Continisio

The intricate textual history of *Hamlet* has always raised the interest of scholars, particularly since the 1980s, when the supposed corruption of Shakespearean 'suspect texts'[1] started to be questioned, and these plays began to be considered legitimate alternative versions. In the space of a twenty-year period, from 1603 to 1623, three completely different versions of *Hamlet* appeared (Q1; Q2, which is almost twice as long as Q1, and with two hundred lines not present in the third version;[2] and F). The nature and origins of Q1 have particularly fascinated textual scholars, from the initial hypothesis that Q1 *Hamlet* was perhaps the so-called *Ur-Hamlet* – altered, abridged or corrupted during its transmission – to arguments defining Q1 as a posterior memorial reconstruction of Q2, allegedly realised by either the rogue actors interpreting the parts of Marcellus, Lucianus

Notes for this section begin on page 189.

and Voltemand (Voltemar in Q1) or the whole cast of a specific production, who might have recited their lines to a compositor as they had been performed. According to Ann Thompson and Neil Taylor, 'the majority of twentieth-century scholars have argued that, despite its being printed after Q1, Q2 records a text which pre-dates the text of Q1'.[3] Nonetheless, in the twenty-first century, that consensus has been challenged by Margrethe Jolly and Terri Bourus,[4] who independently defend Q1 as an early version for the stage later revised by Shakespeare himself in the early seventeenth century.[5]

Whatever the case, Q1 presents us with a rich and vibrant text that is imbued with performative efficiency and dramatic resonances that deserve our attention. My discussion will build on the work of Bourus[6] and Lesser,[7] particularly on how Shakespeare's conception of Hamlet, Gertrude (Gertred in Q1) and Ophelia (Ofelia in Q1) is defined in this first version. By assuming the variation between Q1 and Q2 *Hamlet* regarding the Prince's age, I will try to explore how this supposed textual inconsistency influences some of the canonical traits of Hamlet's personality as we have known it so far, since a younger hero marks a different behaviour towards the female characters of the play (Ofelia and Gertred), and surely discourages a procrastinating attitude.

How old is Hamlet? A discussion on *Hamlet*'s eponymous hero cannot be put forth without mentioning the challenging debate about the age of the Prince. In Q2 (5.1) there is a clear indication that Hamlet is thirty years old.[8] The First Clown has been a gravedigger since 'the very day that young Hamlet was born' (5.1.152); fifteen lines later, he will reveal that he has been a 'sexton' in Denmark for 'thirty years' (5.1.167). Moreover, he recalls how Yorick 'bore [him] on his back a thousand times' (5.1.176) as it 'hath lien you i'th' earth three and twenty years' (5.1.163). This would suggest that Hamlet was seven years old when Yorick died. In spite of this, as a student of Wittenberg, his youth is highlighted on several occasions (for instance, when Polonius labels him 'young' in 1.3, and the Ghost hints at his 'noble youth' in 1.5). Yet – maybe because of Burbage's age at the time of the performance (in 1600, he was thirty-three years old) – this factor was modified, somewhat similarly to the insertion of the bathetic description of his appearance in 5.2.269, which runs counter to any image we might have of the elegant Danish Prince: 'he's fat, and scant of breath'. Q1 is less specific. The Clown's reference to the skull of Yorick ('Look you, here's a skull hath been here this dozen year'; 16.85–86) assumes more practical tones and implies that Hamlet in Q1 would be just a seventeen-year-old youth.[9]

As suggested by Marvin Hunt, in Q2 the focus 'shifts from the plot of *Hamlet* to the character of Hamlet himself'.[10] The Prince emerges as a protean and captivating hero, a man of unparalleled acumen, wit and incomparable eloquence; the straightforward yet refined, extremely sensitive yet inclined to offhandedness student at the University of Wittenberg. The most renowned facet of Hamlet's temperament is his inner sphere, the inward angle of a person who struggles with the impossibility of turning his thought into action. This paradigmatic disunity between his external appearance and inner reality, and his fragmented and depersonalised interiority, are first made apparent in 1.2 of Q2, becoming then more and more convincingly expressed in Hamlet's famous soliloquies (Q2 is the sole version that contains all four) which gradually point towards a crescendo of self-awareness. From an initial imprisonment within the confines of his mind, they reach a climax when memory, thought and language are expressed in a plan of action that struggles to materialise until Hamlet's acceptance of the duel with Laertes, and his resolution to explain his actions, once struck by the venomous sword. As far as this episode is concerned, despite the macrostructural similarities between Q1 and Q2, Q1's dramatic impetus is triggered by the exaggerated rivalry staged for the possession of Ofelia's body when 'Hamlet leaps [into Ofelia's grave] after Leartes' (16.145SD). This erotic triangle, which overcomes death, is clearer in the fewer lines devoted to Hamlet's philosophical implications of the duel: the practical speech of eight lines in Q1 is later expanded in Q2, which may be seen as the umpteenth piece of evidence to Hamlet's pro-active approach to revenge.

A more substantial telescoping of the action may be perceived in the scene where Prince Hamlet plans to unmask King Claudius in the metatheatrical performance of the Mousetrap (Scene 7 in Q1). The fact that the notorious 'To be or not to be' soliloquy is textually dislocated, appearing thus in the equivalent to Act 2 Scene 2 rather than the common Act 3 Scene 1, accelerates Hamlet's desire for revenge: there is no room for being jaundiced and doubtful. In this respect, Kathleen O. Irace points out that 'the neatness of the difference [between Q1 and Q2/F] suggests that this structural change was a deliberate theatrical alteration'.[11] It is hard to deny that the difference is deliberate, but her assumption that the alteration was theatrical is much more dubious. By describing the difference as an effort to 'speed the action', she implies that Q1 is speeding up the action originally represented slowly in Q2, and this infers in turn that Q1 is later than Q2. In eleven lines – against the two hundred of Q2 – Hamlet's initial doubts are dispelled, and the text focuses on his actions and his insistence on decision, rather than procrastination. As may be inferred, the Hamlet of Q1 is not a man who significantly postpones his thirst for revenge, nor is he Q2's somewhat distressed character trapped in his thoughts and contemplation. In Q1, Hamlet gives little evidence of his reflective lucubration and, obviously, less of his bright linguistic and emotional complexity. He is, instead, highly focused on action: a character fit for an audience that was expecting revenge rather than meditation. Hamlet's youthful vehemence and explicitness may be detected also in his encounter with Gertred, when he confronts the Queen about Old Hamlet's assassination. In the same scene, Hamlet explicitly seeks his mother's alliance, which is a distinctive feature of Q1 ('And, mother, but assist me in revenge'; 11.94). Instead, in Q2 Hamlet never asks Gertrude to help him with the vengeful deed, nor do we find there an explicit reference to the equation between avenging the death of Old Hamlet and cleansing Gertred's guilt in marrying the murderer, which is, as Thompson and Taylor point out, another unique trait of Q1.[12]

The implications of Claudius's supposedly heartfelt behaviour towards Hamlet, in both Q1 and Q2, are indissolubly woven with the Prince's (allegedly feigned) lunacy.[13] In both Q2 and Q1, the King displays a wholeheartedly false attitude[14] towards the Prince. But in Q1's much shorter second scene, the King calls Hamlet his 'son' four times;[15] in Q2's much longer scene, he does so only once.[16] In their first encounter, Q1 emphasises, much more than Q2, the King's publicly warm conduct towards the Prince. In Q2, Claudius from the outset invests less in the public claim to fatherhood, and his decision to ship the Prince to England is taken much sooner – the first mention of England occurs after the spying scene, when the King first understands that there may be other causes supporting Hamlet's folly. A parallel conclusion about Hamlet's madness is reached in Q1,[17] but it is separated from the first reference to England, which occurs only after Corambis's[18] assassination (Scene 11), thus postponing the reasoning about the hypothetical feigned folly on the part of Prince Hamlet. Irace claims that in Q1 'the England expedient is a desperate impulse rather than the carefully wrought plan of a clever enemy'.[19] Whether or not her interpretation is correct, in Q1 the King's delayed understanding of the threat posed by Hamlet's madness, and the separation of the initial suspicion from the later decision, may suggest that in Q1 the 'cause and ground of his distemperance' (7.7) is not as significant in terms of dramatic action as it is in Q2.

The Queen's attitude towards Hamlet's counterfeit folly is another prominent difference between Q1 and Q2. In Q2, the Queen explicitly refers to Hamlet's lunacy[20] four times in three different scenes. After Hamlet kills Polonius, she specifically compares his madness to the mighty waves and wind, thus essentialising it as an endless, chaotic struggle between different elements of his nature (or of two of the four elements of humoral theory). In Q1, she refers to his madness only once, much later in the play: 'It is his madness makes him thus / And not his heart, Leartes' (16.167–168). Her single textual reference to Hamlet's madness in Q1 is, in context, clearly intended as an excuse, which may be interpreted as either a deliberate obfuscation or the acknowledgement of a momentary lapse into fury and anguish. It need not indicate a general indictment of sustained mental instability. Likewise, Q1 dramatises the relationship between mother and son, after he murders Corambis in her presence, very differently. In Q1, there is no mention of madness. She focuses instead on his aggressive conduct towards her ('he throws and tosses me about'; 11.108). This physical vehemence, which is unique to Q1, may be a deliberately misleading exaggeration on the part of Gertred, as Thompson and Taylor conjecture.[21]

Neither Gertrude nor Ophelia have a prominent role if compared to Hamlet and the other major male characters, yet they both have great significance in shaping Hamlet's personality and influencing his attitude. Hamlet's conduct towards the Queen and Ophelia and the subsequent overall image stemming from their gestures in Q2 have been extensively debated and thoroughly investigated; what is necessary here is to offer a global account of the differences in these two characters as presented in Q1 and Q2.

Gertrude's first exchange with Hamlet in Q2 (1.2.68–74) is typically considered both a somewhat unpleasant treatment of the Queen (who appears surrounded with a halo of mystery regarding whether she is aware of the murder) and evidence of her genuine love for her son (which is also demonstrated during the episode of Polonius's murder behind the tapestry). With the image of the vein of gold 'among a mineral of metals base' (4.1.25), the Queen seems to be lying for a second time to protect Hamlet. However, her possible knowledge of the facts and the suspicions about her possible implication in the murder of Hamlet's father are never plainly contradicted or confirmed. Although the Queen is shocked by the news of a 'bloody deed' (3.4.26), she does not give an answer. On the other hand, her belief that the cause of Hamlet's madness is her marriage to Claudius is taken by Thompson and Taylor as proof of the Queen's lack of awareness of the murder, as she does not mention it in the Closet scene.[22] The question of Gertrude's involvement in the murder is never clearly answered in Q2, yet she undoubtedly shows a genuine love for Hamlet and his wellbeing, an attitude that is apparent in her last words, when she warns Hamlet of the poisonous drink.

In Q1, the relationship between mother and son assumes slightly different tones. Q1 allows us to understand the Queen not only as a loving mother, but also as someone morally unambiguous. Emphasising 'meekness and silence',[23] the moment when Gertrude in Q2 encourages her son to accept his father's death and, more importantly, to embrace the new ruler, is condensed in Q1 in two lines: 'Let not thy mother lose her prayers, Hamlet, / Stay here with us, go not to Wittenberg' (2.48–49). More surprising is Hamlet's reaction (2.50): he personifies the qualities of a compliant son and, unlike the Q2 hero, by obeying his mother he departs from that outrageous approach which characterises the mother-son argument in Q2 1.2, and mirrors Hamlet's discomposed mind.

Unlike Q2 (3.4), Q1 has Hamlet explicitly accuse his mother of being privy to the murder of his father when describing the King's picture. Gertred's adamant denial of accusation ('But, as I have a soul, I swear by heaven / I never knew of this most horrid murder'; 11.85–86), and her subsequent lines, found solely in Q1 ('Hamlet, I vow by that Majesty / That knows our thoughts and looks into our hearts / I will conceal, consent and do my best'; 11.97–100), together offer us the image of an unambiguous Queen who will resolutely ally herself with Hamlet, plotting against the King. Gertred in Q1 is a 'more sympathetic character',[24] a sorrowful mother (Hamlet never calls her 'Queen' in Q1), a less rounded but more theatrical figure than her counterpart. This side of her character is made explicit in Scene 14, the longest passage found solely in the Q1 version of *Hamlet*. According to Alan C. Dessen, 'the pairing of Gertred and

Horatio in this scene balances the pairing of the king and Laertes in Q1's much shorter, less developed version of 4.7'.[25] I can readily agree with Irace's point, according to which several segments of Q2 that are not present in Q1 are neatly supplied by this brief scene, which still includes all details that are essential for the development of the play.[26] Gertred's support for her son is shown again in her meeting with Horatio: uniquely in the first quarto, the Queen 'inherit[s] Hamlet's role of actor/observer'[27] and clearly perceives that 'there's treason in [the King's] looks' (14.10). Gertred's willingness to unmask her second husband's dishonest appearance (14.12–13) is seen by Thompson and Taylor as clear evidence of her alliance with Hamlet.[28] The scene ends with Gertred thanking heaven for bestowing its blessing upon Prince Hamlet, unequivocally displaying her maternal affection.

Q1 *Hamlet* offers a picture of a multifaceted woman,[29] more prominent than her counterpart in Q2. Gertred's language is less grandiloquent; verbally, she hardly performs the magnificence of a queen. Instead, Q1 emphasises Gertred's role as mother. She is in the full bloom of her fertility (if one assumes, as Bourus suggests, that Gertred 'might be only thirty').[30] This trait is implied also by the stage direction 'Enter the Ghost in his Nightgown', which, charged with sexual innuendoes, presents us with a couple portrayed in their conjugal domesticity. Her fruitful womb ties in with the domestic, maternal and peacekeeping Gertred, whose silence and religious speech[31] ensnare her into the corollary of obedience to male authority. Gertred's motherhood yields in Q2 to Gertrude's royal consorthood: in Q2, Hamlet defines Gertrude according to her political role, thus giving much more emphasis to a status – that of widowhood – which underscores the disruptive effects of feminine agency in a male-dominated world that aims to engender power as masculine.

The relationship between Hamlet and Ophelia in Q2 is profoundly affected by Ophelia's submission to her father and brother. Ophelia's 'I shall obey, my lord' (1.3.135) epitomises the totally submissive personality of a passive and compliant daughter, continually smothered by her father and brother, on whom she depends completely, particularly when decisions are to be made.

As in Q2, in Q1 Hamlet's love for Ofelia is diegetically introduced by her brother. Yet Q1's account is less ambiguous and more direct ('I see Prince Hamlet makes a show of love'; 3.3) than the thirty-three lines in Q2 (1.3.11–44), that demonstrate the philosophical spirit of the mature Shakespeare. Moreover, Leartes in Q1 maintains a comfortable distance from his sister and does not label Ofelia with the bawdy images found in Q2, for example, when he likens sexual intercourse to a 'canker' entering and hurting a delicate flower before its buds have time to disclose. Further evidence of Q2's sexualisation of the character can be found in the contrast between Q1, where she encounters the distracted Hamlet while 'walking in the gallery, all alone' (6.42) and Q2, where the offstage encounter occurs in her 'chamber'.

The Q1 Ofelia is allowed more measured and less eroticised lines than her counterpart in Q2. When commenting on Hamlet's folly, she quite impassively mentions such a 'great alteration in a prince' (6.34), who 'fixed his eyes so steadfast on [her] face' (6.45). By contrast, the Q2 Ophelia is characterised by more hectic and theatrical behaviour ('O my lord, my lord, I have been so affrighted'; 2.1.73) and describes the Prince 'as if he had been loosed out of hell' (2.1.80). In addition, Q1 lacks the sexual imagery found in her Q2 soliloquy, when she heightens the level of intimacy between Hamlet and herself with the famous line 'I ... sucked the honey of his music vows' (3.1.157). As Eric Partridge states,[32] the combination of honey and music is a cross-reference to the sexual act.

The constant intimidation by her brother and father makes her character easier to manipulate, even if Ofelia's bashful and compliant attitude in Q1 turns into resoluteness in the episode of her derangement. The stage direction introducing Ofelia – '*Enter Ofelia playing on a Lute, and her hair down, singing*' – provides noteworthy food for thought. Besides her dishevelled hair, which is an image anchored to a tradition of both insane and virgin women on the Elizabethan stage, Deanne Williams claims that the direction allows for a more 'self-conscious response to her predicament rather than an emotional whirlwind'.[33] In early modern England, the lute implied on the one hand feminine models of daughters submissively ready for marriage, and on the other hand, a somewhat heightened state of general awareness, and a regained trust in their psychological and physical possibilities, likening the lute to female genitalia. The musical instrument thus encapsulates a number of discrepancies – between action and stasis, compliance and disobedience, sexuality and purity – which label the girls' passage from adolescence to adulthood and make us meditate on the stimulating, albeit clichéd, association of madness and music, which reflects the untuning of harmony.

In this case, it shows a conflict within Ofelia, namely between her sexual drive and filial duties, 'torn' – as Williams states – 'between desire for Hamlet and her father's expectations'.[34] The presence of music onstage threatens the boundary between private and public spheres. The female performance of Ofelia's songs, which in Q1 are less fragmented than in Q2,[35] and are thus a sign of a sort of inner and textual consistency, questions her devout image of submissive domesticity and engenders a space and a practice that are typically masculine. It may seem paradoxical, but there is some 'method' in Q1 Ofelia's madness.

In conclusion, Q1 offers a compelling portrait of an adolescent intensely focused on action, whereas Q2, to use Hunt's claim, 'refocuses Hamlet as a figure of immense psychological complexity ... a man working, as it were, from within, motivated as much by the dictates of his own inner reality as by his father's external, objective call for revenge'.[36] Furthermore, the first quarto version of *Hamlet* performs a Gertred siding with her son and determined to deceive the King – an attitude that demonstrates her acknowledgement of the King's guilt and Hamlet's trust in her. Q2 shows none of these features. And the liaison between Hamlet and Ofelia in Q1 is modified by Hamlet's franker and more vigorous displays of affection which collide with Ofelia's silent posture, who yet seems to be less smothered than in Q2. The fictional characterisation in Q1, supported by a close reading of the play, answers the much-debated question about the dramaturgical necessities of Q1's brevity, namely that telescoping of actions at which Lene Petersen hints.[37] If, as George Wright suggests,[38] Q2 *Hamlet* is extensively and rhetorically enriched by hendiadys, something that displays Shakespeare's interest in the potentials of linguistic modes, Q1's brevity may be explained, as Christy Desmet argues, through a 'stylistic concision featuring *brachylogia*' that 'suggests restless action'.[39] This interpretation adds some value to the image of Q1 *Hamlet* as an extremely performative play, and strengthens the possibility that Shakespeare originally wrote a fast and 'plot-driven'[40] play, intended for an audience that was interested in 'less discursive entertainment'.[41]

Tommaso Continisio was awarded the European Doctoral degree in English Literature at the University of Rome Tor Vergata, and is now collaborating with a post-doc scholarship at the University of Verona, under the supervision of Silvia Bigliazzi, on a project about classical reception in early modern English drama. He also contributes to the Verona-based SENS ("Shakespeare's Narrative Sources: Italian novellas and their European dissemination") and CEMP ("Classical and Early Modern Paradoxes in England") digital archives projects. His main research interests lie in early modern English drama and Elizabethan culture. He has published papers on several early modern dramatists, including Shakespeare, Middleton, Heywood and Ford, and has co-edited a collection of essays on female monarchs on the Elizabethan stage (*Queens on Stage: Female Power and Sovereignty in Early Modern English Theatre*, 2008). He is currently on a book-length study on Middleton's tragicomedies, soon to be published.

Notes

'Q1' refers to the 'first quarto' or 'first edition' of *Hamlet*, printed in 1603.

1. Laurie E. Maguire, *Shakespearean Suspect Texts: The 'Bad' Quartos and Their Contexts* (Cambridge: Cambridge University Press, 1996).
2. Melchiori champions Q2 as a text 'intended more for the wiser sort of readers than for the audience of the public theatres'. Giorgio Melchiori, '*Hamlet*: The Acting Version and the Wiser Sort', in *The Hamlet First Published (Q1, 1603): Origins, Form, Intertextualities*, ed. Thomas Clayton (Newark: University of Delaware Press, 1986), 195–210, here 200. The essay has been reprinted in *Memoria di Shakespeare 8*, ed. Rosy Colombo and Daniela Guardamagna (Rome: Bulzoni, 2012).
3. Ann Thompson and Neil Taylor, eds, *Hamlet: The Texts of 1603 and 1623* (London: Arden Shakespeare, 2006), 81. Further references to Q1 and Q2 *Hamlet* will be taken from this edition. Quotations are inserted parenthetically in the text.
4. Margrethe Jolly, *The First Two Quartos of Hamlet: A New View of the Origins and Relationship of the Texts* (Jefferson, NC: MacFarland and Company, 2014); Terri Bourus, *Young Shakespeare's Young Hamlet: Print, Piracy, and Performance* (New York: Palgrave Macmillan, 2014).
5. Alessandro Serpieri went a very long way towards these issues first in his 1996 essay on *Hamlet* Q1, and later in the introduction to his 1997 Italian translation of Q1 *Hamlet*. See Alessandro Serpieri, 'Is *Hamlet* Q1 a Generative or a Degenerate Text?', *Textus* IX (1996), 461–484, http://digital.casalini.it/10.1400/23386; and William Shakespeare, *Il primo Amleto*, trans. Alessandro Serpieri (Venice: Marsilio, 1997), 9–43.

6. Besides the above-mentioned reference to Bourus's seminal study, see also Terri Bourus, 'Enter Shakespeare's Young Hamlet, 1589', *Actes des congrès de la Société française Shakespeare* 34 (2016), 1–14, https://doi.org/10.4000/shakespeare.3736.
7. Zachary Lesser, *Hamlet After Q1: An Uncanny History of the Shakespearean Text* (Philadelphia: University of Pennsylvania Press, 2015).
8. The indication would not be so clear to Rhodri Lewis. In his article 'Young Hamlet', which appeared in the *TLS* on 4 November 2016, Lewis challenges the standard view of Hamlet's age in Q2. I am not at all convinced by his refusal to acknowledge the evidence of the Gravedigger who, according to him, is 'no better at the numerical computation of time than he is at Latin' and whose 'historical measurements of sixteen, thirty, and twenty-three years are empty signifiers – no more than words'.
9. Again, see Bourus, 'Enter Shakespeare's Young Hamlet', which traces the history of the debate about Hamlet's age from mid-nineteenth-century scholarship through A.C. Bradley to Harold Jenkins. In my opinion, this is the most persuasive account of the history of the issue of Hamlet's age.
10. Marvin W. Hunt, *Looking for Hamlet* (New York: Palgrave Macmillan, 2007), 47.
11. Kathleen O. Irace, *Reforming the 'Bad' Quartos: Provenance and Performance in Six Shakespearean First Editions* (Newark: University of Delaware Press, 1994), 27.
12. Thompson and Taylor, *Hamlet*, 135.
13. There is not space in this chapter to consider the long history of debate about how much of Hamlet's madness is real and how much is feigned.
14. As Irace points out, King Claudius is 'little more than a pasteboard villain' in Q1. Irace, *Reforming the 'Bad' Quartos*, 61.
15. Q1 2.26, 32, 40, 51.
16. 'Our chiefest courtier, cousin, and our son' (1.2.117). He also uses the word at the end of the play, when he says 'Our son shall win' (5.2.290). This latter paradoxically hides traces of anxious yet apparently proud fatherhood.
17. 'Some deeper thing is that troubles him' (7.200).
18. The redundancy and tautology of the speeches by Polonius/Corambis are accentuated in Q1 *Hamlet*, where his typical anadiploses and chiasmuses are accompanied by a higher number of *sententiae* (see, for example, this one found solely in Q1 7.66: 'for what we think is surest we often lose').
19. Irace, *Reforming the 'Bad' Quartos*, 61.
20. 'Alas, he's mad' (3.4.102); 'Mad as the sea and wind' (4.1.92); 'his very madness' (4.1.25); 'This is mere madness' (5.1.273).
21. Thompson and Taylor, *Hamlet*, 136.
22. Ibid., 241.
23. Dorothea Kehler, 'The First Quarto of *Hamlet*: Reforming Widow Gertred', *Shakespeare Quarterly* 46, no. 4 (1995), 398–413, here 404, http://www.jstor.org/stable/10.2307/2870979.
24. Irace, *Reforming the 'Bad' Quartos*, 104.
25. Alan C. Dessen, 'Weighing the Options in *Hamlet* Q1', in Clayton, *The Hamlet First Published*, 65–77, here 70.
26. Ibid., 36–37.
27. Tony Howard, *Women as Hamlet: Performance and Interpretation in Theatre, Film, and Fiction* (Cambridge: Cambridge University Press, 2007), 19.

28. Thompson and Taylor, *Hamlet*, 149.
29. Kehler states first that the 'sympathetic' image of the Queen contradicts the entrenched 'prejudice against remarrying widows', but then she acknowledges that the 'reformed lusty widow' is a 'slippery role' by which to label the Q1 Queen. Kehler, 'The First Quarto of *Hamlet*', 399, 409.
30. Bourus, 'Enter Shakespeare's Young Hamlet', 10.
31. G.B. Shand notes that in Q1 she has 'three times the number of references to God and heaven' as in Q2. G.B. Shand, 'Gertred, Captive Queen of the First Quarto', in *Shakespearean Illuminations: Essays in Honor of Marvin Rosenberg*, ed. J.L. Halio and H. Richmond (Newark: University of Delaware Press, 1998), 33–49, here 42.
32. Eric Partridge, *Shakespeare's Bawdy*, 3rd ed. (London: Routledge, 1947), 127.
33. Deanne Williams, *Shakespeare and the Performance of Girlhood* (New York: Palgrave Macmillan, 2014), 73.
34. Ibid., 76.
35. For example, in Q2 *Hamlet* the Queen interrupts Ophelia: 'what imports this song?' (4.5.27).
36. Hunt, *Looking for Hamlet*, 67.
37. See Lene B. Petersen, *Shakespeare's Errant Texts: Textual Form and Linguistic Style in Shakespearean 'Bad' Quartos and Co-authored Plays* (Cambridge: Cambridge University Press, 2010), 117.
38. George T. Wright, 'Hendiadys and *Hamlet*', *PMLA* 96, no. 2 (1981), 168–193, https://doi.org/10.1632/pmla.1981.96.2.168.
39. Christy Desmet, 'Text, Style, and Author in *Hamlet* Q1', *Journal of Early Modern Studies* 5 (2016), 135–156, here 141, 144, http://dx.doi.org/10.13128/JEMS-2279-7149-18086.
40. Thompson and Taylor, *Hamlet*, 16.
41. Anthony B. Dawson, *Shakespeare in Performance: Hamlet* (Manchester: Manchester University Press, 1995), 23.

Chapter 11
Q1 *Hamlet*
The Sequence of Creation and Implications for the 'Allowed Booke'

*Charles Adams Kelly and
Dayna Leigh Plehn-Peavyhouse*

In 1909, Alfred W. Pollard coined the term 'bad quarto' to describe the unauthorised nature of certain early printed texts. Pollard's hypothesis, never universally accepted, is now under greater pressure than ever. The first section of this chapter will briefly review the reconciliation of the authors' findings with selected findings of several others, producing a network of evidence that strongly supports the emerging theory of Q1 *Hamlet* as a text not derived from Q2/F, but related to a pre-Q2 version of the play, specifically a draft of the Q1 text played during 1603. The second section will identify and analyse categories of Q1 vs. Q2 text, and combine this analysis with findings concerning the printing of Q1, which will lead to a conclusion of how Q1 as printed might relate to the non-extant allowed book. This

Notes for this section begin on page 208.

speculative but well-grounded view will represent a perspective useful to stage script planners and editors preparing texts of Q1.

The sequence of creation of the texts

The idea of *reported texts* began around the time James Orchard Halliwell-Phillipps scathingly rebuked the theorised 'inferior and clumsy writer'[1] whom he believed must have provided the text for Q1 *Hamlet*. Subsequently, Alfred W. Pollard coined the term 'bad quarto',[2] and throughout the twentieth century as scholars grappled with the nature of irregular early texts, the theory of bad quartos created by *memorial reconstruction* attracted, like flypaper, a total of forty-one early quartos by Shakespeare and other playwrights. In 1996, however, Laurie Maguire evaluated these forty-one texts and questioned the general theory of memorial reconstruction, while other scholars developed findings challenging the theory as it applied to Q1 *Hamlet*. One of Paul Werstine's conclusions, diminishing the theory of Q1 as a simpler text for provincial audiences, was that 'the standards of provincial performance can scarcely ever again be thought to differ from those of London theatre when the audiences for both contain some of the same people'.[3] If Q1 *Hamlet* was created by actor reporters, the Marcellus actor would have been primary among them, as his Q1 concordance is very high, but he is onstage early in the play only. In 1999, Werstine concluded that 'the failure to discover qualified reporters anywhere in the latter half of the play is one of the most glaring insufficiencies of the memorial-reconstruction hypothesis'.[4]

The hypothesis of the bad quarto of *Hamlet* continued to dissolve in the early decades of the twenty-first century as scholars reconciled their findings with others, current and historical. This process has resulted in an interlocking network of evidence supporting the theory of Q1 *Hamlet* as a pre-Q2 text, and eliminating each of the possible alternatives. The first example of this consolidation of evidence is the relationships between several items of printing and publishing evidence. In July 1602, the printer James Roberts filed for the Elizabethan equivalent of copyright for 'A booke called "the Revenge of HAMLET Prince [of] Denmarke" as yt was latlie Acted by the Lord Chamberleyne his servants'.[5] However, Valentine Simmes was the printer of Q1 in 1603, in seeming violation of the Roberts filing. Roberts was only involved in printing the second quarto, which appeared in late 1604,[6] but curiously, Nicholas Ling was publisher of both Q2 *and* the supposedly unauthorised Q1. When Alfred Pollard included Q1 *Hamlet* in his list of five 'bad quartos', he noted: 'that Ling ... was its publisher may well amaze us'.[7] Pollard theorised that there must have been a 'dispute' between the parties that was subsequently resolved.

However, in recent decades it has become apparent that Roberts, Ling, Simmes and Shakespeare's theatre company had close professional relationships spanning several years before and following 1603, and there is no evidence of any dispute between them. In 1595, Simmes's apprentice transferred to Roberts,[8] and publisher Ling is documented as owning the rights to the play in 1607.[9] Ling could have secured it from Roberts as early as August 1603, there being no record of the date of the transfer. Simmes and Ling were both apprentices to Henry Bynneman, perhaps at overlapping times, and Simmes subsequently received more work from Ling than from any other publisher, twenty-seven titles in total.[10] In 1603, Roberts was very busy[11] and might have been perfectly agreeable to the printing of Q1 by Simmes.

Implicit in the idea of unauthorised bad quartos is the threat that 'good' texts could be printed in response, perhaps immediately. Publishers had to invest in paper, compositors and pressmen, creating an investment that often took more than a year to be repaid.[12] The publisher of each first quarto must have been assured that the theatre company involved would not release and encourage the printing of a 'better' text to render the investment wasted. This economic consideration is a serious obstacle to the general model of early quartos as unauthorised printings of unauthorised texts. In the specific case of Q1 and Q2 *Hamlet*, Ling being the publisher of both represents compelling evidence that the relatively close timing (twelve to eighteen months) of Q2 was not intended to eclipse sales of the so-called bad quarto, but that most of the copies of the first printing of a play popular at least since 1598[13] must have been sold, and that the 1604 Q2 text might be a newly revised version.

In the past, selected printing and publishing evidence was used to support the hypothesis of Q1 as a derived text. Not only does the evidence not support the notion of Q1 as a bad quarto, it indicates that there was nothing unusual in the relationships between Roberts, Ling, Simmes and Shakespeare's company. And, as mentioned, the financial model of Elizabethan publishing argues strongly against the concept of bad quartos for any of Shakespeare's plays.

Turning to the texts themselves, certain elements unique to the text of Q1 have always been at odds with the notion that it derived from a pre-existing Q2. While it might be argued that the twenty-plus minor Q1-unique passages could have been made up by reporters to fill in for parts they couldn't remember, this argument is diminished by two factors. Some of the Q1-unique passages are neatly rhymed and metred (more like the work of a playwright), and there are two Q1 passages, which, when removed, render Hamlet a more isolated character in Q2. The Queen's meeting with Horatio in Q1 is likely a passage that was deleted, and she also explicitly understands that Claudius has murdered old King Hamlet (a fact she does not learn in Q2 until her tragic end in Act 5). Additionally, in the Q1 text she tells Hamlet, 'I vow by the majesty ... that I will conceal ... [your] stratagem'.[14] Similar phrasing '...by that majesty...' is found in Belleforest's (c. 1570) French translation,[15] which is another point of evidence for Q1 as an earlier text.

If the text of Q1 is a product of memory, it is either the memory of actor or audience reporters. If actor reporters were involved, Marcellus would have been primary among them, his lines being 93% concordant between Q1 and Q2 (the highest of any character). But the role of Marcellus was one of the nine most important adult roles, based on line count.[16] Therefore, the Marcellus actor was most probably among the twelve sharers and loyal long-term hired men that were available in Shakespeare's company in 1603,[17] not 'a bit part player who was subsequently discharged', as assumed in the traditional theory.[18] Additionally, the Q1 lines with the highest Q2 concordance are 'not Shakespeare's most memorable lines, and we should reject any theory that makes them the best-remembered lines of the play in performance'.[19] The Marcellus actor theory is even further diminished by the fact that the theorised actor reporter has 'failed to remember' some of his cues.[20] The Marcellus actor is onstage only early in the play, and the high Q1-Q2 concordance occurs early in the play, yet the Marcellus actor has been effectively eliminated as the source of the text of Q1, a paradox that will be resolved.

If the text of Q1 was created by audience reporters, rather than actor reporters, the variations in the reporting style and accuracy indicate that several reporters must have been involved.[21] In the audience reporter hypothesis, the high concordance of the Marcellus actor can be accounted for by the idea that he was simply the player most easily understood. Tiffany Stern makes the best possible case for audience note-takers, but in her conclusion she does not claim the case has been made, stating only that 'if Q1 *Hamlet* is a "noted" text ...'[22] it is more likely the product of audience note-takers than actors. Subsequent to the publication of Stern's analysis, the possibility of audience reporters was undercut by the recognition of a remarkably improbable drop in the concordance of the Q1 vs. Q2 lines of Hamlet and Horatio, early vs. late in the play. Hamlet and Horatio are the two characters with large enough numbers of lines, early vs. late, to provide a sample size large enough to be evaluated statistically.[23] Hamlet's Q1 vs. Q2 concordance drops from 87% to 56%, while Horatio's drops from 93% to 29%. With the Marcellus actor already ruled out as the possible source of the Q1 text, the only remaining alternative would seem to be Q1 as a pre-Q2 text. But, the high early Q1 vs. Q2 concordance is a characteristic of Q1 that must be accounted for. In the second section of this chapter, the vision of Q1 as a pre-Q2 text will come into better focus.

The enigmatic *Brudermord* text (BB) has recently taken a larger role in the analysis of the textual sequence-of-creation issue. Just as Q1 is shorter and less sophisticated than Q2, BB is even shorter and less sophisticated than Q1. Scholarship has generally believed BB to be an abridgement of Q1 and/or Q2, but it is possibly an earlier text, an idea encouraged by the fact that it contains an allusion[24] (early in Act 4 Scene 3) to a disastrous military expedition to Portugal in 1589, which cost the lives of eleven thousand men.[25] In Figure 7, the *Brudermord* text is shown as possibly originating around 1589, because topical allusions tend to enter texts when they are current, and this 1589 allusion was not removed from the 1710 manuscript source of the text. This suggests that the manuscript might have been copied from a very early version of the play. English players (including two of Shakespeare's subsequent partners) are also known to have been in Germany around 1590,[26] and a version of *Hamlet* was known to exist in England at this time.[27] English players are even thought to have played a pre-Q1 version of *Hamlet* in Germany, which the *Brudermord* text may well to be related to.[28]

The textual contribution of BB has always been limited by its being available only from a manuscript in German. However, a valuable finding has emerged from BB by applying an analytical approach utilised by George Ian Duthie in 1941. Duthie recognised that even though vocabulary and nuances of language are lost in translation, essential plot elements and details are not. Duthie con-

The Sequence of Creation and Implications for the 'Allowed Booke' 197

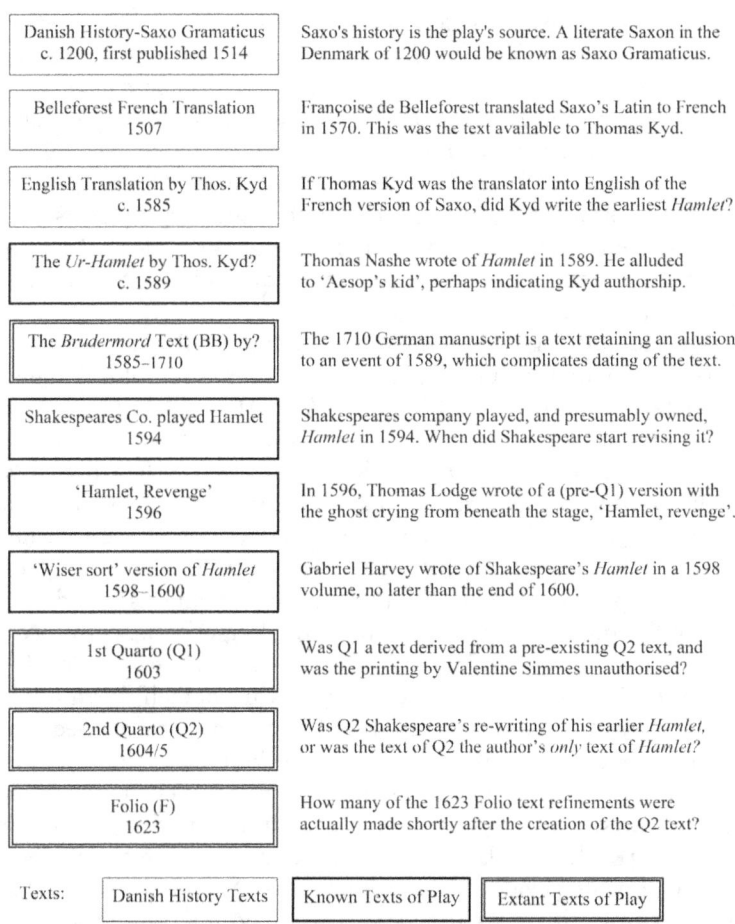

Figure 7. Hamlet from Saxo's Danish History to known texts of the play, through the extant texts. Figure created by the authors.

ducted a laborious search for BB plot elements and details found in Q1 but not in Q2, of which he found twenty-one. His search for BB 'correlates' found in Q2 but not in Q1 produced thirty-six. Duthie concluded that the proportion 21:36 indicated that BB was derived primarily from the memory of players of Q2, with a smaller proportion of contributions from other players working from their memory of Q1 (which Duthie presumed to be a touring text). However, if

BB was not a derivative text, but rather a common ancestor to both Q1 and Q2, scholarship would expect unique correlates to appear in Q1 and Q2 in a ratio close to 21:36, *because 21:36 is approximately the ratio of the total line count of Q1 vs. Q2*. Thus, the emerging value of Duthie's analysis is that BB is *either* derived from both Q1 or Q2 *or* that it *predates both*. Since Duthie's time, the idea of touring scripts has been discounted, and the idea that two groups of players with two different texts would combine their memorial reconstruction efforts adds a burden of complexity to the derivative-text hypothesis that cannot be sustained.

After identifying and cataloguing the unique BB-Q1 and BB-Q2 correlates, Duthie acknowledged that there were a few plot elements and details in BB not to be found in either Q1 or Q2, but he did not seek to identify the total population of them in the same manner as his search for Q1 and Q2 correlates. There are, in fact, over fifty, which we revealed by charting parallel columns of plot elements of BB vs. Q1 vs. Q2.[29] If the text of BB was an abridgement created by people familiar with both Q1 and Q2 texts, BB would not have somehow picked up more than fifty unique elements and details during the process of extraction from the longer texts. No process of abridgement converts the uncertain circumstances of Ophelia's drowning into a blatant suicide by throwing herself down a hill, and no process of abridgement introduces a character named Jens fretting about his taxes and seeking the help of a friend named Phantasmo.[30] These and other details are more likely to have been BB elements that were altered or deleted in the process of revision towards Q1. The very large number of details unique to BB represents compelling evidence that BB predates Q1 and Q2, rather than deriving from them. As it becomes accepted that the *Brudermord* text is most probably related to a very early text of *Hamlet*, that early text will become recognised as the source of the name of the King's counsellor (*Corambus* in BB, *Corambis* in Q1), additional evidence for the theory of Q1 as a pre-Q2 text.

Returning to Q1 vs. Q2/F, editor George R. Hibbard, perhaps noticing the large number of Q2-unique passages that do not appear in Q1, stated that 'the evidence is overwhelmingly in favor of the view that [Q1] stems from the text behind F'.[31] Among the evidence for this are cases where a word in a Folio line appears in a corresponding line in Q1, but not in Q2. Of course, occasional textual omissions, word alterations and other contaminants are known to have been introduced by compositors, and no substantial pattern suggests that Q1 might derive from the Folio text. Hibbard seems to have recognised this when he subsequently wrote, 'Yet since writing those words I have come to doubt their accuracy'.[32] Retaining the widely held belief that Q1 was nonetheless a reported text of some kind, Hibbard concluded that Q1's treatment of certain passages must be 'intermediate between Q2's and F's'.[33] He further acknowledged that 'it has to be admitted that the vagaries of the reporter's memory often defy the laws of probability'.[34] This was not intended to be taken literally, but in 2008 the senior author of this article was startled to note that several passages unique to Q2 (totalling 209 lines), and others unique to F (totalling fifty lines), were *all* missing from the text of Q1. If Q1 was indeed a reported text based on either Q2 or F, all 209 or fifty unique lines were 'missed'. The sample sizes are large enough to be statistically significant, and the resulting finding is that Q1 cannot be demonstrated to have derived from either Q2 or the Folio text.[35] This statistical finding was introduced in the Q1 *Hamlet* Seminar at the Shakespeare Association of America meeting in Boston in 2012. A compact overview of the finding was published in 2016 together with the resolution of a challenge raised in the 2012 seminar. That overview, the 2012 challenge and the resolution of the challenge are paraphrased in the following few paragraphs.[36]

For simplicity, this outline is focused only on Q1 vs. Q2 and evaluates the 209 lines in the ten Q2 passages unique to Q2 vs. the Folio text. The remoteness of the probability that none of the 209 Q2 lines would be remembered (if Q1 is a reported text) can be likened to the probabilities involved in a more familiar situation with an *expected value*. If you toss a coin two hundred times, the *expected value* of heads will be one hundred, and the *standard deviation* will be 10.0. It is *statistically certain* that you would not get zero heads in two hundred tosses. The zero lines 'remembered' in the Q1 *Hamlet* case is similar. The method and rationale are as follows:

- 1,631 Q1 lines are identical or identifiably concordant to lines in Q2.
- 1,631 lines represents 41.8% of the 3,900 lines in Q2.
- Therefore, if Q1 is a reported text, it will contain approximately 41.8% of any sample of Q2 lines that have been identified by a standard independent of Q1.
- There are ten passages (of three or more lines) unique to Q2 vs. F, totalling 209 lines.

- Thus, the 209 lines are identified by a standard irrespective of the existence of Q1.
- The 'expected value' of the 209 lines to appear in Q1 is 41.8% of 209, or eighty-seven lines.
- The 'standard deviation' (σ) is 9.3. Plus or minus three σ gives a range of 59–115.
- It is 99% probable that 59–115 lines would be remembered if Q1 is a reported text.
- The *six sigma*[37] range of 31–143 lines remembered is overwhelmingly probable.
- Yet, *none* of the independently identified 209 Q2 lines have been remembered.
- It is a statistical certainty that Q1 is not derived from Q2 *as printed*.
- A similar calculation for the category of lines unique to F vs. Q2 also effectively rules out the Folio text as printed as a possible source for the text of Q1.

Two additional theoretical post-Q2 texts remain, which must be considered before Q1 as a pre-Q2 text stands as the only practical alternative. In the 2012 Q1 *Hamlet* seminar, when the statistical finding was presented, it was suggested that perhaps 'thoughtful cuts' had been made to the text of Q2 before Q1 was reported by some process. Of course, if the Q2 lines were cut randomly for the purpose of reducing Q2 to an acting-length text, the unlikelihood that the random cutting would happen to *include* 100% of the lines in the ten passages would be statistically the same as the improbability that memory would just happen to *miss* 100% of the lines. Thus, it is a *statistical certainty* that Q1 was not derived from Q2, unless there is some *identifiable rationale* for cutting the 209 Q2 lines involved, in which case the statistical analysis would not apply at all.

Not only does there seem to be no identifiable rationale for producing an intermediate Q2-F text without the 209 Q2-unique lines, but there is evidence against the idea. In 1988, Paul Werstine examined all Q2 cuts and Folio additions,[38] and in his detailed analysis, he identified two such passages. Werstine's purpose was to help establish that Shakespeare did indeed revise his texts, but the same two pairs of passages help illustrate the improbability of an intermediate text. In the first of the unique Q2 passages, 'How all occasions do inform against me', Hamlet concludes that honour demands revenge on King Claudius ('When honour's at the stake'[39]). In the Folio text, *honour* has been replaced by *avoiding damnation* ('... is't not perfect conscience, to quit him with this arm? And is't not to be damn'd to let this Canker of our nature come to further evill'⁴⁰). The Folio passage seems to be a replacement for the Q2 passage. This pair of Q2-Folio passages represents an item of evidence against the idea that an intermediate text existed for Q1 to derive from, for such a text would have neither Hamlet's Q2 nor Folio motive for revenge.

The other Q2-unique passage that is even more certain to have been replaced by a related Folio passage occurs in Q2 at 5.2.188. A lord enters and advises Hamlet that the Queen desires he make peace with Laertes, to which Hamlet replies, 'She well instructs me'.⁴¹ Earlier, Hamlet and Laertes were so incensed they had to be physically separated. Laertes has returned from France with revenge on his mind, and without some indication that their altercation would not continue, the audience might expect it to. In the Folio text, Shakespeare accomplishes this at an earlier point (5.2.80) when Hamlet and Horatio are together. Hamlet simply mentions that 'to Laertes I forgot myself ... I'll court his favors'.⁴² It is as if Shakespeare recognised the need at 5.2.188 as he drafted Q2, and subsequently realised there was a more theatrically economical way to solve the problem earlier in the text.

Scholarship is in general agreement that the text of Q2 is closer to an authorial draft,⁴³ while the Folio text has more marks of performance. Although Werstine's 1988 Q2 vs. F analysis was not undertaken with performance in mind, the second of the above pairs of deletions and additions has implications for staging efficiency, and it adds to the improbability of an intermediate Q2-Folio text. If Q2 is indeed close to the author's draft, one can imagine Shakespeare reaching this point in the text (5.2.188) and recognising the need to divert the audience from expecting violence between Hamlet and Laertes as the time of the fencing match approaches. The unnamed lord advises Hamlet that the Queen desires he make peace with Laertes; Hamlet acknowledges, and the plot goes forward with the audience focusing on the King's intrigue against Hamlet. Now imagine an early review of that Q2 draft, by the author or by the author with his fellow players. They would have noticed the opportunity to accomplish the same objective more efficiently 108 lines earlier (5.2.80). This leads to the idea that much of the Q2-F revision might have been made immediately upon review of the draft of Q2, and that much of Q2, as printed, *may never have been played*. This possibility has not been pursued for at least three reasons: no extant documents support the idea, the replacement of Q2's profane phrasing probably took place in 1606, and the passage referring to Denmark as a prison probably came in after 1619, following the death of Queen Anne (she being the former Anne of Denmark).

With the possibility that many Q2 deletions and many Folio-unique passages may have been created immediately following the drafting of Q2, another passage deleted from Q2 (with no Folio replacement) can be seen in a new light. Hamlet, anticipating his trip to England, states that he will trust his old school companions 'like adders fanged'.[44] Thus, in the Folio text the danger to Hamlet and the tension of the narrative is sharper without Hamlet's overt Q2 suspicion. It is speculation that this Q2 passage may never have been played, and that many other Folio revisions might have been made immediately upon the drafting of Q2, but the possibility adds to the improbability of an intermediate Q2-Folio text for Q1 to derive from. Of course, a post-Folio text, missing all of the Q2-unique and the Folio-unique passages, is equally unlikely to have existed. Among other things, such a text would have neither the Q2 nor the Folio text's motivation for Hamlet's revenge. And, as mentioned earlier, as it becomes accepted that the *Brudermord* text is most probably related to a very early text of *Hamlet*, the name of the King's counsellor (Corambis) in Q1 is more easily accounted for as Q1 becomes accepted as a pre-Q2 text.

Adding to the probability of Q1 as a pre-Q2 text is the likelihood of the Q2 version of *Hamlet* being created in 1604. For more than a century, *Hamlet* (in its Q2/F version), *Othello*, *King Lear* and *Macbeth* have been regarded as Shakespeare's four greatest tragedies.[45] The latter three are agreed to have been written between 1604 and 1606, and as early as 1915, E.C. Black placed the creation of (Q2/F) *Hamlet* 'as near as possible to 1604',[46] without regard to the traditional theory that Shakespeare 'had no call to rework'[47] his plays and that Q1 was a derivative text.

In summary, the statistical findings have eliminated Q2 and the Folio text as possible sources for Q1. Likewise, an intermediate Q2-F text is very improbable, as is a post-Folio text. Turning from the possible *sources* to the possible *processes* of creation of the Q1 text, all narratives involving Q1 as a reported text require reporters. Yet the Marcellus actor and audience reporters seem to have both been ruled out. Therefore, although there is no independent evidence for it, the idea that the text of Q1 predates Q2 is the only remaining possibility. Now, recognising the high probability that Q1 predates

Q2/F, there is a characteristic of the Q1 text, a statistical pattern, that must be accounted for in any theory of Q1. This is the combination of the high Q1 vs. Q2 concordance of the Marcellus lines, which appear only early in the Q1 text, and the drop-off in the similarly high concordance of the lines of Hamlet and Horatio later in the text.

The nature of the text of Q1 and its relationship to the allowed book

Imagine a point early in the existence of the Q1 text, immediately at the time of the censor's review and prior to accommodating any request for a scribal copy. At this point, only two manuscript texts were likely to have existed: the author's draft, and a 'fair copy', the censor-approved 'allowed book' from which the players' lines would have been copied. Does the pattern of early vs. late concordance suggest that Q1 was set from a draft? Something happened to the early portion of the text of Q1 that caused it to have a higher correlation to Q2, higher than could have occurred by chance. Something *caused* it. With the acceptance that Q1 does not derive from Q2, the simplest explanation is that upon drafting Q1 the author went back to the beginning and cleaned up the early portion of his text, resulting in a text with only the early portion containing his second thoughts, thoughts closer to Q2. This simple narrative accounts for the high concordance of Marcellus (onstage only early) and Hamlet's and Horatio's later drop in concordance.

In mid 1603, if no additional copies had yet been made, the text that served as the printer's copy would have been either the author's draft or the allowed book. One can assume Shakespeare's company would not let the valued censor-signed copy out of their possession, so the author's draft (or a copy very close to it) most probably served as the printer's copy. There are at least two points of additional evidence that the type for Q1 was set from a difficult-to-decipher manuscript (the draft described above or something closely related to it).

In 1987, G.R. Hibbard called attention to seventeen lines spoken by Horatio to Hamlet in a Q1 passage beginning at a point corresponding to 1.2.199 and appearing on signatures B4^v and C1^r.[48] Hibbard pointed out that four of the lines were fully stopped in cases where context demanded commas. Compositors often introduced corruptions in punctuation as well as word choice, and Hibbard blamed the compositor and proofreader for their carelessness. But four corruptions in seventeen lines is a high number,[49] and these were all punctuation corruptions at the ends of lines, perhaps evidence that the compositor was struggling to set the type a word at a time from an illegible manuscript, prior to deciphering the following line in each case. In the process of letterpress printing, the compositor selected individual bits of type from the appropriate *type case*. Each letter or symbol was placed in a groove in the *composing stick*. As each line of type was completed, it was placed with other lines of type, in an iron frame (or *chase*) corresponding to a press sheet, and a new line of type was composed. Hence, a single line of type might be thought of as a 'unit of process'. Working with a difficult-to-read manuscript, the compositor might have been forced to judge whether or not each line should be fully stopped without the usual benefit of being able to read the next line. Corruptions in punctuation were among those introduced by compositors, but as mentioned above, four corruptions in seventeen lines is a high number, most probably driven by some extenuating factor. Though the pattern of full stops is not as decisive as evidence for Q1 as a draft, it is consistent with the idea, and it does *not* serve as evidence for Q1 as a reported text.

The case of an unusual word substitution might provide additional evidence of the roughness of the manuscript. Hibbard called attention to a line unique to the text of Q1, just over one hundred lines into Act 5, Scene 1 where Hamlet speaks to the gravedigger. Hamlet speaks of the skeletal remains he supposes to be of a lawyer, and speaking of vouchers and other documents, he asks, '... [does] the honor lie there?'[50] in a context that demands *owner*. But, in a manuscript, an *o* and an *h* cannot be misread in such a way that *owner* can be set as *honor*. Such an error occurs in oral transmission, as Hibbard noted, but Hibbard did not recognise *two* possible points in the oral transmission, stating, 'no blame attaches to [the compositor] for the metamorphosis of *owner* to *honor* ... the word *honor* must have appeared in the manuscript [the compositor] was working from; and it got there because whoever wrote that manuscript misheard the word *owner*'. But Hibbard did not take into account that a reporter in the theatre would have *heard the word* owner *in context as the line was spoken*. Thus, the oral corruption probably occurred in the printing house between a reader (necessitated by a rough manuscript) and a compositor hearing only one word at a time from the most difficult lines. The word *owner* probably appeared in the manuscript and was not changed until the instant it was misheard by the compositor and set in type.[51] It is worth noting that as this older evidence for Q1 as a reported text has become more fully illuminated, it actually tends to support Q1 as an earlier text.

During the 1980s, it became accepted that the variant texts of *King Lear* might represent differing versions of the play, each with some degree of authorial involvement. This encouraged renewed interest in Q1 *Hamlet* and other early variant quartos. To some extent, the interest in these texts 'depended on a recognition of their theatrical potentialities'.[52] Staging experiences with Q1 *Hamlet* during this decade revealed a more straightforward narrative, a fast-paced traditional tragedy that did not suffer for want of Q2's more sophisticated 'interiorisation of action within the tragic subject'.[53] This aspect of *Hamlet*, heretofore considered *missing* from the reported text of Q1, might have simply been *added* when the Q2 version was created.

Accepting that the text of Q1 might have been set from a partially refined 1603 draft, what might be speculated about the textual details of Q1 as played, and what are the implications for editing or staging Q1? We first considered four significant plot element variants: the location of the *To be* soliloquy and the Nunnery scene, the Queen's knowledge and acceptance of the fact that Claudius murdered old King Hamlet, the Queen's vow to conceal Hamlet's plan, and the Queen's meeting with Horatio following Hamlet's return to Denmark. Having no reason to suppose that any of these Q1 elements were altered in the allowed book or on the stage in 1603, we do not plan to alter them in our Q1 editing and script-planning activities.

The greater challenge to editors and script planners will be found in the identifiably concordant (but variant) lines. The lines of Q1 can be divided into three categories as follows:

- 1,054 lines (49% of the text) are *identical* in Q1 vs. Q2 lines, or no more variant than a compositor might cause by very minor alterations.
- 522 lines (24% of the text) are *unique* to Q1. Most are in passages shown in Figure 8.
- 577 lines (27% of the text) are *identifiably concordant*, but altered more than might be caused by the personal choices or careless work of a compositor.

The 1,054 lines that are identical (or nearly so) present few issues to editors or script planners. Regarding the second category, the decision to retain Q1-unique passages is a decision to retain most of the 522 Q1-unique lines. The remaining 577 concordant (but altered) lines will be of the greatest interest to stage directors and perhaps to editors of Q1. As we prepare to develop a Q1 text with a group of theatre students, we face a choice between two assumptions concerning these 577 lines, both influenced by the possibility that Q1 as printed was set from a manuscript closer to the author's draft than the allowed book.

# of Lines	Degrees of Q1 vs. Q2 Concordance in Lines of Q1	% of Q1 Text
522	Lines unique to Q1. Most are in the passages below.	24%
577	Lines recognisably concordant, but seemingly paraphrased	27%
1054	Q1 lines identical or nearly identical to lines in Q2.	49%
2221	Total lines of dialogue in text of Q1	100%

Locations	Descriptions of Passages Unique to the Text of Q1
1.2.51	Laertes' request to Claudius with focus on funeral not marriage
1.2.65	Claudius to Hamlet with Queen's participation minimized in Q1
1.3.140	Corambis' Q1 warning to Ophelia has several unique lines
2.1.73	Ophelia's description of Hamlet is in language unique to Q1
2.2.1	King to Rosencrantz & Guildenstern: Cryptic and unique to Q1
2.2.140	Claudius to Corambis different in Q1, no Queen comment
2.2.190	Unique Q1 location of *To be* soliloquy & Nunnery scene
2.2.230	R&G with none of Q2/F banter or F-unique 'Denmark's a prison'
2.2.375	Hamlet's Q1-unique comment to R&G about players
3.1.1	King, Queen, R&G: Lengthy Q1-unique discussion of Hamlet
3.2.45	Hamlet's Q1 lecture to players might be a dig at Will Kemp
3.2.155	Player Duke and Dutchess: Exchange unique to Q1
3.3.35	King at prayer, passage unique to Q1, including final couplet
3.4.63	Hamlet to Queen, 'face like a vulcan' passage
3.4.151	Queen understands Claudius has killed old King Hamlet
3.4.211	Queen swears to support Hamlet ('vow by … majesty')
4.1.7	Queen describes Hamlet's rant to King in Q1-unique detail
4.1.38	King to Queen: 'Your son … to England'
4.3.67	King's rhymed and metered couplet on Hamlet's intended death
4.5.1	King and Queen discuss Hamlet and popularity of Laertes
4.5.83	Another rhymed and metered couplet unique to Q1
4.6.1	Queen's Q1-unique meeting with Horatio after Hamlet's return
4.7.63	King's plan for Laertes and Hamlet
4.7.145	King's plan finalised in language unique to Q1
5.1.215	Priest's blunt Q1 statement about Ophelia's burial
	King: 'This day shall Hamlet drink his last'.

Figure 8. The nature of the text of Q1 vs. Q2. Degrees of Q1 vs. Q2 concordance and passages unique to the text of Q1. Figure created by the authors.

The assumptions are opposed in their handling of the 577 lines in question. The first is that upon completion of the 1603 draft (Q1 as printed), including the author's second thoughts in the early portion, this text was converted (without further refinement) to fair copy for the censor, perhaps by a scribe. According to this assumption, the allowed book would be essentially the same as the printed Q1. The alternative is that the author himself, perhaps in the process of creating the fair copy, refined the latter part of the Q1 text with his second thoughts as he had with the earlier part. Which narrative is the better assumption is beyond knowing.

Some of our group of theatre students plan to pursue the conservative approach to editing the text of Q1. Having no basis on which to identify which lines might have been revised closer to their Q2 levels, only when they find a Q1 line that is obviously corrupted will they consider the Q2 alternative.

However, other members of the group cite the high Q1-Q2 correlation early in the play as a guide to the handling of many identifiably concordant lines in the latter part of Q1. Assuming that many of these lines might have been heard from the stage in their Q2 form in 1603, the student editors plan to selectively use the Q2 version of many of these 577 lines. This assumption will allow them to develop a Q1 narrative and performance script less encumbered with the unfamiliar and seemingly awkward Q1 versions of lines common to Q1 and Q2.

The 577 Q1 lines that are identifiably concordant yet altered are an enigma that may yield insights and lead to new findings as these lines are compared, line by line and word by word, with their Q2 counterparts. As Q1 becomes more recognised as a pre-Q2 text, these 577 lines may provide scholarship with a significant opportunity to observe Shakespeare at work revising. This will be an aspect of our Q1 *Hamlet* project going forward.

Charles Adams Kelly is Visiting Scholar at the University of Michigan. In 1966, he did pioneering work in digital text graphic research tools at Michigan State University, where he received his MBA, work that has been recognised with four process patents. He founded Howland Research of Ann Arbor in 1995 to further develop this work, and in 2005 shifted his focus to the design of text-graphic research tools for Shakespeare's variant-text plays. He has developed several findings pertaining to Q1 *Hamlet*, and his Q1 *Richard III* project is nearing completion.

Dayna Leigh Plehn-Peavyhouse is a graduate of the University of Michigan. She has been a researcher, editor and designer for Howland Research for over five years, where she develops graphic tools for Shakespeare's variant-text plays. She was responsible for the parallel *text plot element grid* which led to findings pertaining to the *Brudermord* text, and she was co-editor and co-designer of *The Brief Reign and Death of King Claudius, a Play within the Text of Shakespeare's HAMLET*, which won the Independent Publishers "Outstanding Book of the Year" award in 2014.

Notes

'Q1' refers to the 'first quarto' or 'first edition' of *Hamlet*, printed in 1603.
1. James Orchard Halliwell-Phillipps, *Outlines of the Life of Shakespeare*, 5th ed. (London: Longmans, Green & Co., 1885), 170.
2. Alfred W. Pollard, *Shakespeare's Folio and Quartos; a Study in the Bibliography of Shakespeare's Plays 1594–1685* (London: Methuen & Company, 1909), 74.
3. Paul Werstine, 'Margins to the Centre: REED and Shakespeare', in *REED in Review: Essays in Celebration of the First Twenty-Five Years*, ed. Audrey Douglas and Sally-Beth MacLean (Toronto: University of Toronto Press, 2006), 112.
4. Paul Werstine, 'A Century of "Bad" Shakespeare Quartos', *Shakespeare Quarterly* 50, no. 3 (1999), 322. It is significant to note the term *hypothesis* vs. *theory*.
5. Edward Arber, *A Transcript of the Registers of the Company of Stationers of London: 1554–1640 A.D.*, Vol. 3 (London: Privately Printed, 1876), 84b.
6. Three of the seven extant copies are dated 1604, while four are dated 1605.
7. Pollard, *Shakespeare's Folio and Quartos*, 74.
8. R.B. McKerrow, gen. ed., *A Dictionary of Printers and Booksellers in England, Scotland and Ireland, and of Foreign Printers of English Books 1557–1640* (London: Blades, East & Blades, 1910; Printed for the Bibliographical Society), 245.
9. Arber, *A Transcript of the Registers*, 161.
10. Terri Bourus, *Young Shakespeare's Young Hamlet: Print, Piracy, and Performance* (New York: Palgrave MacMillan, 2014), 25.

11. David Scott Kastan, *Shakespeare and the Book* (Cambridge: Cambridge University Press, 2001), 29–30.
12. Peter W.M. Blayney, 'The Publication of Play Books', in *A New History of Early English Drama*, ed. John D. Cox and David Scott Kastan (New York: Columbia University Press, 1997), 408–409.
13. Thomas Nashe, 'To the Gentlemen Students of both Universities', in Robert Greene, *Menaphon* (London: T[homas] O[rwin] for Sampson Clarke, 1589), sig. [A4^r].
14. William Shakespeare, *The Tragicall Historie of Hamlet Prince of Denmarke* (London: [Valentine Simmes] for N[icholas] L[ing] and John Trundell, 1603), sigs. G3^r, G3^v.
15. François de Belleforest, 'The Hystorie of Hamlet', in *Shakespeare's Hamlet-quellen*, ed. Robert Gericke (Leipzig: J.A. Barth, Translation [1570] [1608] 1881), 60–61.
16. T.J. King, *Casting Shakespeare's Plays: London Actors and Their Roles 1590–1642* (Cambridge: Cambridge University Press, 1992), 206–209.
17. Andrew Gurr, *The Shakespeare Company 1594–1642* (Cambridge: Cambridge University Press, 2004), 217–246.
18. G.I. Hibbard, ed., *The Oxford Shakespeare: Hamlet* (Oxford: Oxford University Press, [1987] 1998), 77.
19. Bourus, *Young Shakespeare's Young Hamlet*, 61.
20. Paul Menzer, *The 'Hamlets': Cues, Qs, and Remembered Texts* (Newark: University of Delaware Press, 2008).
21. Tiffany Stern, 'Sermons, Plays and Note-Takers: Hamlet Q1 as a "Noted" Text', in *Shakespeare Survey 66*, ed. Peter Holland (Cambridge: Cambridge University Press, 2013), 1–23.
22. Ibid., 23.
23. Charles Adams Kelly and Dayna Leigh Plehn, *The Evidence Matrix for the 1st Quarto of Shakespeare's Hamlet*, 2nd ed. (Ann Arbor: Triple Anvil Press, 2016), 22–23.
24. When the King advises Hamlet that he will be sent away (to England), Hamlet replies: 'Ay ay, King, send me off to Portugal, that I may never come back again'.
25. R.G. Latham, *Two Dissertations on the Hamlet of Saxo Grammaticus and of Shakespeare* (Edinburgh: Williams and Norgate, 1872), 102.
26. Albert Cohn, *Shakespeare in Germany in the Sixteenth and Seventeenth Centuries: An Account of English Actors in Germany and the Netherlands and of the Plays Performed by Them during the Same Period* (New York: Haskell House Publishers Ltd. Reprint, [1865] 1971), xxv–xxvii.
27. Nashe, 'To the Gentlemen Students', sig. [A4^r].
28. Cohn, *Shakespeare in Germany*, cxx.
29. Kelly and Plehn, *The Evidence Matrix*, 42–44.
30. Cohn, *Shakespeare in Germany*, 278.
31. Hibbard, *The Oxford Shakespeare*, 88.
32. G.R. Hibbard, 'The Chronology of the Three Substantive Texts of Shakespeare's Hamlet', in *The Hamlet First Published*, ed. Thomas Clayton (Newark: University of Delaware Press, 1992), 79.
33. Ibid., 79–80.
34. Ibid., 84.
35. Charles Adams Kelly, *The Evidence Matrix* (Ann Arbor: The Triple Anvil Press, 2008), 19.

36. Kelly and Plehn, *The Evidence Matrix*, Appendix E.
37. 'Six sigma' is a term recognised by statisticians to indicate three standard deviations in either direction from an average or an expected value. It is a statistical certainty that a result outside of the six sigma range will not occur by chance.
38. Paul Werstine, 'The Textual Mystery of Hamlet', *Shakespeare Quarterly* 39, no. 1 (1988), 1–26.
39. Shakespeare, *The Tragicall Historie of Hamlet* (London: J[ames] R[oberts] for N[icholas] L[ing], 1604/1605), sigs. K3^r, K3^v.
40. Shakespeare, *Comedies, Histories, & Tragedies*, (London: Isac Jaggard and Ed[ward] Blount, 1623), sig. pp6^r.
41. Shakespeare, *The Tragicall Historie of Hamlet* (1604/1605), sig. N3^v.
42. Shakespeare, *Comedies, Histories, & Tragedies*, sig. pp6^r.
43. The extra line in a Q2 couplet at 3.2.167 is perhaps the most obvious indication of a draft.
44. Shakespeare, *The Tragicall Historie of Hamlet* (1604/1605), sig. I4^v.
45. A.C. Bradley, *Shakespeare's Tragedies* (New York: MacMillan & Company, 1904), 89.
46. E.C. Black, ed., *The New Hudson Shakespeare: The Tragedy of Hamlet – Introduction and Notes by Henry N. Hudson* (Boston, MA: Ginn & Co., 1915), xxvi.
47. Harold Jenkins, ed., *The Arden Shakespeare, Second Series, Hamlet* (London: Methuen & Company, 1982), 5.
48. Hibbard, *The Oxford Shakespeare*, 70–71.
49. Alan E. Craven, 'The Reliability of Simmes's Compositor A', in *Studies in Bibliography*, Vol. 32, ed. Fredson Bowers (Charlottesville: University of Virginia Press, 1979), 192.
50. Shakespeare, *The Tragicall Historie of Hamlet Prince of Denmarke* (1603), sig. H4^v.
51. Kelly, *The Evidence Matrix*, 24.
52. Graham Holderness and Bryan Loughrey, eds, *The Tragicall Historie of Hamlet Prince of Denmarke* (Boston, MA: Barnes & Noble Books, 1992), 16.
53. Ibid., 24.

Chapter 12
What Doesn't Happen in *Hamlet*

Rory Loughnane

Brevity, 'the soul of wit', is not a feature one regularly associates with *Hamlet*, Shakespeare's longest play (7.90). The protagonist's prolixity is one of his defining characteristics; his seemingly ceaseless series of agonised monologues of self-reproach might be his most memorable stage quality. *Hamlet*, the longer version that most know, provides for its characters a surplus of words and ideas, reasons and motivations. A performance of either the complete second quarto (Q2) or Folio (F) text, or the traditional editorial conflation that combines them both, takes four hours or more. As a piece of theatre, it is long and demanding, resistant to interpretative efforts. With *Hamlet*, Shakespeare offers abundance; his play is consciously expressive and excessive.

Some attendant quandaries produced by such a glut of words and information are familiar to all who encounter the play. As T.S. Eliot observed, *Hamlet*'s 'problems' are many.[1] Why does the protagonist procrastinate? What is the provenance of the Ghost? Is Gertrude an adulteress before the murder? Does Ophelia commit suicide?

Notes for this section begin on page 230.

Realising that the play provides no *one* answer for each of these questions is the first step towards moving past them; understanding that its over-supply of facts, explanations, information is part of the play's *modus operandi* allows us to engage more meaningfully as critics. Ponderousness, verbosity, attention to the act of interpretation and to the production of meaning, are each central to *Hamlet*.

I begin with these points to note that some of the hermeneutical difficulties with *Hamlet* are related to its length. The play provides considerable space for competing interpretations to emerge. Yet an earlier-printed version of the play exists, the much-maligned 1603 first quarto of *Hamlet* (Q1), that is more incisive and energetic, a 'picture in little', perhaps (7.283). At a punchy 15,983 words, it is shorter than any of the texts included in the 1623 first folio collection of Shakespeare's *Comedies, Histories, & Tragedies* and some 44% shorter than the Q2 *Hamlet* text. *Hamlet* at speed – 'most wicked speed', indeed – it follows almost exactly the structure of the longer Q2 and F texts (2.156). It includes one additional scene, an exchange between the Queen and Horatio, that does not appear in the longer versions; what it does not include, broadly considered, are the long chunks of meditative material familiar to readers of Q2 and F. Poetically, the longer versions of *Hamlet* are undeniably the finer works. Few teachers of Shakespeare would send their students to the Q1 version first. But, theatrically, Q1 can be a highly effective work. It tells a story succinctly, if bluntly, without committing an audience to the sort of slow-burn meditation about life, love, familial duty, revenge and mortality for which the longer play is renowned. Q1 offers a short, action-packed tale, wherein almost everything that *happens* pushes along the revenge narrative towards its bloody conclusion.

In John Dover Wilson's landmark study of the play, *What Happens in Hamlet* (1935) – by which he means a conflated text – he writes at length about the sort of interpretative difficulties raised by the play. Chapter titles include 'Ghost or Devil?' and there are appendices on 'The adultery of Gertrude' and 'The funeral of Ophelia'.[2] Central to his discussion, and of course central to all three versions of *Hamlet*, is the play-within-the-play.[3] Wilson's fifth chapter, 'The Multiple Mouse-trap', offers an invigorating account of the staging difficulties of this scene. Within this chapter, and of course within all three versions of *Hamlet*, is the dumb show that precedes the play-within-the-play. Wilson's subtitle, channelling Eliot and responding to the critical work of W.W. Greg, reads 'The problem of the dumb-show'.[4] The familiar 'problem', first identified by Greg, is whether Claudius sees the dumb show, and, if so, why might he not react? Wilson presents a list of explanations, some of which we will consider later.

Dumb shows, as a theatrical device, are a kind of compressed action. Through mime-like action, they communicate an extended narrative in a compact stylised way, speedily supplying significant information but often in a manner that lacks nuance and detail. Brevity need not necessarily be uninformative. But at some point, economy of statement becomes an enemy to understanding. To engage with an idea, a concept, we must be supplied adequately with the tools required for its explication. If we fail to understand, we are more prone to misinterpretation; we, as interpreters, impose our own meaning on what we see, read or hear to make sense of what it is that we are engaging with. With Peter Quince and company's 'tedious brief scene', Shakespeare shows himself aware that somewhere along the spectrum from 'brief' to 'tedious' there must be an optimal length (7.56).[5]

The dumb show in *Hamlet*, by which at first I mean all three versions of the play, is an exercise in economy of statement, and, in preceding *The Mousetrap*, a theatrical exemplar of interpretative difficulty. We, as an actual or imagined audience, watch as those on the stage fail to understand the meaning of the dumb show. Its mysteries, though questioned, are never explicated by Hamlet or another for the onstage audience. This is the exact opposite of what happens next, where the play performance of *The Mousetrap* is supplemented by Hamlet's frequent interruptions as an interpreter (he is 'as good as a chorus', according to Ophelia [9.219]), a role he actively refuses for the dumb show. During the play performance, Hamlet provides a wealth of detailed additional information that would be unattainable from the performance itself: the setting, character names, relationships, motivations and so on. Comparatively, the dumb show's brevity and non-verbal form produces an information deficit for audiences both on and off the stage; the actors' movements gesture towards a detailed narrative not yet communicated.

Analysis of dumb shows fell out of vogue until recently. Perhaps never the most arresting of topics, the dumb show in *Hamlet* – meaning invariably Q2's or a Q2/F amalgam in a conflated text – has always received a disproportionate amount of critical attention.[6] Yet dumb shows were abundant in the period and the phrase evidently held significant cultural resonance at the time.[7] In what follows, we will first consider this wider usage of 'dumb show', before discussing how the dumb show in *Hamlet* fits within the dramatic tradition. Our analysis will then focus on variant readings between the three extant early versions of *Hamlet*, before considering more broadly the dumb show's importance to our interpretation of the play(s).

Dumb show as metaphor

In a telling comparison with emblems, another abstract representation of compressed meaning, Rosemary Freeman observes that both emblems and dumb shows are 'somewhat removed from reality and that [in both] the visible scene is only a vehicle for some deeper meaning'.[8] Emblems are typically comprised of three parts: a title (*inscriptio*), image (*pictura*) and a written explanation (*subscriptio*). Where dumb shows separate the text (silently prescribing the mimed performance) from the image (performed on stage), with emblems the reader must concurrently connect the image to the text provided. The formalised action of interpreting the dumb show, often found in early modern drama though missing from *Hamlet*, offers a similar function to the *subscriptio* of the emblem. Freeman proposes that 'the *dumb show* of the stage is in both form and function only a more elaborate version of the pictures in an emblem book'.[9] We might do more to tease out the connections between emblems and dumb shows in terms of supply and deficit of meaning; both are prone to be misinterpreted or too narrowly interpreted.

Early modern emblematists were certainly aware of this danger. George Withers describes as follows an emblematic image of a snake wrapped around an upright sword at the beginning of the *subscriptio*:

> A *Sword unsheathed*, and a *strangling-Snake*,
> Is figur'd here; which, in *dumbe-shewes*, doe preach,
> Of what the *Malefactor* should beware;
> And, they doe *threaten too*, as well as *Teach*.[10]

The emblematic form is an exercise in prudence for those whose hearts are 'inclin'd / to any kind of *Death-deserving-crime*' but it is both didactic and an image of 'death' to keep them 'in awe'.[11] In other words, multiple meanings converge between image and text and, invoking the dumb shows of the theatres, Withers warns against a singular interpretation. Francis Quarles uses the conceit of the structure of a play to describe the 'life and death of man', and, rather miserably, observes that our first breath on this earth is but a dumb show, a foreshadowing but not a full realisation, of the griefs to come; our new born cries are but the 'prologue' to the pitiful play of our lives.[12]

Early modern authors working outside the emblem tradition often use dumb shows as a metaphor in similar ways. In his plague pamphlet, *The Wonderful Year* (1603), Thomas Dekker observes that upon the death of Elizabeth I the country was in great mourning and the 'English Nation' had never seen so much black clothing as worn on the day of her funeral. But, Dekker notes, in a metaphor drawn from the theatre, the funeral was 'but the dumb shew' for 'the Tragicall Act hath bin playing euer since'.[13] Similarly, in *News from Hell* (1606), Dekker describes the pitiful actions of Monsieur Money-monger on the banks of the river Styx, as wordless and not knowing what to say, like a player who has forgotten his lines, turning away from hope and towards evil.

> In such a strange language was this *vltimum vale* sent forth, that Mounsieur Mony-monger stood onely staring and yawning vpon him, but could speak no more: yet at the last (coniuring vp his best spirits) he onely in a dumb shewe (with pittifull action, like a Plaier, when hees out of his part) made signes to haue a Letter deliuered by the Carrier of condemnation, to his sonne, (a yong Reueller, prickt down to stand in the Mercers books for next Christmas,) which in a dumbe shewe likewise being receiued, they both turnde backe the Vsurer, looking as hungrily, as if he had kist the post.[14]

More notably, what is emphasised here is that the communication is partial, incomplete; that the visual sign does not make up for the unspoken message; that gesture is not entirely redundant but is still somehow lacking. The longer texts, the letter and the mercer's book, both contain the same matter but in longer forms. The dumb show can gesture towards the fuller text but it cannot 'deliver' it in full.

Similarly, in *The Merchant of Venice*, when Portia discusses her potential suitors, she laments that though Fauconbridge, the young Baron of England, 'is a proper mans picture', his understanding of 'neither Latine, French, nor Italian' means she cannot communicate with him: she says, 'alas who can conuerse with a dumbe show?' (1.2.51–54)[15] Though she continues to mock him for his clothing – a gentle mockery of the fashions of early English dandies – Portia's primary frustration is with the dissonance between image and text (via language). In the anonymous *Euerie woman in her humor* (1609), Flavia, also overburdened by the affections of suitors, says she is better pleased with the 'dumbe shewe of all their pictures' than with being with any of them in person.

> Teren.   Why *Flauia* you haue many suitors.
> Flau.   Oh I am loaden with suitors: for indeede I am faine to beare with any of them, I haue a dumbe shewe of all their pictures, each has sent in his seuerall shadow, and I sweare I had rather haue them then the substance of any of them.[16]

Here, Flavia prefers the insubstantial abstract of the pictures, her suitors' 'dumbe shewe', to the real 'substance' of their presence.[17] A more dismissive comment about dumb shows occurs in Jonson's *The Case is Altered* where Onion praises Antonio as being the 'best plotter' (an appraisal, by the by, reserved for Anthony Munday in Meres' *Palladis Tamia*), and Antonio rejects this, saying, 'I might as well ha bene put in for a dumb shew too'.[18] What Antonio seems to mean is that for all the good his writing did him, he might as well have just composed a dumb show, the implied simpler activity.

Another recurring feature of such allusions is that there might be something less than sincere about dumb shows. For example, Barnabe Rich, in *Faultes faults* (1606), distinguishes between 'outward appearance' of religious devotion to 'satisfie the world' without dedicating oneself fully to Christ.

> We speake of *Honestie*, but it is with halfe a lip; and for *Vice*, we seeme to shut it out at the broade gate, but we priuily take it in againe at the Wicket: we make a gappe where the gate stands open, and we seeke to enter by force, where the high way lyes by fauour. We desire to come to Christ by night with *Nichodemus*, that no bodie might see vs for feare of worldly losses, and it is a point of wisdome to take Christ in one hand, and the world in another, and to make some outward appearance a litle to satisfie the world, if it be but with a dumb shew.[19]

The idea of false outward show recurs in Thomas Adams' sermon *The White Deuil, or The Hypocrite Vncased* (1612), where he proposes that 'monstrous pride ... turns hospitallity into a dumbe shew: that which fed the belly of hunger, now feedes the eie of lust'.[20] More sinister yet, let us consider an excerpt from the trial of John Dorrell, who was accused of fraudulently 'deluding the people by counterfeyt miracles'.[21] Together, Dorrell and his co-conspirator Sommers perpetrated a hoax whereby Sommers feigned demonic possession and

Dorrell pretended to cure him. Sommers, however, confessed and gave up Dorrell to the authorities.

> *Dorrell did interpret the sinnes which Sommers acted in a dumb shew, saying hee had seene others possessed doe the like.*[22]

Dumb show here is not an abstract representation of some greater truth, but a hoaxster's efforts to deceive through blunt mimed action subject to interpretation; the focus of fraud here is the interpretation of the action.

But dumb shows can still be as effectively affective as any primary method of storytelling; the signifier can carry similar weight to the sign. For instance, in his *Anatomy of Melancholie* (1621), Robert Burton warns that even a dumb show of a 'terrible object, heard or seen', such as a ghost story or tragedy, is to be avoided for those suffering from melancholy.

> If the party be sad, or otherwise affected, *consider* saith *Trallian, the manner of it, and all circumstances, and forthwith make a sudden alteration,* by remouing the occasions, avoide all terrible obiects, heard or seene, *monstrous and prodigious aspects,* tales of diuels, spirits, ghosts, tragicall stories, to such as are in feare they strike a great impression, and renew many times, and recal many chimeras and terrible fictions into their mindes. *Make not so much as mention of them in private talke, or a dumbe show tending to that purpose, such things* saith *Galateus, are offensiue to their Imagination.*[23]

What seems evident from such early modern references is that the meaning of 'dumb shows', alluding to either their supply and/or deficit of meaning, was unfixed in the period, and I would argue that we require a much broader conception of dumb show within the early English literary tradition; it is not simply stylised mime (though it could be), but can be understood as part of a wider cultural preoccupation with representation and misrepresentation, knowing and unknowing.

Dumb show as performance

The first dumb show to be found in an English play appears in Thomas Sackville and Thomas Norton's *Gorboduc* (1561). The play, an otherwise fairly staid oratorical showpiece, is punctuated by a series of dumb shows before each Act. Early English dumb shows vary significantly in form. Often the shows are highly abstract, offering a symbolic comment on what has just happened or will happen next (for example, the series of kindermords in *Gorboduc* in the dumb show before Act 4), but sometimes they provide important information (like the plot exposition before the beginning of the play proper of Thomas Hughes' et al. *The Misfortunes of Arthur*, or vital plot information like the 'moor's murder of his brothers to gain the throne for himself in the first dumb show of George Peele's *The Battel of Alcazar*).[24] Dumb shows can be reliably deployed to convey a huge amount of plot information in a conveniently short amount of time. This tradition continues in later drama. For example, in John Marston's *Antonio's Revenge*, the sequel to his *Antonio and Mellida*, the play opens with an extended summarising dumb show that informs the audience quickly of what has happened since the end of the previous play.[25] I will consider here some examples of how dumb shows supply information to (and deprive information from) audiences, and the difference in experiencing the dumb show as either a playgoer or as a reader.

Dumb shows may be accompanied by a 'presenter' who interprets and articulates the meaning of the stylised presentation. The most familiar of dumb shows before *Hamlet*, and perhaps the most influential due to the play's enduring popularity, appears in Thomas Kyd's *The Spanish Tragedy* (c. 1587). The character of Revenge acts as the presenter:

> *Enter a dumme shew.*
> Ghost. Awake Reuenge, reueale this misterie.
> Reuenge. The two first the nuptiall Torches boare,
> As brightly burning as the mid-daies sunne:
> But after them doth Himen hie as fast,
> Clothed in sable, and a Saffron robe,
> And blowes them out, and quencheth them with blood,
> As discontent that things continue so.
> Ghost. Sufficeth me thy meanings vnderstood ...[26]

We will note here that the action of the dumb show itself is not prescribed by a stage direction, but rather revealed in the ensuing interpretation of its 'misterie'. Kyd's dumb show is an excellent example of an inset performance that privileges the experiences of an audience member over the reader. The audience member sees the dumb show while its meaning is being explicated by Revenge: the cue 'Awake Reuenge, reueale...' informs us that the dumb show is not performed before this act of interpretation, but rather concurrently with it. The reader, on the other hand, is given no clues to the action of the dumb show until they have retroactively pieced together the dialogic explication.

In John Webster's *The Duchess of Malfi* (c. 1612–1613) we encounter a stylised pantomimic performance that, contrariwise, privileges the reader over an audience member. This is not a dumb show *per se*, but has significant crossovers with the tradition. A reader of the 1623 quarto would note that:

> *Here is discouer'd, (behind a Trauers;) the artificiall figures of Antonio, and his children; appearing as if they were dead.*[27]

Here, in performance, the apparently dead bodies of Antonio and his children with the Duchess are revealed to an audience. An audience has no reason to believe that what they are seeing is not real.[28] But a reader is immediately let in on this trick: the bodies are mere '*artificiall figures ... appearing as if they were dead*'.

Turning now to a more complicated case, in *Pericles*, Gower says 'what need speake I[?]' because all that needs to be known will be shown in the upcoming dumb show:

> [GOWER]
> ...
> But tidings to the contrarie,
> Are brought your eyes, what need speake I.
>
> *Dombe shew*
> *Enter at one dore* Pericles *talking with* Cleon. *all the traine with them: Enter at an other dore, a Gentleman with a Letter to* Pericles, Pericles *shewes the Letter to* Cleon; Pericles *giues the Messenger a reward, and Knights him: Exit* Pericles *at one dore, and* Cleon *at another.*
> Good *Helicon* that stayde at home,
> ...
> Sau'd one[29] of all, that haps in *Tyre*:
> Howe *Thaliart* came full bent with sinne,
> And had intent to murder him;
> And that in *Tharsis* was not best,
> Longer for him to make his rest ...[30]

During the dumb show, Pericles receives a letter from a gentleman, the contents of which neither audience nor reader can discern from the dumb show itself. Thus Gower, after the dumb show ends, is forced to inform the audience or reader about the letter's contents.

Recalling Dekker's *News from Hell*, here the dumb show, through the onstage letter (itself a textual object), is demonstrably inadequate in its supply of meaning, and more text, delivered via Gower's monologue, is required for its explication. Thus, neither audience member nor reader is privileged – they must wait and wait until their curiosity is sated.

Something similar occurs in Thomas Heywood's *Four Prentises* (1615), where the dumb show is first prepared for when a character says 'we will make bold to explane it in dumbe Show'.[31] The dumb show that is prescribed by stage direction is highly detailed, eighty-one words in length, and involves a series of interactions between '*certaine Spaniards*' and '*certaine Citizens of Bullen*'. But when the dumb show ends, the 'Presenter' realises that nothing could be discerned from the dumb show unless the participants are identified. Thus, he must note that:

> Those Cittizens you see were *Bullonoyes*,
> Kept vnder bondage of that tyrannous Earle[32]

By doing so he retrospectively provides both reader and audience with information that could not possibly be gained by the mimed performance alone.

Sometimes dumb shows can seem an utterly redundant concession to visual performance. In R.A.'s *The Valiant Welshman*, the character of the Bard or Welsh Poet, who acts as presenter, introduces a dumb show in a way that makes it feebly repetitive.

> Now *Cornewall*, *Gloster*, twinnes of some *Incubus*,
> And sonne and heyre to hells Imperiall Crowne,
> The Bastard *Codigune*, conspire the death
> Of olde *Octauian*. Those that faine would know
> The manner how, obserue this silent show.
>> *Enter a dumbe show, Codigune, Gloster, and Cornwall at the one dore: After they consult a little while, enter at the other dore, Octauian, Guiniuer, and Voada, the sister of Caradoc: they seeme by way of intreaty, to inuite them: they offer a cup of wine vnto Octauian, and he is poysoned. They take Guiniuer and Voada, and put them in prison. Codigune is crowned King of Wales.*
> Bardh. The trecherous Bastard, with his complices,
> *Cornewall* and *Gloster*, did inuite the King,
> Fayre *Guiniuer* and beautious *Voada*,
> The sister of renowmed *Caradoc*,
> Vnto a sumptuous feast...[33]

First, we hear that Cornwall, Gloucester and Codigune 'conspire' to kill King Octavian. Then the dumb show shows the murder – he is poisoned when he partakes of an offered cup of wine. Then the Bard reappears to repeat what we have just seen. There is no explication, just a summarising of the facts. The only privilege for the reader is that they are more easily able to first identify each character in the dumb show (who are thereafter carefully identified by the Bard).

Finally, sometimes dumb show is used as a form of shorthand for a type of unspoken onstage action not formally recorded as a dumb show. For example, in the anonymous *The True Chronicle History of King Leir*, Ragan is infuriated by a letter given to her by a messenger from Goneril. She does not, and would not, tell the Messenger the contents of the letter, so the Messenger calls attention to her displeasure by noting aside to the audience that her anger will mean 'more worke and more crownes' for him.

> RAG. How fares our royall sister?
> MES. I did leaue her at my parting, in good health.
> *She reads the letter, frownes and stamps.*
> See how her colour comes and goes agayne,
> Now red as scarlet, now as pale as ash:
> She[34] how she knits her brow, and bytes her lips,
> And stamps, and makes a dumbe shew of disdayne,
> Mixt with reuenge, and violent extreames.
> Here will be more worke and more crownes for me.[35]

The Messenger here verbalises what we can deduce – Ragan's displeasure – but we share in the Messenger's lack of knowledge. We are as underprivileged as those watching on the stage.

The dumb show in *Hamlet* aligns exactly with none of these preceding models. It is highly unusual in that it is a dumb show for an inset play performance, and not the play-at-large itself. It is also unusual in that there is no presenter, no explication. Finally, it is unusual in that the larger audience is already deeply familiar with the plot it mimes out. It is important to remember that the dumb show is not for the audience of *Hamlet*; it is for the audience of *The Mousetrap*. As such, it does not provide us, the larger audience, with plot exposition for the longer work. And we already know the conditions of the murder from the Ghost's report. We already know more than any other of Hamlet's audience watching onstage. Rather, we are watching an onstage audience watching a dumb show for a play to be performed. The ostensible purpose of the dumb show in the play-world of Elsinore is to set out the play plot for the onstage audience. It fails miserably in this task. The ostensible purpose of the dumb show in *Hamlet*, the larger play, is, as we shall see, quite different. So, too, is the result.

Hamlets' dumb shows

Before *The Mousetrap*, Ophelia plays the role of an unhappily confused audience member in all three versions of the text. A dumb show is performed, its meaning is oblique for her, and Ophelia (or 'Ofelia' in Q1) asks Hamlet several times about its import. Hamlet, who knows the plot and is evidently unhappy that the events of the play are at least partially revealed in dumb show, tosses aside Ophelia's repeated queries, using the interaction to further insult his one-time love. Yet Ophelia's queries are not our own. We, as either audiences or readers, are in the privileged position of Hamlet, not Ophelia, in that we understand that the dumb show reflects the conditions of the murder and seduction previously only verbalised during the Ghost's revelation. Once verbalised, now visualised, but ne'er the twain will meet.

The following displays the dumb show and subsequent commentary upon it as it appears across all three texts. Passages in bold reveal substantive differences between the three texts. What is emboldened in Q1 is what occurs there but not in Q2. What is emboldened in Q2 is what is not found in Q1. What is emboldened in F is what is present there and not in Q2. Original settings and orthography are preserved in each case, though ligatures are not retained.

Q1 *Hamlet* (1603; STC 22275), sig. F3^r
Substantive variants from Q2 are marked in bold.

*Enter in a Dumbe Shew, the King and the Queen, **he sits downe in an Arbor**, she leaues him: Then enters **Lucianus with poyson in a Viall**, and powres it in his eares, and goes away: Then the Queene commeth and findes him dead: and goes away with the other.*

OFEL.   What meanes this my Lord?
             Enter the Prologue.
HAM.   This is myching Mallico, that meanes **my chiefe**.
OFEL.   What does this mean my lord?
HAM.   **you shall heare anone**, this fellow will tell you all.

OFEL.	Will he tell vs what this shew meanes?
HAM.	I, or any shew you'le shew him,
	Be not **afeard** to shew, hee'le not be **afeard** to tell:
	O these Players cannot keepe **counsell**, thei'le tell all.
PROL.	For vs, and for our Tragedi,
	Heere stowping to your clemencie,
	We begge your hearing patiently.
HAM.	I'st a prologue, or a poesie **for** a ring?
OFEL.	T'is **short** my Lord.
HAM.	As womens loue.

Enter the Duke and Dutchesse.[36]

Q2 *Hamlet* (1604–1605; STC 22276), sig. H1ᵛ
Substantive variants from Q1 are marked in bold.

The Trumpet sounds. Dumbe show followes.
*Enter a King and a Queene, **the Queene embracing him, and he her**, he takes her vp, and declines his head vpon her necke, he lyes him downe vpon a bancke of flowers, she seeing him asleepe, leaues him: anon come in **an other man**, takes off his crowne, kisses it, pours poyson in **the sleepers** eares, and leaues him: the Queene returnes, finds the King dead, **makes passionate action**, the poysoner with some three or foure come in againe, seeme to condole with her, the dead body is carried away, the poysoner wooes the Queene with gifts, shee seemes harsh awhile, but in the end accepts loue.*

OPH.	What meanes this my Lord?
HAM.	Marry this munching *Mallico*, it meanes mischiefe.
OPH.	**Belike this show imports the argument of the play.**[37]
HAM.	We *shall* know by this fellow,
	The Players cannot keepe, they'le tell all.
	Enter Prologue.[38]
OPH.	Will a tell vs what this show meant?
HAM.	I, or any show that you will show him, be not you **asham'd**
	to show, heele not **shame** to tell you what it means.
OPH.	**You are naught, you are naught, Ile mark the play.**
PROLOGUE.	For vs and for our Tragedie,
	Heere stooping to your clemencie,
	We begge your hearing patiently.
HAM.	Is this a Prologue, or the posie of a ring?
OPH.	Tis **breefe** my Lord.
HAM.	As womans loue.

Enter King and Queene.

Folio *Hamlet* (1623; STC 22273), sig. Oo6ʳ (p. 267)
Substantive variants from Q2 are marked in bold.

*Hoboyes Play. The dumbe shew **enters**.*
*Enter a King and Queene, **very louingly**; the Queene embra-*
*cing him. **She kneeles, and makes shew of Protestation unto**
***him.** He takes her up, and d[e]clines his head upon her neck.*
Layes him downe upon a Banke of Flowers. She seeing him
*a-sleepe, leaves him. Anon comes in a **Fellow**, takes off his*
Crowne, kisses it, and powres poyson in the Kings eares, and
Exits. The Queene returnes, findes the King dead, and
*makes passionate Action. The Poysoner, with some **two or***
***three Mutes** comes in againe, seeming to lament with her.*
The dead body is carried away: The Poysoner Wooes the
*Queene with Gifts, she seemes **loath and unwilling** awhile,*
but in the end, accepts his love.   **Exeunt**

Ophe.	What meanes this, my Lord?
Ham.	Marry this is Miching *Malicho*, that meanes Mischeefe.
Ophe.	Belike this shew imports the Argument of the Play?
Ham.	We shall know by **these Fellowes**[39]: the Players cannot keepe **counsell**,[40] they'l tell all.
Ophe.	Will they tell vs what this shew meant?
Ham.	I, or any shew that you'l shew him. Bee not you asham'd to shew, hee'l not shame to tell you what it meanes.
Ophe.	You are naught, you are naught, Ile marke the Play.

       Enter Prologue.
       For vs, and for our Tragedie,
       Heere stooping for your Clemencie:
       We begge your hearing Patientlie.

Ham.	Is this a Prologue, or the Poesie of a Ring?
Ophe.	'Tis briefe my Lord.
Ham.	As Womans loue.

       Enter King and his Queene.

Let us begin by noting what is common to all three texts. In each, there is a dumb show enacted, which involves the characters of a King and Queen who enter to a setting in nature. In each, the Queen departs from the King. Then another man enters. This man kills the King. He does so by pouring poison into the King's ears. The poisoner then leaves. Next, in each, the Queen returns. She finds the King dead. She then interacts with the poisoner who has returned.

The dumb show ends with the Queen in the company of the poisoner. In each, it is Ofelia/Ophelia who responds first to the dumb show, and in each version she is puzzled by its meaning. Hamlet, in each, seems angered by the performance, lamenting that the players will 'tell all'. In each a prologue follows, mocked by Hamlet as but a 'P/po(e)sie' that might be found in a ring. Hamlet compares the prologue's duration to a woman's love. Then, in each, the married male and female protagonists of the to-be-performed play enter.

Such self-evident correspondences in language and scene structure would alert any reader to the fact that they are encountering different versions of a similar episode. But we should not overlook the significance of some of the differences, and the consistent nature of the differences between the versions. Our chief focus here will be on variants between Q1 and Q2, but I will also note variants found in F.

Q2 and F include most of the action prescribed by Q1. Even the four substantive variants in Q1's dumb show are largely unremarkable – the explicitly stated entrance of the characters 'in a Dumbe Shewe' (implicit in Q2 but also stated in F), the specification of an arbour (it is a natural setting in Q2 and F also), the named receptacle for the poison (the poison has to be carried in something), and the naming of the poisoner (a detail provided in the larger play).[41] What is more remarkable is the action only prescribed in the later texts. The directions for Q2 and F are not simply longer; with the additional information they supply, they produce significantly different versions of the scene:

1. In Q1 no reason is initially given for the murder of the King; in Q2 and F the murderer takes up the crown and kisses it.

That is, in both longer versions the murderer clearly signals his ambition to gain the crown, an aspect omitted in the Q1 text.

2. In Q1 the Queen goes away with the murderer immediately after finding the King's body; in Q2 and F she at first resists but then accepts the murderer's love only after receiving gifts.

There are two significant points of difference here. One, leaving with the murderer in Q1 after the murder might reasonably imply cooperation. Two, leaving with the murderer in Q1 might reasonably imply a pre-existing love relationship. Neither implication could be plausibly communicated given the stage action prescribed by the stage directions in Q2 and F.

3. In Q1 the King's body is left on the stage when the Queen and the murderer leave; in Q2 and F, followers of the murderer carry the body away *before* the courtship begins.

Q1 is a tad messier here, with the body left on the stage. Q2 and F are tidier, and again absolve the Queen of any culpability in the murder plot, as the love plot is made temporally and spatially distinct.

Each of these points of difference between Q1 and Q2/F relates significantly to the Queen; what is expanded upon in the prescribed action of the stage directions in Q2 and F minimises the Queen's involvement with the crime. In Q2 and F the poisoner (a) displays his ambition for the crown, (b) has a cohort of other followers who help him dispose of the body ('three or foure'; 'three mutes'), (c) condoles or laments with the Queen on her loss (which obviously indicates the Queen's lack of awareness), and (d) woos the Queen with gifts and, only eventually, wins her over. In Q1, the nature of the Queen's involvement is much more ambiguous, but perhaps tending towards accusatory. This is not the only place in Q1 where greater emphasis is placed on the Queen's culpability. As the Arden Three editors Anne Thompson and Neil Taylor note, the line 'None weds the second but she kills the first', a variant reading on Q2/F's 'who kild the first', makes Q1 'more explicit in the accusation of the Queen'.[42]

Dumb shows and *mise en abyme*

Critics have expended much effort on the question of why the dumb show is included at all, noting (often exasperatedly) that it gives away the plot before it is performed and that it seems absurd that Claudius would not respond to such an obvious act. Directors have often sought to evade this problem by having Claudius miss the dumb show somehow, perhaps distracted by Gertrude or others. Edward Dowden thought that Claudius might assume that the dumb show included material not 'developed through dialogue'.[43] A.W. Pollard famously coined the 'second tooth' theory, suggesting that Claudius could endure the first sighting of his murder but reacts upon the second (akin to having more than one tooth removed at a dentist).[44] Dieter Mehl, noting that dumb shows were so stylised as to make them 'so different from the rest of the play and real life', thought it reasonable to assume that Claudius would not react to something that only vaguely reminded him of his guilt.[45] Stanley Cavell, in his typically contrarian way, proposed that Claudius did not react because Hamlet had the details of the murder wrong.[46] I care little about whether Claudius 'sees' the dumb show. He may, he may not; that is a director's prerogative – none of the early versions of the play make it explicit so we cannot say whether he does or not. What seems more important is to attempt to understand Shakespeare's intention, as a dramatist of great experience and understanding, in including the dumb show in the play given it creates such problems. Through Hamlet's annoyed response – the players 'tell all' – Shakespeare clearly, openly, adverts to the awkwardness of including this device. So why does he do it?

The dumb show does not advance the action of the main play through the supply of information; rather, it visually summarises what might potentially be performed. As such, the dumb show has been considered to be anticipatory and to lack emblematic quality. Resisting this, Tiffany Stern argues that because the dumb show is never interpreted and 'remains undirected' it is able to 'convey one set of symbolic messages to the fictional courtier audience, another to Claudius, another to Hamlet, and a further set to us, the actual audience'.[47] Stern, who has no problem with Claudius watching the dumb show, thus argues that the device 'ruins' Hamlet's plans in two ways: 'On the one hand, it forewarns Claudius, who does not respond to the play as intended; on the other, it forces an overwrought Hamlet, disastrously, to become interpreter himself'.[48] Stern acutely observes that various groups onstage and off experience the dumb show and subsequent play differently. However, Stern's analysis falls into a familiar critical trap. The critical response to the 'seeing' issue seems misguided.[49] By saying that the dumb show reveals a plot to be performed, critics are assuming that there is an *entire* play to be performed. That is, they are placing real-world expectations on what is a fictional construct. John Dover Wilson fell into this trap, too. Discussing the dumb show, Wilson notes that the typical usage of such a device is to either 'foreshadow the contents of a play (or an act) by means of a *symbolical* or *historical* tableau' or 'to save the dramatist the trouble of composing dialogue for part of the action by presenting it in pantomime' that might then be interpreted by a choric figure or presenter.[50] (Wilson here relies upon the work of Wilhelm Creizenach, and, as we have seen above, dumb shows can actually serve a much wider variety of purposes.) Wilson then notes that the dumb show in *Hamlet* fits neither category: 'it is an anticipation in full action of the spoken scene that follows, and as such would be entirely superfluous in any ordinary drama'.[51] But, of course, there is no 'spoken scene that follows' that exactly mirrors the dumb show which precedes it; only half of what is promised from the dumb show is ever performed. Shakespeare, in writing *Hamlet*, knows that the play-within-the-play will not be played to completion. Shakespeare writes a passage of a 'play' – a 'play' that, in the play-world, is ostensibly adapted by Hamlet from another 'play' – that he knows will be concluded abruptly by his character Claudius before it is completed. There is no 'complete' *The Murder of Gonzago* or *The Mousetrap*. This may seem so obvious as to be inane, but the critical history of the dumb show makes it necessary to spell this out word by word: *all that exists of the 'play' is what is written and performed.*

But this is why the dumb show is so significant, so necessary for Shakespeare: it offers us a version of the extended, imagined 'play' that is never to be performed or, indeed, written. It shows us what doesn't happen in *Hamlet*. It provides us with an answer to the 'what happens next' for a dramatic sequence that is already complete at its moment of interruption. Without the dumb show, we would not know what Hamlet plans for the character of the Queen after the King's death with his little play. All we would have is, as is present in all three versions, a Queen character who protests that she would never marry again once widowed. But in Q1 the ambiguity present in dumb show alerts us to the hypocrisy of these protestations within the fictional world of the play, and, moreover, the play-world of *Hamlet* itself. In Q2 and F, we might at once reasonably believe the Queen's protestations while still knowing that she will go back on her word.

So much critical thought has gone into answering the question of whether or not Claudius sees the dumb show. But, for our purposes, perhaps the more interesting question is whether or not Gertrude does. After all, Hamlet's focus (as a would-be presenter, directing the reception and interpretation of what is performed) falls so often upon Gertrude and not Claudius. The majority of *The Mousetrap* in all three versions is taken up with the Queen's protests to the King. After the Queen/Duchess exits, the first extended exchange between Hamlet and the others present is about the Queen/Duchess's behaviour. Even after the introduction of Lucianus, 'nephew to the King', Hamlet's most bitter barbs are directed towards his mother forgetting her duties towards his dead father ('looke how cheerefully my mother lookes', Q1 reads). The significant difference between Q1 and Q2/F is that in the latter Hamlet appears to be viciously but redundantly haranguing Gertrude for her post-funeral actions, and thereby rejecting his Ghost father's request to 'leaue her to heauen' (as Q2 reads); in the former, Hamlet seems to be asserting and thereby testing her guilt in the murder plot.

Or, at least, this might be the case. Such a reading is drawn from an information shortfall in Q1's dumb show. In the fifty-one words of this dumb show, we can glean nothing about the existing relationship of the King and Queen, and therefore, given the incomplete nature of *The Mousetrap*, nothing about what Hamlet plans for his mother. The Player King and Player Queen enter. He sits down, she leaves. Consider for a moment all of the information that Q2 and F supply between this first entrance and exit. In the later, longer texts, the pair embrace, and there is prescribed the exact stage action of the King placing his head upon the Queen's neck. In F, mirroring the to-be-performed passage from the play, the Queen must visibly make a 'shew of Protestation'.[52] In Q1 only the barest details of performance are prescribed. Its paucity of detail, its deficit of information, deters us from advancing the sort of critical readings that the dumb shows of Q2 and F encourage, and that more readily 'anticipate' *The Mousetrap*. Encountering such a shortfall, with nothing else to go on, we might then supply our own interpretation for what this lack of information means. Thus, I could propose earlier that 'Hamlet seems to be asserting and thereby testing her guilt in the murder plot'. But not because the text suggests this, only because the text does not tell us otherwise. In an instant, we have returned to the realm of 'but did Claudius see the dumb show?' and other such questions of an unproductive nature. *Horror vacui*, as we know.

So, we have versions of the play that is *Hamlet* and each of these versions includes its own skewed, partial versions of the backstory producing *Hamlet* via, first, the dumb show and, second, the play-within-the-play. *Hamlet*, in this sense, is endlessly recursive, a representation of a representation, a reflection of a reflection, *ad finitum*. Or rather, *Hamlet* in its three early texts offers us a set of representations of a representation, reflections of a reflection. Perhaps we should not reflect upon this for too long or it may become tedious.

Rory Loughnane is Reader in Early Modern Studies and Co-Director of the Centre for Medieval and Early Modern Studies at the University of Kent. He is an Associate Editor of the *New Oxford Shakespeare*, a General Editor of The Revels Plays series and *The Oxford Marlowe*, and a Series Editor of Routledge's Studies in Early Modern Authorship and Cambridge's Shakespeare and Text.

Notes

1. T.S. Eliot, '*Hamlet* and His Problems', in *The Sacred Wood: Essays on Poetry and Criticism* (London: Metheun & Co. Ltd., 1920), 87–94. Eliot thought the play an 'artistic failure' (90). Swayed by the work of J.M. Robertson, who argued that the play included George Chapman's rewriting of passages originally written by Thomas Kyd (as the supposed author of the ur-*Hamlet*), Eliot held that it was better to think of *Hamlet* as 'superposed upon much cruder materials which persists even in the final form' (88). Robertson's work had a similar title to Eliot's essay, *The Problem of Hamlet* (New York: Harcourt, Brace, & Howe, 1920). All citations to *Hamlet* are taken from John Jowett's edition of the play in *The New Oxford Shakespeare: Modern Critical Edition: The Complete Works*, gen. ed. Gary Taylor et al. (Oxford: Oxford University Press, 2016). Jowett's edition is based upon the second quarto text of 1604–5.
2. John Dover Wilson, *What Happens in Hamlet* (Cambridge: Cambridge University Press, 1935).
3. Indeed, it was W.W. Greg's discussion of the dumb show in *Hamlet*, and whether Claudius sees it, that Wilson identifies as the inspiration for his entire study. See his 'epistle dedicatory' to Greg, 4–5. Greg's initial article study was published in 1917: 'Hamlet's Hallucination', *MLR* 12 (1917), 393–421. This, in turn, inspired a flurry of correspondence in print between Greg and Wilson; see William Witherle Lawrence, 'Hamlet and the Mouse-trap', *PMLA* 54, no. 3 (1939), 709–735, for a summary account of this exchange.
4. Ibid., 144–152. Wilson, however, seriously disagreed with Eliot's assessment of the play.
5. All citations are to Terri Bourus's edition of *A Midsummer Night's Dream* in *The New Oxford Shakespeare: Modern Critical Edition. The Complete Works*, gen. ed. Gary Taylor et al. (Oxford: Oxford University Press, 2016).
6. Dieter Mehl's *The Elizabethan Dumb Show* (London: Methuen, 1965) remains the standard-bearer study for the evolution of the form. For the dumb show in *Hamlet*, see, for example: William Witherle Lawrence, 'The Play Scene in Hamlet', *The Journal of English and Germanic Philology* 18 (1919), 1–22; Andrew J. Green, 'The Cunning of the Scene', *Shakespeare Quarterly* 4, no. 4 (1953), 395–404; John Doebler's 'The Play Within the Play: *Muscipula Diaboli* in *Hamlet*', *Shakespeare Quarterly* 23, no. 2 (1972), 161–169; Alfred Mollin, 'On Hamlet's Mousetrap', *Interpretation* 21, no. 3 (1994), 353–372; Charles Edelman, '"The Very Cunning of the Scene": Claudius and the Mouse-trap', *Parergon* 12, no. 1 (1994), 15–25; and Steve Roth, 'Who Knows Who Knows Who's There? An Epistemology of *Hamlet*

(Or, What Happens in the Mousetrap)', *Early Modern Literary Studies* 10, no. 2 (2004), 1–27. Lee Sheridan Cox devoted an entire book to *Hamlet*'s dumb show: *Figurative Design in Hamlet: The Significance of the Dumb Show* (Columbus: Ohio State University Press, 1973). Two recent essays by Jeremy Lopez and Tiffany Stern, heralding a not unwelcome return to these dramatic devices, both make the dumb show in *Hamlet* central to their arguments: see Tiffany Stern, '*Hamlet*: The Dumb Show', in *Shakespeare Up Close: Reading Early Modern Texts*, ed. Russ McDonald, Nicholas Nace and Travis Williams (London: Methuen, 2012), 273–281, and Jeremy Lopez, 'Dumbshow', in *Early Modern Theatricality*, ed. Henry S. Turner (Oxford: Oxford University Press, 2013), 291–305. Tiffany Stern has since written another study about dumb shows, 'Inventing Stage Directions; Demoting Dumb Shows', which also touches on some differences between the versions of the dumb show in the texts of *Hamlet*: in *Stage Directions and Shakespearean Theatre*, ed. Sarah Dustagheer and Gillian Woods (London: Bloomsbury, 2018), 19–45.

7. An *EEBO-TCP* trawl for the bigram 'dumb show' produces 173 hits across 134 texts printed between the opening and closing of the professional theatres (1576–1642). Search completed in March 2017. In Dieter Mehl's landmark work, he lists some 150 dumb shows across seventy-three plays. Leslie Thomson expands the definition of dumb show much further to include any 'action without dialogue – pantomime – typically by at least two (and usually more) figures'. Her count gives 186 dumb shows appearing in ninety-eight plays written between 1580 and 1642. See Leslie Thomson, 'Dumb Shows in Performance on the Early Modern Stage', *Medieval and Renaissance Drama in England* 29 (2016), 17–45, here 18–19.

8. Rosemary Freeman, *English Emblem Books* (London: Chatto & Windus, 1948), 14–15.

9. Ibid., 15.

10. George Withers, *A collection of emblemes, ancient and moderne* (1635; STC 25900a), sig. L2^v.

11. Ibid., sig. L2^v.

12. Francis Quarles, *Diuine fancies* (1633; STC 20530), sig. A2^v.

13. Thomas Dekker, *The wonderfull yeare* (1603; STC 6535), sig. B2^r.

14. Thomas Dekker, *Newes from Hell* (1606; STC 6514), sig. G4^v.

15. All citations are to Rory Loughnane's edition of *The Merchant of Venice* in *The New Oxford Shakespeare: Critical Reference Edition. The Complete Works*, gen. ed. Gary Taylor et al. (Oxford: Oxford University Press, 2017).

16. Anonymous, *Euerie woman in her humor* (1609; STC 25948), sig. E4^r.

17. A similar reference to dumb shows as something to be more desired and relished occurs in *Much Ado About Nothing*. The Prince tells Claudio: 'Let there be the same nette spread for her, and that must your daughter and her gentlewomen carry: the sporte will be, when they holde one an opinion of an others dotage, and no such matter, thats the scene that I woulde see, which wil be meerely a dumbe shew: let vs send her to call him in to dinner'. *Much adoe about nothing* (1600; STC 22304), sig. D3^r. These two examples show that dumb shows might, for certain purposes or certain audiences, be preferred. In the same way that, in modern films, certain spectators may be more impressed by action sequences than dialogue.

18. Ben Jonson, *His* (i.e. *The*) *Case is alterd* (1609; STC 14757), sig. A3^v.

19. Barnabe Rich, *Faultes faults, and nothing else but faultes* (1606; STC 20983), sig. R1ᵛ.
20. Thomas Adams, *The white deuil, or The hypocrite vncased* (1613; STC 131), sig. D1ʳ.
21. Samuel Harsnett, *The Triall of Maist. Dorrell* (1599; STC 6287), sig. A2ʳ.
22. Ibid., sig. D1ᵛ.
23. Robert Burton, *The Anatomy of Melancholy* (1621; STC 4159), 367.
24. In a short article, Eric Rasmussen argues that the unusual (though not anomalous) use of the past tense in the dumb shows in the play indicates that they were memorially reconstructed (a theory of textual provenance and integrity that has since been hotly contested); see his 'The Implications of Past Tense Verbs in Early Elizabethan Dumb Shows', *English Studies* 67 (1986), 417–419.
25. This functional purpose may be usefully compared to the use of anonymous omniscient gentlemen characters in the plays of the period, more frequently used by Shakespeare towards the end of his career. For example, think of the two Gentlemen who begin *Cymbeline* or the two brothel-going Gentlemen in *Pericles*, or the two Gentlemen who recount the downfall of Buckingham in *Henry VIII* (or *All is True*). For more on this choric function, see Rory Loughnane, 'Semi-choric Devices and the Framework for Playgoer Response in *King Henry VIII*', in *Late Shakespeare, 1608–1613*, ed. Andrew J. Power and Rory Loughnane (Cambridge: Cambridge University Press, 2012), 108–123.
26. Thomas Kyd, *The Spanish Tragedie* (1592; STC 15086), sig. I2ᵛ–I3ʳ. Rather surprisingly, Leslie Thomson proposes that 'Dumb Shows require stage directions', when, as we see in this example from Kyd's play, that is not the case. Stage movement can also be prescribed by dialogue.
27. John Webster, *The Tragedy of the Dvtchesse of Malfy* (1623; STC 25176), sig. I1ᵛ.
28. In fact, as I have argued in print elsewhere, the actors playing the parts of Antonio and his children most likely performed in the role of the 'artificiall figures'. See Rory Loughnane, 'The Artificial Figures in Webster's *Duchess of Malfi*', in *The Arts of Remembrance in Early Modern England*, ed. Andrew Gordon and Thomas Rist (Farnham, Surrey: Ashgate, 2013), 211–228.
29. The phrase 'Sau'd one' is likely corrupt, and can be usefully emended to 'Sends word'. See Rory Loughnane, ed., '*Pericles, Prince of Tyre*', in *The New Oxford Shakespeare: Complete Works: Critical Reference Edition*, gen. ed. Gary Taylor, John Jowett, Terri Bourus and Gabriel Egan (Oxford: Oxford University Press, 2017), 1374 (6.22).
30. Shakespeare and George Wilkins, *Pericles, Prince of Tyre* (1609; STC 22334), sig. C1ʳ⁻ᵛ.
31. Thomas Heywood, *The foure prentises of London* (1615; STC 13321), sig. C1ʳ.
32. Ibid., sig. C1ʳ.
33. R.A., *The valiant Welshman* (1615; STC 16), sig. C4ᵛ.
34. A clear error in the quarto text: 'She' should read 'See'.
35. Anon., *The True Chronicle History of King Leir* (1605; STC 15343), sig. E1ʳ⁻ᵛ.
36. The character designations change from the dumb show to the play performance. In the dumb show they are a 'King' and 'Queene'; in the performance, a 'Duke' and 'Dutchesse' (and consistently with speech prefixes also). Reinforcing such inconsistency, Hamlet later identifies the 'Duke' as Albertus before identifying Lucianus as 'nephew to the King'.

37. Note how Ophelia's second question becomes much more sophisticated in the Q2 text (also in F); in Q1 she essentially asks the same question twice, presumably because Hamlet does not answer it the first time she asks. The repetition in Q1 calls attention to Hamlet's refusal to answer.
38. The stage direction for '*Enter Prologue*' drops down two lines in Q2.
39. An interesting variant which (correctly) pluralises the number of actors onstage, though Q1 and Q2 might highlight the role of the poisoner in the dumb show's action (or even possibly by the Prologue who is about to appear).
40. The phrase 'keepe counsell' also occurs in Q1.
41. Of these, the 'arbour' is perhaps the most interesting as it recalls the setting of Horatio's murder in Kyd's *Spanish Tragedy*. Whatever the provenance of Q1, about which there is little agreement, this is a detail that might have been borrowed from Kyd's play (either by the author, if we presume that Q1 represents an early version of the play, or by a reporter, if we presume that Q1 represents a corrupted text of the later versions).
42. Anne Thompson and Neil Taylor, ed. *Hamlet, The Texts of 1603 and 1623*, The Arden Shakespeare (London: Thomson Learning, 2006), 119n.
43. Edward Dowden, ed., *The Tragedy of Hamlet* (London: Metheun and Co., 1899), 116n.
44. John Dover Wilson attributes the coinage to A.W. Pollard (Wilson, *What Happens in Hamlet*, 151), though it is uncertain whether Pollard advocated such an interpretation. He did not publish on the theory, and the first reference to it (and most likely to Pollard also) appears in a footnote to W.W. Greg's article 'Hamlet's Hallucination': 'a theory (dubbed by a friend the "second tooth" theory)' (398). Roth, 'Who Knows Who Knows Who's There?' discusses this in further detail (n13).
45. Mehl, *The Elizabethan Dumb Show*, 118.
46. Stanley Cavell, *Disowning Knowledge: In Seven Plays of Shakespeare* (Cambridge: Cambridge University Press, 1987), esp. 182–183.
47. Tiffany Stern, 'The Dumb Show in *Hamlet*', in *Shakespeare Up Close: Reading Early Modern Texts*, ed. Russ McDonald, Nicholas D. Nace and Travis D. Williams (London: Metheun, 2012), 273–81, here 276.
48. Ibid., 276.
49. In his article 'Did the King see the Dumb-Show' (*The Cambridge Quarterly* 6.4 [1975], 303–26) W.W. Robson offers a remarkably sustained study of this 'problem', detailing the various critical explanations offered and adding his own two cents ('there is no sign that the King was *publicly* exposed' to the dumb show, 320).
50. Wilson, *What Happens in Hamlet*, 147.
51. Ibid., 147.
52. This is a detail especially resistant to interpretation: how might it be effectively communicated through mime what it is that she is protesting against? Here, if anything, F seems to follow the opening speeches of *The Mousetrap* too closely, losing sight of the constraints of mimed performance.

Afterword
Q1 *Hamlet*

Graham Holderness and Bryan Loughrey

We are delighted to publish this volume devoted to contemporary studies of the first published text of Shakespeare's *Hamlet*, the first quarto (Q1), and grateful to Terri Bourus for bringing together such an important resource for future scholarship and criticism.

We are particularly gratified to see that so much has changed since 1992, when we published the first accessible paperback edition of Q1, as part of a series of diplomatically edited texts under the generic title of *Shakespearean Originals*. The first text to be published, and the text that generated the most controversy, was indeed a version of the 'first quarto' of Hamlet: *The Tragicall Historie of Hamlet Prince of Denmarke (1603)*.[1]

The main objectives of the *Shakespearean Originals* series were: the recuperation of discrete textualisations, and their liberation from canonical authority; the introduction of historic textual variety to a wider audience of students and scholars; the acknowledgement of early printed texts as reliable historical documents, the only 'originals' that exist; the opening up of pedagogic and theatrical possi-

Notes for this section begin on page 242.

bilities released by the provision of accessible and usable editions that retain in their foreground some at least of the linguistic and dramatic traces of the 'originals'; and the interrogation of modern editorial traditions and their ideological underpinnings.

Today these principles are widely accepted. Not so in 1992. The publication of *Q1 Hamlet* in the series was greeted by Brian Vickers in the *Times Literary Supplement* as 'Hamlet by Dogberry', and as a 'perverse reading' of the text.[2] Most of Vickers' long review was taken up with defending the 'memorial reconstruction' hypothesis and the status of Q1 as a corrupt, performance-derived 'bad quarto'. It was generally conjectured, from the early twentieth century onwards, that the first quarto was reconstructed from memory, possibly by one of the actors who performed in it, and published without permission of the author or his company. The second quarto (some copies of which are dated 1604, some 1605), which bears on its title page the description 'Newly imprinted and enlarged to almost as much againe as it was, according to the true and perfect Coppie', would then have been a publication by dramatist and company of an authorised text. If that were the case, it would be reasonable to assume that the second quarto represents both Shakespeare's 'intended' text and the version the company used for performances.

Thus, the basis of Vickers' critique of *Shakespearean Originals* in the *TLS* was a defence of the traditional bibliographical judgement on the 'bad quarto' of *Hamlet* as an unauthorised 'memorial reconstruction' of a contemporary performance; and his deepest objection to the *Shakespearean Originals* edition of *The Tragicall Historie of Hamlet Prince of Denmarke* was that it failed to comply with this traditional view of the text as the 'inauthentic' shadow of an 'authentic' original. The 1603 quarto is, he argued, as Duthie and Hart 'incontrovertibly confirmed', a memorial reconstruction, based on performance, corrupted and contaminated, full of senseless language and bad verse, and above all manifestly and irrefutably inferior as a text to the 1604/1605 quarto version and the 1623 folio text. To argue against this orthodoxy could only result in a 'perverse reading'.

Despite Vickers' robust defence, the 'memorial reconstruction' theory was losing its status of orthodoxy, as subsequent correspondence in the *TLS* (4 and 11 February 1994; 4 March 1994; 1, 8, 15 and 22 April 1994) abundantly demonstrated. And many other scholars have shown that this use of the term 'bad quarto' to identify a dramatic text supposedly reported or reconstructed from a theatrical performance permits a pervasive strategic dispersion of the attribution of 'badness', from a description of a particular mode of transmission (illegitimately copied from a performance rather than derived from some supposedly more authoritative source such as an authorial manuscript, a scribal copy of the manuscript or an authorially 'approved' prompt-copy) to ascriptions of artistic or even moral 'badness' on the part of both the text and its conjectural producers.[3] A 'bad quarto' can readily be received as not only bad in itself, but the product of bad men, the unscrupulous Elizabethan 'pirates', the ubiquitous 'playhouse thieves'. But since we have no means of knowing the extent to which authorial influence (as distinct from the influences of actors, theatre entrepreneurs, scribes, printers, pirates) uniquely determined the shape and contents of the printed texts, we are left with a self-evidently and irredeemably collaborative cultural production.

As it is now widely agreed that the early modern drama was a highly collaborative cultural form, such collectively processed scripts would seem accurate and appropriate products of its collective methods. In practice, however, this general acceptance of the 'Shakespearean' drama as a collaborative rather than an individual cultural form has not finally dislodged the rigid hierarchy of functions implicitly assumed by traditional editorial practices: what the writer writes, others (actors, theatre entrepreneurs, scribes, printers, pirates) corrupt, mangle and pervert to illegitimate uses. The privileging and hypostatisation of the authorial role is a retrospective anachronism, and the pervasive assumption of hierarchical precedence between the various functions an entirely inappropriate model of the historical conditions of early modern culture (Shakespeare, for one, belonged to at least three of the categories listed here: writer, actor, entrepreneur). If 'corruption' could be purged of its aura of moral transgression and translated as the collaborative, overdetermined productivity of the early modern theatre, in which the authentically Shakespearean input fruitfully coexisted with a diversity of other influences, then Q1's validity as an 'original' text could hardly any longer be questioned.

In Vickers' review, *The Tragicall Historie of Hamlet Prince of Denmarke* was referred to as 'corrupt', 'rubbish', 'horribly jumbled', 'garbled', 'dross', 'contaminated', 'unintelligible'; and the pirate-actors responsible for expropriating it, and all others involved in its reproduction, dismissed as 'inept'. This 'inauthentic' text stands in Vickers' theoretical model in sharp contradistinction to an 'authentic' text. Oddly, however, there seem to be three quite separate definitions of which text is the authentic one:

> The pirated version of *Hamlet* [Q1] came out in 1603, Shakespeare's company issuing an *authentic* version [Q2] in the following year ... the 1623 Folio [F1] offer[ed] this almost complete edition as the *authentic* work of Shakespeare ... Graham Holderness and Bryan Loughrey reject ... all attempts by modern editors since the eighteenth century to establish an *authentic* text [my italics].[4]

Thus, the quality of 'authenticity' is shared by three textualisations of this play: Q2, F1 and those modern editions that have sought – usually by merging Q2 and F1 – to re-establish Shakespeare's 'authentic' text of '*Hamlet*'. Q2 is assumed 'authentic' because closest to the authorial manuscript (though since the title page of Q2 makes no mention of the company, there is no evidence that it was issued by the company). The Folio collection is also however 'authentic' because the editors claimed it was based on Shakespeare's own papers. Yet Q2 and F1 are quite different texts. This confusion is worse confounded when a third text is claimed as 'authentic', this time the text that modern scholars 'establish' as an emulation of the manuscript original, the ideal text of *Hamlet* that appears in most standard editions. If Q2 and F1 are both 'authentic', why was it necessary for modern editors to 'establish' an 'authentic' text? Vickers attributed to Q2 and F1 a quality of 'authenticity' based on *OED* sense 6, 'really proceeding from its reputed source or author'. But another kind of 'authenticity', that defined in *OED* senses 3 ('reliable, trustworthy') and 5 ('real, actual, genuine'), has to be inserted by the editor. It is the editor, acting as the author's agent, who confers authenticity and guarantees to restore the text to a form approximating Shakespeare's intended artistic vision, by correcting the errors introduced into its variant forms in the course of performance and printing. Here nothing much has changed since Nicholas Rowe.

Vickers' review is a reaffirmation of the very editorial theory, embodied particularly in New Bibliography, that the series was set up to destabilise. For him, the criminalised status of *The Tragicall Historie of Hamlet Prince of Denmarke* had already been settled beyond dispute, and the text itself was sufficiently available in texts appropriately framed by this orthodoxy. By way of illustrating these related points, Vickers recommends Howard Mill's book *Working with Shakespeare*, which addresses the Q1 text, and which contains in its 'specimen analyses' of the different texts of '*Hamlet*' an 'admirable comparison' likely to command 'wide agreement'.[5] In fact, Mills' book disqualifies both of Vickers' arguments. Enjoying a common access to all those old facsimiles and editions, Mills nonetheless employed, for his comparative discussion, the *Shakespearean Originals* edition itself, which he explicitly applauds and from which he quotes several pages. And he does so partly in order to challenge the categorisation of Q1 simply as a 'bad quarto'.

> The first Quarto is often dismissed out of hand as 'the Bad Quarto', quoted in Riverside's notes only to 'help the reader in appreciating its debased nature'. All power, therefore, to the editors of a 1992 reprint [i.e. *Shakespearean Originals*], which I gratefully use as my source, whose introduction 'attempts to view the play as a work of art in its own right rather than as an analogue to the received text'.[6]

The primary objective of our edition of *The Tragicall Historie of Hamlet Prince of Denmarke* – 'to make the play generally available, for the first time since the early seventeenth century, for the kind of practical experimentation and theoretical mobilisation which alone can genuinely test the validity of that scholarly consensus that has kept this play on the margins of editorial reproduction, critical debate and theatrical performance' – therefore appeared even then, at least from the example cited by Brian Vickers, on its way to being achieved.

Shakespearean Originals was also challenged by some commentators particularly interested in the dramatic and theatrical issues raised by the reproduction of 'original' texts.[7] Janette Dillon's *Shakespeare Quarterly* essay 'Is There a Performance in this Text?' quickly became something of a *cause celebre*, and has been extensively cited as a useful 'antidote' to the 'excesses' of *Shakespearean Originals*.[8] Dillon's essay generously acknowledged the value of the series:

> The aim of the series, to make available in cheap paperback these early printed versions of plays more familiar to students in conflated editions, is a worthy one ... the price and format of these new editions does increase their availability ... The value of *Shakespearean Originals: First Editions* lies in the extent to which the editors foreground difference and warn against the false idea of the singular text, often a conflated text pretending to be singular and authentic. The point that these editions underline, and from which there can be no going back, is the plurality of the extant material objects, the undeniable existence of, in the case of *Hamlet*, at least three texts of the play so different from one another that their difference should be recognised by the printing of separate editions. The appearance of *Shakespearean Originals* marks the end of the notion of correctness.[9]

On the other hand, Dillon attacked the series by questioning the publisher's promotional material, criticising evident inaccuracies and apparent errors, and then dispersing assumptions derived from the advertising copy across the series' critical parameters:

> The title of the series makes a claim for authenticity, a claim central to the way the texts are advertised ... The slippery and undefined notions of authenticity and originality, which underwrite not only the advertising copy but also the general introduction to the series and the introductions to specific play texts, stands in urgent need of questioning.[10]

Later in the article, discussing the quality of evidence supplied by early modern title pages, Dillon undermines the very method on which her critique is based. She rejects the claim to a performance history contained in the title page of the 1603 quarto of *The Tragicall Historie of Hamlet Prince of Denmarke*, on the grounds that 'Title pages are devised in order to sell books, not to make precise scholarly statements about the texts they preface'.[11] The original title page of *Hamlet* has no status at all as evidence, yet she found it legitimate to read the Harvester Press Catalogue's reference to 'Shakespeare's real *Hamlet*' as such a 'precise scholarly statement'.

The primary focus of Dillon's interrogation is on the particular status she imagines the series attributes to *The Tragicall Historie of Hamlet Prince of Denmarke*:

> The thrust of the editorial argument, as set out in the introductory material, is not towards a plurality of authentic texts but towards an insistence on the superior authenticity of Q1.[12]

This assertion is incorrect. The critical introduction naturally, in the light of the text's historical marginalisation, argues for a revaluation. But that is not a revaluation vis-à-vis the other Jacobean texts of *Hamlet*, but against the modern editorial tradition. Nowhere does the introduction argue that Q1 has more value as a text than Q2 or F1, only that it is a *better* text in absolute terms *than is generally acknowledged*. Indeed, the 'Introduction' explicitly disavows such comparative judgements between 'original' texts:[13]

> In a hierarchical configuration of texts separated by principles of moral discrimination, priority is automatically given to those texts adjudged 'good'. On a level playing-field of textual plurality, variant readings can be objectively compared and apprehended as different from one another, without any establishing of discursive hierarchy.[14]

The main objective of the introduction to *The Tragicall Historie of Hamlet Prince of Denmarke* was to test a hypothesis. Since the text is generally accepted as a 'bad' text, how could it produce a 'good' performance? The problem arises, the introduction goes on to suggest, from a 'current diplomatic alliance of scholarship and theatre studies',[15] which is put under some pressure when an effective performance arises from a text judged to be 'bad'. Dillon worries about this term 'diplomatic alliance', which seems to her to suggest 'a calculated interdependence for mutual profit'. She goes on to point out that such 'alliance' between theatre and scholarship is 'not really so new', citing the instance of William Poel's 1881 production of Q1 '*Hamlet*'. Poel's production is actually discussed in some detail in the 'Introduction' to the edition; and the word 'diplomatic' was employed to foreground the historical relativity of that symbiosis of stage and study which clearly exists today, and is quite different from the equivalent relations in (to cite an extreme example) the Restoration and eighteenth century. The problem posed would not have been an issue in eighteenth-century culture, where scholars were attempting to fix the Shakespearean text, while the theatres excelled in free adaptation and rewriting.

When Nicholas Shrimpton saw a production of Q1 *Hamlet* at the Orange Tree Theatre in Richmond, he was shocked at the success of the performance because of his prior negative opinion of the play as a text.[16] If, on the other hand, it is accepted that the text is in its own right 'authentic', and possesses both historical and contemporary interest and value, then its capacity for performability will not surprise. The issue remains a paradox only for those who are convinced by practical demonstration of the text's performability, yet wish to retain the dismissive aesthetic category of 'bad quarto'. As editors we did not need to 'authenticate' the text by reinstating a theatrical 'authenticity factor', and in fact the edition attempted to show, by only a few illustrative examples,[17] how the 'distinctive poetic' qualities of the play have remained unrecognised by a scholarship generally disposed to view the text as a garbled imitation of something better.

Dillon argues that *The Tragicall Historie of Hamlet Prince of Denmarke* theoretically eliminates the author only to re-authenticate the text by reference to the criterion of performance, and that Q1 is asserted to be, by virtue of its historical theatricality and modern performability, demonstrably superior to both Q2 and F1. But this is not the case. It is the common consensus that this text comes very close to actual stage practice in Shakespeare's lifetime, which is why some of its striking stage directions (*'Enter Ofelia playing on a lute, and her hair downe, singing'*), together with other theatrical features, are frequently borrowed for modern editions and performances.[18] Dillon makes much of the fact that the basis of that consensus is a general acceptance of the theory of 'memorial reconstruction', which in turn underlies the designation of 'bad quarto'. So the edition appears to be using symptomatic evidence derived from a theory it disavows. But those characteristics of the so-called 'bad quartos' that are consonant with the 'memorial reconstruction' theory – graphic and detailed stage directions, self-evidently theatrical devices (such as the complete Christopher Sly-frame of *The Taming of a Shrew*), a certain 'levelling' populism – could equally point to some other performance-related origin.[19] At the same time, the edition explicitly states that F1 also bears many traces of playhouse influence, and even concedes that from the evidence of Q2's title page, it would be reasonable to assume that the second quarto represents a version the company may have used for performances.

The main issue, then, is not, as it is for New Bibliography, the relation between text and author. All these early modern dramatic texts have been transmitted in printed forms that effectively *conceal* specific elements of indebtedness to their several and various contributors. The dramatist naturally played a central, even an 'originating' role in this process of multiple and collective 'authorship'.[20] But if there is an 'authenticity factor' in play, it is neither the author as sole originator, nor the theatre as proxy-author, but rather that collective process of cultural production now widely acknowledged as the source of the drama, and whose precise causal configuration, and particular divisions of labour, remain to such a large extent hidden from us.[21]

Nor is it necessary to invoke a hypostatised and unitary conception of theatre to validate the text. Dillon argues that 'there is a slippage toward a more unitary notion of Jacobean stage practice which judges some texts as more authentic than others',[22] producing a privileging isolation of Q1 *Hamlet*. But the edition says something quite different:

> It is becoming clear that within Elizabethan and Jacobean culture, around each 'Shakespeare' play there circulated a wide variety of texts, performing different theatrical functions and adopting different shapes in different contexts of production.[23]

The existence of three '*Hamlet*' plays is evidence supporting that theoretical premise, while to the post-Malone editorial tradition such variants testify only to the pristine unity possessed by the authentic original before it disintegrated into its constituent textual fragments. Differing texts arise from 'different contexts of production', and although it is often difficult to link specific texts to particular contexts, the very fact of textual multiplicity disposes of any 'unitary' notion of 'the Jacobean stage'. Nor can it reasonably be said that the agency of 'historical performers' is occluded in an edition that explicitly acknowledges their determining, though indeterminate, contributions.

It is perhaps inevitable that an initiative in the re-individuation of texts long since incorporated into a tradition of combination should be mistaken for a strategy of idealisation, a ring-fencing of such texts as the 'bad quartos' to accord them a more privileged status.[24] The very isolation of the historic text might seem calculated to suggest authorial authenticity. This remains unfortunate, for the required emphasis is precisely the opposite of textual isolation and singularity. What we had hoped we could achieve via *Shakespearean Originals* was a focus on historical contingency: that is, a restoration of these texts not to uniqueness, but to the plural and multiple histories from which they derived. In divesting the texts to some degree of validation by authorship ('Shakespearean'), we had hoped that more readers might be enabled to experience them in terms of the multiple, collaborative authorship proper to a highly collectivised theatre industry; and to see in them, in the depth and thickness of their material textuality, something of their authorship by history.

Graham Holderness is a writer and critic who has published, as author or editor, more than sixty books, many on Shakespeare, and hundreds of chapters and articles of criticism, theory and theology. His more recent work has pioneered methods of critical-creative writing, exemplified by *Nine Lives of William Shakespeare* (Arden Shakespeare, 2011); *Tales from Shakespeare: Creative Collisions* (Cambridge University Press, 2014); and *Re-writing Jesus: Christ in 20th Century Fiction and Film* (Bloomsbury, 2014). His work has been translated into French, German, Italian, Spanish, Turkish, Arabic and Chinese. He has published several works of fiction: *The Prince of Denmark* (University of Hertfordshire Press, 2001; EER, 2021); *Ecce Homo* (Bloomsbury, 2014); *Black and Deep Desires: William Shake-*

speare Vampire Hunter (Top Hat Books, 2014); and *Meat, Murder, Malfeasance, Medicine and Martyrdom: Smithfield Stories* (EER, 2019). Recently his work has taken an autobiographical turn, as in his *Samurai Shakespeare: Early Modern Tragedy in Feudal Japan* (EER, 2021). His new novel *Ancestors: Adventures in a Foreign Country* will be published by EER in 2022. He was General Editor, with Bryan Loughrey, of the series *Shakespearean Originals*, published by Harvester Wheatsheaf and Prentice-Hall.

Bryan Loughrey (1952–2021) was from 1987 Editor, General Editor and lately Editor Emeritus of *Critical Survey*. He served as Lecturer in English, and later Director of Research, at Roehampton University, and afterwards worked as a Director for Oakley Consulting in the Middle East. His many publications included editions of Shakespeare, John Gay, Izaak Walton, and Thomas Middleton, and he served as a senior commissioning editor for Penguin, Longman and the British Council. He was General Editor, with Graham Holderness, of the *Shakespearean Originals* series, published by Harvester Wheatsheaf.

Notes

This afterword is based on material from Graham Holderness's forthcoming book, *Textual Shakespeare: Writing and the Word*, 2nd ed. (Edward Everett Root, 2020).

1. *The Tragicall Historie of Hamlet Prince of Denmarke*, ed. Graham Holderness and Bryan Loughrey (Hemel Hempstead: Harvester Wheatsheaf, 1992), 9–10.
2. Brian Vickers, '*Hamlet* by Dogberry: A Perverse Reading of the Bad Quarto', *Times Literary Supplement*, 24 December 1993, 24–25. See also Vickers' letters in *TLS*, 4 March 1994 and 15 April 1994.
3. See especially Random Cloud (Randall McLeod), 'The Marriage of Good and Bad Quartos', *Shakespeare Quarterly* 33 (1982), 421–431; Steven Urkowitz, 'Good News about "Bad" Quartos', in *Shakespeare Study Today: The Horace Howard Furness Memorial Lectures*, ed. Georgianna Ziegler (New York: AMS Press, 1986), 189–206; Paul Werstine, 'Narratives about Printed Shakespearean Texts: "Foul Papers" and "Bad" Quartos', *Shakespeare Quarterly* 41 (1990), 65–86; and Peter Blayney, 'The Publication of Playbooks', in *A New History of Early English Drama*, ed. John D. Cox and David Scott Kastan (New York: Columbia University Press, 1997), 383–422. Much new work on Q1 was published later in the 1990s, including new editions, such as Kathleen O. Irace, *The First Quarto of Hamlet* (Cambridge: Cambridge University Press, 1998), and Paul Bertram and Bernice Kliman, *The Three-Text Hamlet: Parallel Texts of the First and Second Quartos and*

First Folio (Studies in the Renaissance, no. 30) (New York: AMS Press, 1991). Other critical studies include Laurie E. Maguire, *Shakespearean Suspect Texts: The 'Bad Quartos' and Their Contexts* (Cambridge: Cambridge University Press, 1996); Steven Urkowitz, 'Back to Basics: Thinking about the *Hamlet* First Quarto', in *The 'Hamlet' First Published: Origins, Form, Intertextualities*, ed. Thomas Clayton (Newark: University of Delaware Press, 1992); Maxwell E. Foster, *The Play Behind the Play: 'Hamlet' and Quarto One* (London: Heinemann, 1991); and Eric Sams, *The Real Shakespeare* (New Haven, CT: Yale University Press, 1995), 125–135.
4. Vickers, '*Hamlet* by Dogberry', 24.
5. Brian Vickers, letter to *TLS*, 4 March 1994.
6. Howard Mills, *Working with Shakespeare* (Hemel Hempstead: Harvester Wheatsheaf, 1992), 62, quoting Holderness and Loughrey, *Tragicall Historie*, 27.
7. See also Alan Posener, 'Materialism, Dialectics and Editing Shakespeare', *New Theatre Quarterly* 39 (1994), 263–6 (which was a response to Graham Holderness and Bryan Loughrey, 'Text and Stage: Shakespeare, Bibliography and Performance Studies', *New Theatre Quarterly* 34 [1993], 179–191); Andrew Spong, 'Bad Habits, "Bad Quartos" and Myths of Origin in the Editing of Shakespeare', *New Theatre Quarterly* 45 (1995), 65–70.
8. Janette Dillon, 'Is There a Performance in this Text?', *Shakespeare Quarterly* 45 (1994), 74–86.
9. Dillon, 'Is There a Performance', 85.
10. Ibid., 74–75.
11. Ibid., 79.
12. Ibid., 75.
13. Interestingly, Chris Hopkins in *Thinking About Texts* (London: Palgrave, 2001) explicitly deploys the *Shakespearean Originals* text of Q1 in a comparative exercise, arguing that such critical judgements can still be made, on grounds other than moral discrimination, between texts accepted as equally 'authentic' (85–89, especially 85n3).
14. Holderness and Loughrey, *Tragicall Historie*, 22–23.
15. Ibid., 13.
16. Nicholas Shrimpton, 'Shakespeare Performances in London and Stratford-upon-Avon 1984–5', *Shakespeare Survey* 39 (1987), 197. See also Bryan Loughrey, 'Q1 in Recent Performance', in Clayton, *The 'Hamlet' First Published*, 123–136; and Andrew Stott, '"Bad Quartos" in Performance: Charles Calder in Conversation with Graham Holderness and Bryan Loughrey', *Studies in Theatre Production* 14, no. 1 (1996), 48–58.
17. Holderness and Loughrey, *Tragicall Historie*, 21–22.
18. Examples listed by Irace, *The First Quarto*, 20–23.
19. A point well made in *William Shakespeare: The Complete Works*, ed. Stanley Wells and Gary Taylor with John Jowett and William Montgomery (Oxford: Oxford University Press, 1988), xxvii. See also Stanley Wells, 'Multiple Texts and the Oxford Shakespeare', *Textus* 9 (1996), 2. Irace in *The First Quarto* lists other specifically theatrical features (4–5, 8–20), and discusses modern performances of Q1 (23–27), including a staged reading of the *Shakespearean Originals* edition.
20. Holderness and Loughrey, *Tragicall Historie*, 6–7.
21. Ibid., 16.
22. Dillon, 'Is There a Performance', 77.

23. Holderness and Loughrey, *Tragicall Historie*, 7.
24. 'The opponents of emendation fetishize the printed text as an object in itself, and in doing so they occlude both the process whereby it came into being and the very reason why it came into being.' John Jowett, 'After Oxford: Recent Developments in Textual Studies', *The Shakespearean International Yearbook* 1 (1999), 71. See also Gabriel Egan, 'Myths and Enabling Fictions of "Origin" in the Editing of Shakespeare', *New Theatre Quarterly* 49 (1997), 41–47.

Index

Abjection, 25
Actor-playwright, 46
Allusion, 22, 61, 110, 113, 116, 117, 122, 138, 156, 157, 196
Amlethus. Amleth. Amleto. 1, 171, 173, 175, 177
Aeneas, 158
The Aeneid, 150–1, 153–8
Ariel, 11
Artaud, Antonin, 25
Authorial
  Authenticity, 242
  Canon, 145
  Draft, 201
  Influence, 236
  Involvement, 205
  Markers, 15
  Manuscript, 236–7
  Role, 236
  Signature, 10

bad quarto, 5, 17, 19, 26, 90, 91, 95, 96, 103, 193, 194, 241, 242
bad folio, 96
Bales, Peter, 167
Bandello, Matteo
  Certain Tragical Discourses, 18
Banquo, 8
Batman upon Bartholme, 23
Belleforest, François, 1, 2, 23, 84, 173, 195,

Belsey, Catherine, 8–11, 24–5
Bertram, Benjamin, 116
Bertram, Paul, 164–5, 168–9, 171–2
Beowulf, 23
Booksellers, 17, 92, 102
Bookshop, 93, 98, 100–2
Book trade, 74, 92, 105
Bourus, Terri, 1, 4, 5, 8, 10, 11, 14, 90, 114, 118, 123, 144, 147, 158, 166, 175, 181, 186, 234
Bowers, Fredson, 154
Boyle, A.J., 9
Bullen, A.H., 154
Burbage, Richard, 68, 114–5
Burrow, Colin, 156
Bynneman, Henry, 194

Caliban, 11
Cambridge University, 8, 10, 97
Canon, 17–8, 22, 115, 145, 156
Canonical authority, 234
Canonical form, 138
Canonical play, 134
Canonical relationships, 155
Canonical Shakespeare plays, 15
Canonical shape, 143
Canonical text, 12, 16, 19, 144, 156
Canonical traits, 181
Canonical version, 21, 56, 130
Cavell, Stanley, 226
Caxton, William, 150–1, 153

Céline, Louis-Ferdinand, 25
Chamberlain's Men. *See* Lord Chamberlain's Men.
Chapman, George, 15, 19
  Bussy D'Ambois, 15
  May Day, 15, 19
Character(s), 5, 9,11, 20, 22, 39, 40, 44, 45, 55, 56, 58–60, 62, 64–68, 78, 82, 110, 111, 146, 149, 150, 163, 171, 174, 177, 181, 182, 183, 184, 185, 187, 195, 196, 198, 212, 213, 218, 220, 221, 224, 225, 228
Christianity, 9, 116,
Chronology, 10, 110, 113, 119, 148, 156, 162–4, 176
classical literature, 9
Cnut, 18
Collier, Jeremy, 25,
Collier, John Payne, 92, 97, 147, 148, 152, 154, 163
Compositor A, 78, 80–1, 83
Gunthio, Ambrose, 163
Conflated editorial text, 11
Conflated edition, 2, 238
conflated editorial version, 2
Conflated text, 212, 213, 238
Conflated, 152
Correr, Gregorio, 9
  Procne, 9
Creede, Thomas, 85
  The True Tragedy of Richard III, 85
  The Famous Victories of Henry V, 85–6
Creizenach, Wilhelm, 227
Cunningham, Francis, 154
Cynthia's Revels, 113

Danes, 23
Data point, 15, 17, 18
Database, 14–5, 17–8, 92, 93, 112
Dekker, Thomas, 13, 15, 18, 109, 215
  News From Hell, 215, 220
  Old Fortunatus, 15, 18
  The Wonderful Year, 215

Dering, Sir Edward, 26
Description, 4, 8, 25, 91–2, 94, 111, 114–5, 121, 126, 149, 150, 181, 235–6
Desmet, Christy, 188
Dessen, Alan C., 185
Dialogue, 4, 11, 20, 22, 36, 61, 74, 77–8, 81–2, 141, 173, 226–7,
Dido, Queen of Carthage, 144–55, 156, 158
The Division of the Kingdoms, 11
Dostoyevsky, Fyodor, 25
Dramatic texts, 15–19, 82, 241
Dramatist, 109, 112, 227, 235, 241
Dramaturgy, 4, 22
Drayton, Michael, 5, 15, 18, 99, 101, 102, 105
  The Owl, 99
dumb show, 212–22, 224–29
Dyce, Alexander, 146–7, 154
Dynastic collapse, 23

Early English Books Online (EEBO), 92–4, 101, 112, 117, 169
Early English Books Online-Text Creation Partnership (EEBO-TCP), 17, 29
Early modern, 4, 14, 26, 150
  Authors, 215
  Bookbuyer, 74
  Books, 94–5, 98
  Book trade, 92
  Culture, 236
  Discourse, 149
  Drama, 9, 214, 236
  Dramatists, 19
  Emblematists, 214
  England, 156, 187
  London, 73, 83,
  Maps, 23
  Performance practices, 25
  Period, 165
  Play quartos, 94
  Plays, 13
  Printed books, 92
  Printing, 103

Publishing, 103
References, 217
Romanitas, 133
Stage, 144, 155
Theatre, 3, 236
Texts, 13, 144, 241
Title page, 239
Edition, 2–4, 8, 13, 21 23–6, 63–4, 747, 79, 83, 85, 87, 91–8, 101–5, 116–7, 126–7, 145, 154, 156, 234–5, 237–42
Edward IV, 15, 18
Elizabeth I, 14, 127–8, 215
Elizabethan
 Clothing, 37
 Copyright, 193
 Costumes, 37
 Culture, 241
 Dress, 37
 England, 133
 Ghosts, 9
 Hamlet, 8
 London, 118
 Pirates, 236
 Plays, 25
 Publishing, 194
 Satires, 109
 Settings, 37
 Stage, 187
 Students, 133
 Theatre, 40, 120
 Theatregoers, 120
 Texts, 23
 Writers, 7
England, 9, 18, 23, 26, 50–1, 83, 133, 135, 156, 183, 187, 196, 202, 215
Enlightenment, 25
Erne, Lukas, 13, 57
European, 9, 24

F1. F. The Folio. First Folio, 2, 11, 15, 24, 36, 42, 45–7, 49, 51–3, 57, 77, 86–7, 95–6, 104, 112, 136, 143, 162, 168, 198–9, 200–2, 211–2, 224, 235, 237, 239, 241

Fabyan, Robert, 23
 Fabyan's Chronicle, 23
Fireside stories and tales, 8
first *Hamlet*, 1, 2, 3, 10, 141
first quarto, Q1, 2–4, 9–16, 18–20, 22–3, 25–7, 35–6, 40–53, 55–58, 60–2, 65–8, 73–87, 90–5, 97–105, 112, 114–5, 117–20, 122–3, 126–135, 137–8, 141–9, 152–4, 156–8, 162–77, 180–88, 192–207, 212, 222–3, 225–6, 229, 234–41
Fletcher, John, 13, 15
Florio, John, 5, 127–8, 137–8
Folio, 95, 96, 138
Folk tales, 10
French Civil Wars, 130

Geats, 23
Ghosts, 7, 8, 11, 24–5, 49, 80, 113, 142, 158, 175, 212
 of Andrea, 8
 of Hamlet, 7–12, 25–7
 Lore, 8,
 play, 7
 stage, 9
 story, 8, 11, 217
Gibson, William, 26
Gibson, H.N., 111
Gill, Roma, 154
Gothic, 20, 24–6
Goths, 23
Grafton, Richard, 18
 Grafton's Chronicle: Or, History of England, 18
Grammaticus, Saxo, 1, 8, 23
Greene, Robert, 18, 19
 A disputation between a hee coney catcher and a she-coney catcher, 18
 Friar Bacon and Friar Bungay, 18, 19
Grimeston, Edward, 18
 History of France, 18
 History of the Netherlands, 18
Groatsworth of Wit, 110, 112

Grossart, Alexander, 154
Gurr, Andrew, 13

Hamlet, characters
  Barnardo, 25, 55–6
  Claudius, 21, 40, 50–1, 116, 138,
    182–3, 185, 195, 200, 205,
    213, 226–9
  Corambis, 40, 44, 47–8, 66, 73,
    163, 165–7, 169–76, 183–4,
    198, 202
  Fortinbras, 23
  Guildenstern, 40, 51
  Gertrard, 168
  Gertred, 8, 11–2, 40, 181, 183–6,
    188
  Gertrude, 21, 40, 50–2, 168,
    172–3, 181, 183–6, 211–2,
    226, 228, 229,
  The Ghost, 7, 8, 9–12, 25, 39–40,
    45–6, 55–6, 115, 141–3,
    157–8, 173, 181, 186, 211,
    221–2, 229
  Hamlet, 1, 7, 10–12, 15, 21, 23,
    38, 40, 42, 44–53, 58–68, 77,
    112, 114–6, 127, 131, 134–8,
    141–2, 150, 154, 158, 165,
    170–4, 176, 181–8, 195–6,
    200–4, 213, 222, 225, 227–9,
    234
  Horatio, 12, 21–2, 25, 40, 49–51,
    53, 56, 104, 135, 176, 186,
    195–6, 201, 203, 205, 212
  King of Denmark, King Hamlet,
    195, 205
  Laertes, 21, 38, 52, 114, 167–9,
    182, 186, 201
  Leartes, 21, 167, 169, 170–4, 182,
    184, 187
  Lucianus, 164, 180, 222, 228
  Marcellus, 25, 55–6, 164, 168,
    180, 193, 195–6, 202–3
  Ofelia, 22, 44, 58, 60–2, 65–8, 77,
    87, 168, 170–4, 181, 186–8,
    222, 225, 241
  Ophelia, 43–5, 51–3, 58–68, 87,
    168, 171–2, 181, 184, 186–7,
    198, 211–3, 222, 225
  Polonius, 40, 47, 163, 167, 171–2,
    174–5, 181, 184
  Reynaldo, 166–7
  Rosencrantz, 40, 51
  Voltemand, 167, 181
  Voltemar, 164, 167, 181
  Yoricke, 77–80, 82
  Yorick, 181
Harvey, Gabriel, 5, 109–10, 113–8,
  122–3
Hecuba, 151–4
Heywood, Thomas, 13, 15, 18, 26,
  166
  If you know not me, you know
    nobody, 15, 18, 166
Holderness, Graham, 4, 76
Holy Trinity Church, 26
Horror, 25
Horror vacui, 229
Hybrid, 4, 11, 41

Imperial nationalism, 9
Interpretation, 2, 9, 11, 59, 76, 96,
  115, 120, 134, 184, 188, 212, 214,
  217–8, 228–9
Interruption, 55–64, 66–8, 228

Jacobean
  Culture, 241
  Era, 81
  Satires, 109
  Stage, 241–2
  texts, 239
James I, 5, 144
Jonson, Ben, 5, 13, 15, 23, 109–13,
  122, 137, 144
  Every Man Out of His Humor,
    110–13, 144
  Haddington Masque, 15
  King's Entertainment, 15
  Poetaster, 15, 110
  Volpone, 137

Jordanes, 23
  Getica, 23

Kazan, Elia, 110
  On the Waterfront, 110
Kliman, Bernice, 164–5, 168–9, 171–2
Knight, Charles, 148
Kristeva, Julia, 8, 24–5
Kyd, Thomas, 3, 5, 8–11, 13, 15, 25–7, 84, 113, 144, 168–9, 218,
  Spanish Tragedy, 8, 25, 84, 94–5, 105, 113, 144, 168–9, 218

Lesser, Zachary, 3, 56, 73, 103–4, 97–101, 142, 163, 181
Lexical sequences, 15
Ling, Nicholas, 78, 84, 92, 97–103, 105, 193–4
Literary
  Achievement, 105
  Allusions, 110
  Attacks, 117
  Criticism, 25
  Domain, 73
  Drama, 97
  History, 7, 155
  Imagination, 156
  Inheritance, 155
  Insiders, 113
  Marketplace, 83
  Nature, 97
  Objects, 95
  Production, 155
  Scene, 109
  Taste, 95
  Text, 57, 97
  Tradition, 150, 217
  Quarrels, 110
  Quartos, 97
Literature Online, 14–5, 17
Lodge, Thomas, 1, 3, 5, 10–11, 15, 25, 118, 148, 175
London, 10, 17, 73, 74, 83, 84, 93, 94, 100, 118, 119, 120, 121, 122, 193

London Theatre, 17, 120, 193
Lord Chamberlain's Men, 1, 2, 10, 13, 118–20
Loughnane, Rory, 4, 123
Lute, 22, 58, 121, 187, 241,
Lydgate, 150–1, 153

Malone, Edmond, 3, 7
The Mariners Mirror, 23
Marlowe, Christopher, 5, 13, 117, 144–6, 148, 150, 154–5
Marlowe, Kit. *See* Christopher Marlowe.
Marriage, 24, 40, 67, 185, 187,
Marston, John, 109, 110
  Antonio and Mellida, 218
  Antonio's Revenge, 10, 110, 218
Martyr, Peter, 23
  History of Travayle, 23
McKerrow, R.B., 154
Medieval, 1, 8, 11, 23–4, 26, 150
Memorial reconstruction, 12, 19, 43, 45, 50, 57, 142–3, 147, 163–4, 168, 176, 180, 193, 198, 235, 241
Menaphon, 110, 113
Meyerhold, Vsevolod, 115
Micro-attribution techniques, 13
Middleton, Thomas, 13, 15, 19, 94
  Trick to Catch the Old One, 19
Miller, Arthur, 110
  The Crucible, 110
Miola, Robert, 156–7
Modern audiences, 21
Montagu, Elizabeth, 8, 24–5
Montaigne, Michel de, 127, 130, 132, 134, 136–38
The Mousetrap, 182, 213, 221–2, 228–9
The Murder of Gonzago, 48, 176, 228

N-gram, 13, 16
Nashe, Thomas, 1–4, 10–11, 13–4, 23, 25, 109, 113–8, 122, 148, 150, 154
Neoclassical critics, 20

New Bibliographers, 163
New Bibliography, 237, 241
The New Oxford Shakespeare (NOS), 20, 59, 128, 155, 164
Newington Butts, 1, 118–9
Norwegians, 23

Oliver, H.J., 154
Oral, 8, 24–6, 57, 204,
Original, 11, 13–4, 22, 23–25, 37, 39, 40, 43, 77, 96, 98, 113, 144–5, 148, 157, 173, 222, 235–9, 242
Oxford University, 8, 10, 97, 104, 166

Painter, William, 18
　Palace of Pleasure, 18
Partridge, Eric, 187
Patriarchal, 9, 11, 68
Peele, George, 13
Phaer, Thomas, 150–1, 153, 156
Pica roman, 91
Play quarto, 92–4, 102
Play, 1–5, 7, 9–26, 35–7, 40–2, 44, 46–9, 53, 55, 58, 60, 77–8, 82–4, 86, 92–4, 97, 99, 102, 105, 110, 113–4, 116–22, 127, 134–5, 142–50, 153–58, 162–168, 170, 172, 174–7, 181, 184, 186, 188, 192–7, 205, 207, 211–5, 217–8, 221–229, 237–41
Petersen, Lene, 188
Playbook, 73–4, 78, 83–4, 86
Playbook-buyers, 17
Player-dramatist, 110
Playwright, 8, 13, 15–7, 19–20, 22, 24, 26, 58, 110, 122, 155, 175, 177, 193, 195
Poetic texture, 20
Polites, 150
Popular culture, 155
Postmodern, 4, 25
Priam, 145–8, 150–4, 158
Protestant Reformation, 9
Proust, Marcel, 25
Purgatory, 8, 39
Pyrrhus, 147–51, 153–4, 158

Radcliffe, Anne, 8, 24
Reception, 3, 53, 59, 73, 97, 104, 142, 228
Renaissance, 9, 14, 23, 36
Retailers, 102–3
Revenge, 1, 3, 10, 23, 45, 84, 127, 130, 132, 136–7, 150, 158, 168–70, 173–77, 182–3, 188, 193, 200–2, 212, 218
Ritson, Joseph, 145
Roberts, James, 77, 84, 92, 95, 98, 127, 193
Robin Goodfellow, 11
Robinson, George, 145
Roman Empire, 9
Rowe, Nicholas, 237
Rowley, William, 13, 15
Rupture, 55–7, 59–61, 64, 67

Scene 14, 4, 12–6, 19, 40, 50, 185
　The Mysteries of Udolpho, 24
Scholarly tradition, 9, 11
Second quarto, Q2, 2, 4, 11, 15–6, 18, 24, 36, 42, 44–7, 49, 51–3, 57–68, 73, 75, 77, 80–1, 86–7, 92, 97–105, 112, 114, 126–8, 130–5, 137–8, 141–4, 147–8, 153, 156–8, 162–5, 167–176, 180–7, 192–203, 205–7, 211–3, 222–6, 228–9, 235, 237, 239, 241
Seneca, 4, 8–9, 11, 25, 84, 110, 113–6, 118, 133, 144
Seville, Isidore of, 23
Shakespeare as Literary Dramatist, 57
Shakespeare, William, plays of
　2 Henry VI, 15, 17, 78
　3 Henry VI, 15–8, 110
　A Midsummer Night's Dream, 96
　Antony and Cleopatra, 16, 156,
　As You Like It, 86, 110
　Cymbeline, 156
　Henry IV, 26, 78, 83, 86, 96, 175
　Henry V, 156
　Julius Caesar, 15–7, 121
　King Lear, 21, 24, 80, 202, 205

Love's Labour Lost, 18, 96
Macbeth, 8, 156, 202
The Merry Wives of Windsor, 84, 86
Much Ado About Nothing, 15–6, 18, 78, 83, 86, 96
Othello, 21, 202
Pericles, 15, 219
Richard II, 15–6, 18, 21, 37, 78, 83–4, 96
Richard III, 37, 78, 83, 85, 96
Romeo and Juliet, 15, 21, 96
Taming of the Shrew, 15, 17, 111, 241
The Tempest, 127, 136, 156
Titus Andronicus, 19, 20–5, 96, 156
Troilus and Cressida, 110, 156–7
Twelfth Night, 37, 110
Two Gentlemen of Verona, 15, 17–8, 24
Two Noble Kinsmen, 15,
Venus and Adonis, 83–4, 103, 156,
The Winter's Tale, 16,
Shakespearean Originals, 76, 234–5, 238, 239, 242
Shorthand, 2, 13, 92, 211, 221
Simmes, Valentine, 78, 91–2, 94–5, 97–100, 193–4
Stage directions, 165, 225–6, 241
Stallybrass, Peter, 78, 97
Stanyhurst, Richard, 150–1, 153, 156
Stationers' Register, 96
Steevens, George, 145
Stemma, 84–6, 96
Stemmata, 84, 86
Stern, Tiffany, 163, 165–70, 195, 227
Stratford-upon-Avon, 26

Taylor, Gary, 123, 264
Textual
   Agreement, 148
   Apparatus, 60
   Authority, 96
   Consistency, 188
   Contribution, 196
   Criticism, 11–2, 90
   Details, 205
   Editing, 12
   Field, 144
   Fragments, 242
   History, 7, 56, 87, 126, 133, 180
   Hits, 35
   Hypothesis, 9
   Interruption, 57
   Inconsistency, 181
   Isolation, 242
   Issues, 11
   Matchups, 36
   Multiplicity, 242
   Notes, 3
   Object, 220
   Omissions, 198
   Processes, 163
   Question, 127
   Reference, 184
   Revision, 134
   Scene, 143
   Scholars, 180
   Scholarship, 96, 157
   Sequence, 196
   Stemma, 96
   Studies, 143
   Succession, 144
   Touchstones, 35
   variety, 234
   Witness, 97
The Tain of Hamlet, 163
The Theatre, 11, 118–9, 175
Theobald, Lewis, 13
title page
   Tragoedia der Bestrafte Brudermord oder Prinz Hamlet aus Dännemark, 2
   Tragicall Historie of Hamlet Prince of Denmark, 2, 100–1
transmission, 5, 26–7, 46, 84, 86, 103, 142, 156, 162–3, 175–6, 180, 204, 236
Troy, 145–6, 148–58

Trundell, John, 78, 84,
Tucker Brooke, C.F., 154

Unauthorised texts, 17, 194
Unauthorised transmission, 27
Unique parallels, 15–19
Ur-*Hamlet*, 7, 15, 19, 143, 148, 180

Variants, 4–5, 12 166, 175, 205, 222–5, 242
Venus, 151, 158
Vickers, Brian, 235–38
Violence, 20–2, 68, 130–1, 152–3, 201
Virgil, 4, 150–1, 153, 156–8

Voltaire, 20, 24–5

War of the theatres, 110, 113, 157
Warwickshire, 8, 10
Webster, John, 8
Wells, Sir Stanley, 19–22, 24
Werstine, Paul, 164, 193, 200
Wilkins, George, 8
Wilson, John Dover, 25, 212, 227
Wright, George, 188

Xylographic, 100

Young Shakespeare's Young Hamlet, 11, 123, 163, 166

www.ingramcontent.com/pod-product-compliance
Lightning Source LLC
Chambersburg PA
CBHW072149100526
44589CB00015B/2145